Teacher Training and Education in the GCC

Expansion and Internationalization of Higher Education in Asia, North Africa, and the Middle East

Series Editors: Hassan Bashir and Kevin Gray

This series is an interdisciplinary examination of the development of Western-style educational institutions outside Europe and North America. It welcomes approaches across academic disciplines, but most notably politics, economics, sociology, and educational theory, which focus either on the development of higher education in specific regions, or similarities and differences between educational projects between regions. Volumes in the series may choose to interrogate the history of the development of these branches and foreign campuses, the political impetus for their development, the sociological effects of the rise of foreign campuses in Asia and Africa, and/or the specific pedagogical challenges faced by practitioners in these institutions. This series particularly welcomes critical reflections about the role of these institutions as imperial projects or as expansions of Western hegemony, or, conversely, reflections on the relationships between universities and non-democratic regimes, including texts which engage with how the norms of academic life have been modified by the locus of education abroad.

Recent Titles

Teacher Training and Education in the GCC

Unpacking the Complexities and Challenges of Internationalizing Educational Contexts

Edited by
Naved Bakali and Nadeem A. Memon

LEXINGTON BOOKS
Lanham • Boulder • New York • London

Published by Lexington Books
An imprint of The Rowman & Littlefield Publishing Group, Inc.
4501 Forbes Boulevard, Suite 200, Lanham, Maryland 20706
www.rowman.com

6 Tinworth Street, London SE11 5AL, United Kingdom

British Library Cataloguing in Publication Information Available

Library of Congress Cataloging-in-Publication Data

Names: Bakali, Naved, editor. | Memon, Nadeem A. (Nadeem Ahmed), 1980- editor.
Title: Teacher training and education in the GCC : unpacking the complexities and
    challenges of internationalizing educational contexts / Edited by Naved Bakali and
    Nadeem A. Memon.
Description: Lanham : Lexington Books, [2021] | Series: Expansion and
    internationalization of higher education in Asia, North Africa, and the Middle East |
    Includes bibliographical references and index.
Identifiers: LCCN 2021031450 (print) | LCCN 2021031451 (ebook) |
    ISBN 9781793636737 (hardback) | ISBN 9781793636744 (epub)
Subjects: LCSH: Teachers—Training of—Research. | Teachers—In-service training—
    Research. | International education. | Education and globalization. | Education,
    Higher—International cooperation.
Classification: LCC LB1707 .T4241 2021 (print) | LCC LB1707 (ebook) |
    DDC 370.71/1—dc23
LC record available at https://lccn.loc.gov/2021031450
LC ebook record available at https://lccn.loc.gov/2021031451

Contents

List of Tables

Acknowledgments

This work has been the culmination of the hard work and effort of many individuals whom we have had the pleasure of working and collaborating with over the years. Here, we would like to acknowledge their help and support in developing this volume. First, we would like to thank those who have mentored us over the years. Through their kindness, support, dedication, and advice, we have been able to chart a course toward knowledge production relevant to this present volume. These individuals include Dr. Aziz Choudry, Dr. Shirley Steinberg, Dr. Anila Asghar, Dr. Ronald Morris, and Dr. Sheheen Shariff. We would also like to thank our cherished colleagues at our respective institutions, particularly Dr. Catherine Hill, Dr. Nadera Alborno, Dr. Jessica Tsimprea Maluch, Dr. Matthew Ingalls, Dr. David Schmidt, and Dr. Sabrina Joseph at the American University of Dubai. Your candor, support, and collegiality will always be greatly appreciated. From the University of South Australia, sincere appreciation to Dr. Deborah Price, Dr. Deborah Green, and Dylan Chown for a memorable trip to the Middle East pre-COVID in 2020 and to the Department of Foreign Affairs and Trade (DFAT) and Council of Australian-Arab Relations (CAAR) for funding our research trip. Thank you also to the individuals, schools, and universities in the UAE and Qatar that hosted us on that trip. Finally, and most importantly, we would like to thank all of the students that we have had the pleasure and honor of working, teaching, learning, grow, and develop with over the years. You have all served as a tremendous inspiration for us in putting this volume together.

Introduction

GCC Teacher Education: Mapping Challenges and Complexities

Naved Bakali and Nadeem A. Memon

TEACHER EDUCATION IN THE GCC

Contemporary educational discourse across teacher training programs globally advance learner-centered, inquiry-based, and constructivist approaches to teaching and learning. This approach to teacher training informed by critical scholarship challenges positivist educational notions of standardization, overreliance on measurement, and a "one-size-fits-all" approach to learning and teaching. For Schools of Education in the Gulf Cooperation Council (GCC) nations, many of which are in their infancy stages, critical educational discourse combined with positivist pressures of performativity both embedded within a local context of existing cultural and social norms for schooling has been complex. Traditional approaches to teaching and learning in the region relied heavily on rote memorization, employed a top-down teacher-centered structure, and placed strong emphasis on storytelling and the oral tradition (Freimuth 2014). There have been reforms across schools of education in the GCC to work toward educational transformation. These calls to reform come at the heels of a burgeoning expat population fervently growing in the region, as well as to meet the needs and expectations of twenty-first-century student skills development and learning outcomes (Alhashmi, Bakali, & Baroud 2020). This has been reflected by the transitioning away from recruitment of teachers in the Middle East and North Africa (MENA) region, to a greater reliance on Western educators for primary and secondary schools, as well as in schools of education since the early 2000s (Gallagher 2019).

This multidisciplinary volume highlights some of the challenges and complexities that inevitably arise from this paradox. Ultimately, the themes discussed in this volume serve as a tool kit to navigate the complex educational landscape faced by preservice and in-service educators, as well as provide important insights for teacher development in the GCC region.

In this volume, contributors consider important themes in teacher education including: Arabic language acquisition; K–12 Islamic education; inclusive and special needs education; teaching for diversity and equity education; and advancing teaching practices through professional development. The contributors of this volume argue that the establishment of critical educational practices in teacher training programs create opportunities for K–12 education development in the GCC.

A number of journal articles and book chapters have been written about various aspects of teacher education and training in the GCC; however, these works are independent studies that are not compiled as a comprehensive guide to serve as a resource that can be used to assist and develop teaching practices. Teacher training programs in the region rely heavily on textbooks and resources that have been developed in Western contexts. Few, if any of the programs to date have incorporated textbooks or resources that have been developed within the contexts that GCC preservice and in-service teachers are working in. Given the prevailing regional educational complexities and challenges highlighted above, this volume aims to address this gap by providing locally contextualized scholarship on a number of pressing issues facing educators in the GCC, specifically focusing on the themes of cultural barriers in teacher education; pedagogical approaches and praxis in teacher education; and ways forward in teacher education and development. To better understand the relevance and importance of these themes, it is pertinent to discuss current global discourses that have become operationalized in the field of educational studies, which have helped construct our approach to teacher training and development in the region.

GLOBAL TRENDS IN EDUCATIONAL DISCOURSE

Three global educational discourses inform our collective reading of teacher education in the GCC. The first is a push toward responsive/inclusive/asset-based pedagogies that is influenced by broader educational discourses in "New Pedagogy Studies." New pedagogy Studies are grounded in critical theory and critical pedagogy specifically, but call for an enactment of educational renewal that is pedagogically driven (Green 2003; Hattam and Zipin 2009; Connelly 2015). Such approaches demand pedagogies that are justice-oriented, embedded in local contexts and realities, and that draw on the lived experiences, perspectives, and cultural assets of learners—commonly referred to as lifeworld knowledges of learners. From this perspective, the learning is not solely "learner-centered" in the sense that learner interests inform curricular choices but rather the lifeworlds of learners are viewed as "learning assets" that are drawn upon to deepen curricular choices. What is commonly referred to as Culturally Responsive Pedagogy (CRP) or also known as Culturally Relevant Pedagogy or Culturally Sustaining Pedagogy (CSP) are emerging as critical theoretical shifts from previous emphases on multicultural education, intercultural understanding, and equity and inclusive education to name a few. In many cases, discourses of responsive pedagogies were a reaction to rampant deficit perceptions of the home cultures of minoritized learners in Black American and Indigenous Canadian communities (Morrison et al. 2019). Over the past two decades, however, responsive and asset-based pedagogies have emerged as a reframing of equitable and inclusive educational practice to nuance the ways in which diversity within classrooms is understood and pedagogically responded to across the globe. Conceptual understandings of "critical reflexivity," "cultural humility," and "critical reflection" more commonly inform pedagogical discourses and innovation in schools today. Previous ideas of encouraging educators to become "culturally competent" are now increasingly being challenged with a call toward responsive, reflective, and reflexive pedagogies that emphasize the humility of not knowing.

A second and in many ways overlapping educational discourse is a push toward fostering critical consciousness in learners. Equally rooted in the broader discourse of critical pedagogy, educating for critical consciousness relates to preparing learners to "read the world." Learning from this perspective is about having the agency as educators to facilitate meaning-making and for learners to make meaning of the local realities that define who they are and the global discourses that inform them. Learning from this perspective is also highly political and thereby intended to be personally and sociopolitically transformational (Freire 2015; Giroux 2001). Such an approach inherently challenges didactic pedagogies that teach to assessment or that view learners as passive recipients of knowledge. Teaching for critical consciousness demands a heightened self-awareness of learners and by virtue an engagement with the social, political, and economic structures that shape the world around them. The implications of an education system committed to fostering critical consciousness requires educators to be seen as experts in their own contexts—to have the agency to be active decision-makers in their classrooms (Priestly, Biesta and Robinson 2015). Amidst pressures to conform and perform in the Global Educational Reform Movement (GERM) that places a priority on measurable learning, high-stakes accountability, and prescriptive curricula, such commitments to fostering critical consciousness remain aspirational at best (Lingard and McGregor 2014).

A third and yet also complementary trend in educational discourse that informs this book is the increasing awareness for social emotional learning

(SEL) and well-being. Enhancing pedagogies as practices linking educators and learners in cultural contexts with implications on human development must attend to whole-child development. The Collaborative for Academic, Social, and Emotional Learning (CASEL) define SEL as "the process through which children and adults understand and manage emotions, set and achieve positive goals, feel and show empathy for others, establish and maintain positive relationships, and make responsible decisions" (CASEL. org). With complementing overlaps, well-being focuses on respecting individual, family and community values, beliefs, values, and experiences (Price and McCullum 2016). Together, the more forthright push toward educational programs and initiatives that foster SEL and well-being are becoming commonplace in schools. It reinforces the fact that teaching is a relational profession and that within pressures to learn "intellectually," developmental domains of spiritual, physical, interpersonal, cultural, and social cannot be forgotten. Research is increasingly showing that integrating SEL, for example, within curriculum contributes to both the attainment of these broader core competencies as well as academic growth (Durlak, Dymnicki, Taylor, Weissberg & Schellinger, 2011).

For the GCC, a context that has witnessed a rapid growth of the education sector particularly with the influx of expatriate educators and students, these three educational discourses describe the interplay between aspiration and reality. Educators in the GCC grapple between multiple worlds. For expatriate education, they straddle educational norms that inform their educational practice from their country of origin; an educational context in the Middle East that is distinct to their own; and an educational policy context informed by global educational discourses. Local educators, on the other hand, experience their own version of straddling these multiple educational expectations between a rapidly internationalizing education system defined by a dominant global education policy context and a devaluing or at minimum decentering of local cultures, heritages, and languages. The educational realities in the GCC require an urgent consideration of responsivity and reflexivity to challenge dominant discourses in education.

THE COMPLEXITIES AND CHALLENGES SURROUNDING CURRENT EDUCATIONAL TRENDS IN THE GCC

The rapid economic transformation of the GCC is well documented with a heavy reliance on unskilled migrant workforce tied to a sponsorship system, the exacerbation of social hierarchies and disparities between educated and not, visa holder types, passports, language, culture, religion, and race.

This transformation has had implications on the social, political, economic, and education sectors. In the education sector particularly, the ambitious internationalization of system-wide changes and initiatives have had critical implications on education systems, schools, educators, and learners. Internationalization has meant expanding the private education sector, which in many cases across the GCC now exceeds the number of schools in the public sector. As such, private education has increasingly become the sector of choice even for locals, placing a primary reliance on international assessments to measure performance. This situation produces a heavy reliance on an expatriate teaching force and has created a host of tensions and challenges for the education sector. Among these challenges is the growing concern over the loss of local culture and heritage. Most, if not all, GCC governments have made it a national priority within the education sector to find ways to preserve local culture and heritage—namely the Arabic language and Islamic values. However, with English Language as the de facto language of instruction in the blossoming private education sector and arguably also infiltrating public sector schools particularly in subject areas considered "core" such as Math and Science—the place, relevance, and efficacy of Arabic is increasingly unclear. In places like Qatar, decisions to overturn English as the medium of instruction in public schools may have been welcomed by some; however, it remains a point of contention for others. The plight to ensure public schools are able to provide a globally competitive education remains. Low levels of literacy, underachievement of boys, inconsistent teacher qualifications, and continued reliance on and high turnover of expatriate educators are just some of the challenges associated with K–12 public education in GCC nations, in addition to the language debate.

In the private schooling sector, the preservation of local culture and heritage are equally challenging. With a plethora of international education providers, international curricula, and increasingly diverse learners and educators, GCC private schools are feared to becoming cultural enclaves or cultural bubbles within an existing local culture. Schools are arguably the best suited to serve as the conduit for achieving national priorities among GCC states to foster an appreciation for local cultures and heritages but also to foster social cohesion. However, to what extent will an international British or American curriculum school go beyond tokenistic national celebrations or mandated cultural interventions? In most private schools, the teaching of Islamic studies remains on the periphery, Arabic language no more than a necessary hurdle, and intercultural understanding celebratory. The primary focus for schools in the GCC private education sector is competition. The pressures on private schools (and by virtue educators and students) in the GCC to perform is indicative of the impacts of internationalization that cannot be understated. The high-stakes performativity and accountability educational culture where schools are publicly ranked, where inspection results hold implications for licensure and tuition, and where test scores on international assessments determine teaching effectiveness hold serious implications for how learning and teaching takes place in the GCC. National priorities of aspiring for educational global competitiveness are undoubtedly important. However, with the pace at which GCC education systems have evolved in the recent past, significant pressures have been placed on educators to be rapidly upskilled and/or perform; for a new educational policy culture to be defined, implemented, and renewed; for the overabundance of international curricula to be assessed, evaluated, and supported; and in the end for students to adapt to a seemingly ever-evolving system of education that at times feels incessantly in a flux.

ORGANIZATION OF THIS BOOK

In light of the aims and goals of this volume in addressing the challenges and complexities of internationalizing education and teacher training in the GCC, the chapters of this volume have been separated into three themes: cultural barriers in teacher education; pedagogical approaches and praxis in teacher education; and ways forward in teacher education and development. The first section of the volume is composed of three chapters and aims to contextualize a number of obstacles posed by preserving the culture and identity of the region through schooling systems, which have predominantly given preference to the English language as a mode of instruction and have framed Western cultures and ways of knowing as normative. This section of the volume has included chapters which explore the challenges and complexities of religious and language instruction in GCC nations. Both language and religion are cultural elements and identifiers, which are central to the identities of the citizenry of the GCC. However, in practice, these aspects of culture have been relegated as subjects of lesser importance and continue to be underdeveloped components of the curricula in most GCC nations (Bakali, Alhashmi, & Memom 2018). The three chapters in this section examine the opportunities and gaps in religious instruction in the United Arab Emirates (UAE), the development of reflexive teaching practices of Islamic education teachers in Qatar, and the shifting paradigms of Arabic language pedagogy and the associated opportunities and challenges in developing Arabic language instruction in the UAE. These chapters highlight a number of critical issues associated with religious and language instruction, discuss approaches for cultural preservation, and provide an overview of the current state of educational praxis and teacher training in the fields of Islamic pedagogy and Arabic language instruction in the GCC.

The second section of the volume shifts focus toward pedagogical challenges and opportunities associated with teaching practices employed by schools of education in the GCC. This section consists of four chapters that cover a range of teaching approaches promoted in GCC schools of education including special needs education, educational leadership, and teacher identity development. More specifically, this section of the volume will provide valuable insights on the preparedness of Omani educators for teaching inclusive education and how gaps in this field can serve as an impetus for educational reform in Oman. This section will also explore pedagogical development needs of preservice and in-service educators in the UAE, with regard to their abilities in teaching children with special educational needs. Furthermore, the section will examine the notion of teacher quality in the context of the 2020–2021 COVID-19 pandemic through the dimensions of teacher education, educational leadership, and student recruitment, using a Bahraini teacher education program as a case study. The final chapter of this section will discuss the intangible qualities and experiences that need to be fostered and developed in teacher education, through reflections from a teacher training program in the UAE. These chapters cover a diverse range of topics; however, they are all bound by the common theme of exploring the practices of teaching promoted in schools of education in the region and how these practices can be further developed.

The final section of the volume provides guidance and suggestions, drawing from the critical challenges and complexities outlined in the previous two sections, to chart a course moving teacher training and development in the GCC forward. Here, important discussions and insights will be presented on theoretical approaches for transformative educational praxis and how these frameworks can be taken up within schools of education. This section consists of four chapters. The first of these chapters focuses on the importance of promoting critical consciousness or conscientization within teacher training programs to enable GCC educators to face the challenges of internationalizing education. Building on the first chapter of this section, the second chapter explores the potential for incorporating the notion of critical consciousness in technical and vocational education and training (TVET) teacher professional development in the GCC. These two chapters provide a theoretical bedrock for developing transformative teaching praxis in GCC schools of education and teacher training. The final two chapters aim to address the cultural barriers that have arisen from internationalizing education in the GCC between schools of education and preservice and in-service teachers who attend these schools. This will be accomplished by discussing the potential and need for an asset-based and culturally responsive pedagogy being promoted in the region, with particular emphasis on the UAE as a model for such an approach.

This book will present a nuanced appreciation of specific themes that critically engage with the complexity and evolution of teacher education in the GCC. It will provide up-to-date accounts and analysis of the challenges and complexities of internationalizing education in the GCC through exploring the cultural barriers, teaching practices, and educational reforms present in various country contexts in the region. There are a number of schools of education in Saudi Arabia, Kuwait, the UAE, Qatar, Bahrain, and Oman. Professors, researchers, and specialists working in these nations have contributed to this volume with the intent of empowering educators with authentic and contextualized research and insights to advance collective understanding of the complexities and challenges of teacher education and training in the GCC. Ultimately, we hope that this work will serve as a practical tool and resource that will be employed by schools of education to provide authentic insights, strategies, and research to further develop teacher training in the GCC and globally.

REFERENCES

Alhashmi, Mariamm, Bakali, Naved, & Baroud, Rama. 2020. "Tolerance in UAE Islamic Education Textbooks" *Religions*, 11(8), 377. https://doi.org/10.3390/rel11080377.

Bakali, Naved, Alhashmi, Mariam, & Memon, Nadeem. 2018. *Islamic education in the United Arab Emirates: an assessment of the challanges, gaps, and opportunities*. Policy Report, Abu Dhabi: Tabah Foundation.

Collaborative for Academic, Social, and Emotional Learning (CASEL) https://casel .org/what-is-sel/.

Connelly, L. M. 2015. "Life-Worlds in Phenomenology." *Medsurg Nursing*, 24(2), 119–120.

Durlak, J. A., Dymnicki, A. B., Taylor, R. D., Weissberg, R. P., & Schellinger, K. B. 2011. "The impact of enhancing students' social and emotional learning: A meta-analysis of school-based universal interventions." *Child Development*, 82(1), 405–432. doi:10.1111/j.1467-8624.2010.01564.

Freimuth, H. 2014. "Who are our students? A closer look at the educational and socio-cultural influences that have shaped Emirati students." *The KUPP Journal*, 3, 37–48. Retrieved December 30, 2020, from http://www.kustar.ac.ae/source/academics/prepprogram/kupp-journal-issue3-june2014.pdf 2014.

Freire, Paulo. 2015. *Pedagogy of Hope: Reliving Pedagogy of the Oppressed*. New York, NY: Bloomsbury.

Gallagher, Kay. 2019. "Challenges and Opportunities in Sourcing, Preparing and Developing a Teaching Force for the UAE." In *Education in the United Arab Emirates* edited by Kay Gallagher, 127–145. Singapore: Springer.

Giroux, Henry A. 2001. *Theory and Resistance in Education: Towards a Pedagogy for the Opposition.* Westport, CT: Bergin & Garvey.

Green, B. 2003. "An unfinished project? Garth Boomer and the pedagogical imagination." *Opinion: Journal of the South Australian English Teachers' Association,* 47(2), 1324.

Hattam, R., & Zipin, L. 2009. "Towards pedagogical justice Discourse Studies in the Cultural Politics of Education: 'Symposium 1: Global/National Pressures On Schooling Systems. *The Andrew Bell Lecture Series'* and *'Symposium 2: Re-Designing Pedagogy,'"* 30(3), 297–301.

Lingard, Bob & McGregor, Glenda. 2014 "Two contrasting Australian Curriculum responses to globalisation: what students should learn or become," *Curriculum Journal (London, England),* 25(1), pp. 90–110.

Morrison, A., Rigney, L.-I., Hattam, R., & Diplock, A. 2019. "Toward an Australian culturally responsive pedagogy: A narrative review of the literature." Retrieved from Australia: https://apo.org.au/sites/default/files/resource-files/2019/08/apo-nid 262951-1392016.pdf.

Price, D. & McCallum, F. 2016. Wellbeing in education (Chapter 1). In *Nurturing Wellbeing Development in Education: From Little Things Big Things Grow,* edited by F. McCallum, & D. Price. London & New York: Routledge. ISBN: 978-1-138-79382-8.

Priestley, M, Biesta, M. R., & Robinson, G. 2015. *Teacher Agency: An Ecological Approach / by Mark Priestley, Gert Biesta, and Sarah Robinson.* London; New York: Bloomsbury Academic, an imprint of Bloomsbury Publishing, Plc.

Part I

CULTURAL BARRIERS IN TEACHER EDUCATION

Chapter 1

The Challenges and Complexities of Religious Education in the UAE

Naved Bakali and Mariam Alhashmi

INTRODUCTION

In the context of globalization, Gulf Cooperation Council (GCC) nations have become increasingly multicultural societies. The United Arab Emirates (UAE) is a country composed of more than 200 nationalities with various religious and ethnic communities (Chaudhry 2016). In light of this, promoting the values of moderation, mutual respect, and acceptance of other cultures within an Islamic worldview is essential for fostering a pluralistic and cohesive society (Bakali & Alhashmi 2021). Muslim youth residing in the UAE are required to take Islamic education classes at every grade level throughout their primary and secondary schooling. As such, this program can profoundly impact and shape everyday Muslim youth identities in the country. The Islamic education curriculum in the UAE is offered in Arabic or English, depending on students' first language. Both curricula are identical, as the English program is translated based on the locally developed Arabic curriculum. This chapter explores the challenges and complexities of religious education in UAE private and public schools through an ethnographic approach. By engaging in open-ended and semi-structured interviews with UAE Islamic education teachers and parents of Islamic education students, this study aimed to: (1) examine important societal values promoted in the UAE to see how/if they are in alignment with Islamic education programming; (2) explore the lived experiences of teachers of the Islamic education program; and (3) discuss the gaps and opportunities that exist in further developing and enhancing Islamic education programming in the UAE. This analysis is of particular importance as Islamic education is sometimes accused of having limited relevance for students, with the potential of fostering intolerant attitudes toward others (Elbih 2012). The insights gleaned from

3

this study challenge such perceptions and further provide a nuanced understanding of the role of Islamic education in forming a meaningful aspect of Muslim children's formal schooling in the UAE.

CONTEXTUALIZING THE UAE ISLAMIC EDUCATIONAL LANDSCAPE

Islamic education, like most forms of religious instruction, is intended to foster a strong sense of identity, inculcate values rooted in a religious tradition, and nurture the student's responsibility toward self, community, and humanity broadly (Zine 2008). An essential component of Islamic education is imparting *adab*, often translated as "etiquette" or character education, but also entails a sense of civic responsibility and moral values (Al-Attas 1979).

The terms "Islamic education" and "values" have been frequently exploited and misconstrued in various contemporary discourses related to Islam, Muslims, and global affairs. This has led many mainstream religious institutions to qualify normative understandings of Islam with the description "moderate" that is rooted in Quranic Arabic words signifying balance, moderation, and the middle path (Alhashmi, Bakali, & Baroud 2020). UAE government documents commonly precede the terms "Islam," "Islamic education," or "Islamic values" with "moderate," in order to distinguish a national perspective on Islamic education and values:

> Ambitious and responsible Emiratis will successfully carve out their future, actively engaging in an evolving socio-economic environment, and drawing on their strong families and communities, *moderate Islamic values*, and deep-rooted heritage to build a vibrant and well-knit society. [Emphasis added] (Government of the UAE 2020)

The Ministry of Culture, Youth, and Community Development (now known as the Ministry of Culture and Knowledge Development) defined an "Ideal Citizen of the UAE" as being loyal, religious, educated, fluent in Arabic, connected to the Arab world, open and interactive to the whole world, positive and able to take initiative, empowering of women, productive, ethical, aware of one's history, endowed with a strategic vision, family-oriented, and hospitable (Ministry of Culture, Youth, and Community Development 2009). Furthermore, the country's vision statement for 2021 states that the UAE aspires to foster "deep rooted heritage to build a vibrant and well-knit society," one that embraces "moral values," "in the face of multiculturalism" (Government of the UAE 2020). Piecing these and other statements together illustrates that religious values are indeed an important aspect of UAE national identity and one that schools play a significant role in imparting.

The Islamic education curriculum taught in all public and private schools across the UAE is regulated by the Ministry of Education. All Muslim students in the UAE are provided with Islamic education as part of the school daily program with the allocated time ranging between 90 and 180 minutes weekly depending on the type of school and the grade level. The Islamic education curriculum attempts to maintain the interaction of the presented concepts with real-life issues, while fostering the development of the students' thinking skills. As the official 2011 UAE National Islamic Education Curriculum document asserts, "the Qur'an and the Prophetic tradition are not dealt with as materials to be memorized only, rather, they are also the material for generating topics and constructing ideas and arguments" (UAE Ministry of Education 2014, 9). The curriculum employs a value-based approach and states that "values are an aim for every component of this curriculum and are a behavioral objective for every part of it" (UAE Ministry of Education 2014, 9). Consequently, values and attitudes are highlighted in every lesson of the Islamic education textbooks. The curriculum is also based on "a practical vision of Islam that nurtures a human being who is an active citizen and who makes positive contributions to their society" (UAE Ministry of Education 2014, 9). Within this vision, the value of tolerance is placed as a core tenant of the developed curriculum. The curriculum textbooks and teaching guides are produced and provided to all schools by the Ministry of Education and are aligned with the developed standards. An exception to this was the Islamic education curriculum provided to the Muslim non-Arabic-speaking students. The adopted English Islamic education curriculum, up to the academic year 2016–2017, was the "I Love Islam" series, a North American developed K–12 Islamic educational curriculum (I Love Islam Books 2017). However, starting from the academic year 2017–2018, the Ministry of Education made an English version of the locally developed curriculum available to all schools. Islamic studies textbooks serve as a guide for instruction, including the means and ends of instruction. Additional teaching and assessment strategies are included in separate teachers' manuals.

The seven areas under which the learning outcomes of the Islamic education curriculum are organized are "Islamic values and purposes, divine revelation, Islamic rules and character, mentality of faith, biography, identity and belonging, and the human and the universe" (UAE Ministry of Education 2014, 17). These categories do not resemble traditional approaches to Islamic sciences. Rather, they indicate an attempt to apply a concept-based curriculum through the use of discipline aligned concepts. The use of these conceptual lenses adds depth to the material and fosters synergetic thinking—a situation where there is a strong interplay between factual and conceptual knowledge (Erickson 2002). The curriculum standards reflect an approach toward a concept-based curriculum as opposed to a facts-based curriculum at a high level as resembled by the seven curricular themes. The themes and standards were further detailed in a separate document, published in 2014 (UAE Ministry of Education 2014). This separate curriculum document identified what students should know and be able to do in a particular discipline of knowledge (Ornstein & Hunkins 2009).

The considerable expatriate community in the UAE has fueled the need for a massive private education sector, which includes British, American, and other Western curriculum-based schools, in addition to the public school system. Islamic education in the public school system is strictly regulated by the Ministry of Education, with stringent rules in place to ensure strong standards of teachers, adequate time allotment for the subject, as well as a general culture that gives importance to the subject matter. Islamic education in the private system is also regulated by the Ministry of Education, which enforces similar rules to the public sector. However, in the private sector, the level of importance given to Islamic education is greatly influenced by the school's culture and the administrative teams within the schools (Bakali, Alhashmi, & Memon 2018). Some private schools place a high priority on engendering Islamic values in their student body. Such schools will make strident efforts to integrate Islamic teachings and values throughout their curricula in addition to offering students the Islamic education curriculum that is mandated in the UAE. Hence, Islamic education and values are integrated within the school through a cross-curricular approach to inculcate a sense of Islam as a lived reality. Islam forms an essential component of the DNA of such private schools and is instilled within the administration of the school, which provides the vision for the educational landscape, through to the teachers who develop lessons that are ingrained with Islamic values. At the other end of the spectrum, some schools have a culture that emphasizes STEM subject areas (science, technology, engineering, and mathematics) and may not promote Islamic values as a part of their core identity (Alhashmi, Bakali, & Baroud 2020). Such schools view their institution as responsible for providing academic tools and training that will lead to the pursuit of higher education. Although these schools may not promote the notion that Islamic values are incompatible with academic success, they have ultimately devalued the importance of Islamic education in the process of attaining academic excellence. Most private schools in the UAE fall somewhere between these two types of school culture in relation to their promotion of Islamic education and values. Based upon these contextualized realities, this study aimed to explore the challenges and complexities of religious schooling in the UAE.

THEORETICAL FRAMING OF ISLAMIC EDUCATION

To better understand the positionality of the participants in this study, it is useful to briefly touch on conceptualizations of Islamic education and pedagogy. Islamic education has traditionally been derived from the concept of *ta'līm* (learning). An important author on this topic was Al-Zarnuji (d. 1223 CE), who wrote the foundational work *Ta'līm al-Muta'allim-Ṭarīq at-Ta'-allum* (*Instruction of the Student: The Method of Learning*). This treatise was a reference for this study because it was one of the first written works on education in the Islamic tradition. It is not intended to be an exhaustive framework but is an exemplary text that reflects the features of learning in the Islamic tradition, which helped us to understand traditional worldviews related to Islamic education and pedagogy. Al-Zarnuji (2003) focused on the learning process rather than the teaching methods. This approach differentiated him from previous Muslim authors on the subject of Islamic education. The features of *ta'līm* based on Al-Zarnuji's work include some of the following aspects: the obligation of seeking knowledge, which states that learners are required to seek knowledge relating to the work that they are engaged in, as whatever leads to the fulfillment of duty is in itself a duty; the notion of continuity, which entails that a Muslim is required to institutionalize learning as a daily form of worship throughout their life; purposefulness, which indicates that the process of learning is mainly constructed based on the learner's intention; perseverance, which emphasizes the requirement of hard work and the dedication of ample time to master the learned knowledge; and mastery, which implies the learner should aim to achieve a deep understanding of their chosen subject and gradually attain a firm grasp of the material by exerting themselves efficiently without bypassing or overlooking any knowledge.

One drawback to the work of Al-Zarnuji is that there is little discussion on the importance of the application of learned knowledge. However, one can find that the aspect of the application is extensively discussed in many other Islamic traditional texts such as 'O dear beloved son!' by al-Ghazali (d. 1111). The above-mentioned features of *ta'līm* (learning) provided a grounding for understanding how teachers of Islamic education in this study conceptualized and approached the subject matter, as well as provided insights as to how they perceived this topic in relation to their students.

METHODOLOGY

This exploration was an ethnographic study, which involved interviewing private and public Islamic education teachers, as well as parents of students who attended Islamic education classes in the UAE. Interviewing of teachers and parents took place between August 2018 and May 2019. In total, nine teacher participants were interviewed (seven women and two men), across five private schools and four public schools in the UAE. Four parent participants were interviewed to provide additional insights about their own and their children's experiences with the Islamic education program in the UAE. Interviews were semi-structured offering open-ended questions relating to participants' experiences with Islamic education in schools, their views regarding challenges and opportunities for Islamic education in the region, and their insights on areas of concern. Upon completion, participant interviews were transcribed. Interview transcripts along with audio-recorded interviews served as primary data sources that formed the basis of our analysis for this study. Through this analytical process, emergent themes were codified through the transcripts.

EXPLORING THE LIVED REALITIES AND COMPLEXITIES OF ISLAMIC EDUCATION IN THE UAE

Having described the context of Islamic education, some of the details relating to the curriculum, and the methods employed for data collection, the chapter now turns to a thematic analysis of key findings through the interview process. The key themes that emerged from interviews included discussions about societal values within the UAE and how they impact the Islamic education curriculum, the structural dynamics of Islamic education in the public and private school systems, and Islamic educational curricula in relation to students. The chapter will now discuss these emergent themes in more detail.

Societal Values within the Islamic Education Curriculum

Participants interviewed in this study strongly felt that the promotion of diversity and multiculturalism in the UAE was essential to promote cohesiveness in society. Participants in both public and private schools felt that multiculturalism and tolerance were essential values that needed to be promoted to reflect the differences and diversity of UAE society. They described how these topics were addressed through the textbooks at various grade levels of the Islamic education program. Participants particularly discussed the value of "tolerance" and its promotion in the UAE. They explained how tolerance was promoted by the state through various initiatives, such as designating 2019 as the Year of Tolerance, the building of religious structures by the state for minority faith groups, and events taking place in the country to celebrate diversity as a strength. Participants understood the notion of tolerance in UAE society as reflected through the promotion of religious plurality. Therefore, a number of them described how Pope Francis's visit to the UAE in February 2019 was an indication of how the UAE was tolerant, as Christianity is a minority faith in the country and the papal visit was a historic event in the region. Furthermore, the Pope held mass in the capital to an estimated crowd of over 100,000 UAE residents. Participants felt that UAE culture had evolved through the diverse populations living in the country, which partially explained why tolerance was needed and beneficial to society. In addition to supporting cohesiveness, participants discussed how tolerance was essential to enriching the UAE. Tolerance was essential because they felt there needed to be an acknowledgment that other cultures have differing ways of doing things, which may enable members of the host society to learn from these differences. In other words, through a process of promoting tolerance, there could be a healthy and respectful exchange of ideas and views. This had the potential of bringing about positive change in one's community, even if these changes may be perceived as "strange" at the outset. Furthermore, participants felt that diversity in the student body in their schools promoted the exchange of different ideas, expressing different views, as well as learning to accept and respect the "other."

When participants were asked if they felt that the theme of tolerance formed a major or foundational component of educational curricula in the UAE, most participants felt that the theme of tolerance represented a meaningful portion of the Islamic educational curriculum. A number of participants discussed how there were entire chapters in the Islamic education textbooks at various grade levels, particularly at the senior levels, which were dedicated to the topic of tolerance. Furthermore, related themes to tolerance and multiculturalism, such as civic engagement, religious plurality in the UAE, globalization, and equity in Islam also formed meaningful themes in the Islamic education curriculum. Participants mentioned how discussion of these topics in the Islamic education program helped provide an authentic Islamic discourse to frame these issues as "Islamic" concepts. In addition to important societal values being discussed in the Islamic education curriculum, participants also discussed the central role of the teacher in providing a meaningful Islamic educational experience in UAE schools.

Teaching, Structural Dynamics, and Challenges of Islamic Education in the UAE

Overwhelmingly, all stakeholders who participated in this study described the paramount importance of the role of the teacher in Islamic education. Teachers who were described as the most effective in teaching the program and in achieving its objectives had deep Islamic knowledge and awareness and were highly skilled in teaching methods. They were able to connect the course content with real-life situations. These teachers were able to demonstrate how Islamic education was not simply a theoretical form of knowledge, but had practical and relevant applications for students' daily lives. Furthermore, effective teachers, according to participants, incorporated differentiation in their teaching activities. These teachers avoided teacher-centered approaches, such as lecturing or showing a video for the full class period. Rather, they incorporated multiple approaches to engage students as active participants in the learning process. This included undertaking group activities, creating spaces for children to demonstrate what they have learned, engaging in group discussions, incorporating audiovisuals, offering variations in assessment techniques—such as oral testing and producing original content—challenging students to use higher order cognition, providing websites and other online tools for supplemental materials, and finding ways for students to practically apply Islamic education in their daily lives. Good teachers, according to participants, were not only passionate about the subject matter, but viewed the topic as an immense responsibility with which they had been entrusted. These beliefs expressed by teacher participants resonated with Al-Zarnuji's views on the obligatory nature of Islamic knowledge and its continuity, as much of the content taught in Islamic education classes related to personal obligations within the faith. Unfortunately, many teachers that we interviewed were not able to be as dedicated as they wished because of the impracticalities and challenges inherent in the way their schools' structured Islamic education classes. Participants frequently described the structuring of Islamic education in the private school system as posing a number of challenges.

The inherent dynamics of private and public schools create different practicalities for Islamic education in these settings. As many private schools have a smaller Muslim student population than public schools, there are fewer sections of Islamic education courses taught at each grade level compared to the public system. As such, in order for Islamic education teachers to have a complete workload, they are usually required to teach multiple grade levels. Some participants explained that they had to teach as many as seven different grade-level groups. In this scenario, teachers needed to be familiar with multiple curricula for the various grade levels, as opposed to being able to specialize in one or two grade levels. Many private school teachers were overburdened with course preparation and learning the content of the different curricula and seldom had the time or energy to employ differentiated practices in their classrooms. As such, it comes as little surprise that school inspection results from the Knowledge and Human Development Authority (KHDA) and the Department of Education and Knowledge (ADEK) over the past few years in both Dubai and Abu Dhabi reveal that no private schools have achieved an "outstanding" rating in Islamic education, including the top tier schools in the country (Abu Dhabi University Knowledge Group 2017).

Islamic education teachers' workloads were less of an issue in the public school system, which had larger student populations and were composed almost entirely of Muslim students. This meant that they had more students at each grade level and, therefore, more sections for Islamic education at each grade level. Hence, many public school teachers were able to teach multiple sections in fewer grade levels and could specialize, as well as fully familiarize themselves with the course content for these classes. As less time was spent on class preparation, due to the fewer grade levels taught, public school teachers theoretically had more opportunities to create engaging and differentiated lessons for their students.

Another factor, which brought about challenges was that teachers across subject areas had very high turnover rates and were mostly expatriates, particularly in private schools. Therefore, they were more likely to be risk averse and reluctant to try innovative and differentiated practices out of fear that they may be violating cultural norms or face reprisal for their actions. Many teachers of the Islamic education program avoided trying new and innovative approaches and opted to employ placid techniques to avoid drawing unnecessary attention to themselves. Teachers also discussed how there was a lack of opportunities available to them for professional development, which was theoretically built into their work schedules. This allocation toward professional development would appear in their spare periods when they were not teaching. As such, the responsibility for engaging in professional development fell squarely on the teachers themselves. However, due to their burdensome workloads, teachers would often use time slotted for professional development toward preparing their lessons or catching up on other tasks. Participants mentioned that in order for professional development to be meaningful it would require ongoing collaborative programs with opportunities for application and feedback. It should also address sensitive questions or objections that face Islamic education teachers such as those related to the areas of women's rights, differences between Muslim sects and in jurisprudence rulings, and rulings related to contemporary issues. Most teachers were only allotted an hour and a half in the week for professional development, which was not enough time to learn and practically incorporate meaningful knowledge and skills. Beyond the complexities inherent in the dynamics and structure of Islamic education programming, participants also described challenges associated with teaching their students.

Islamic Educational Curriculum in Relation to Students

As previously mentioned, the UAE is a very diverse and multicultural society. Many Islamic education classes in the country reflect this diversity, as students came from differing backgrounds with regard to religiosity and adherence to religious traditions. This was more pronounced in private schools. A number of private schools visited for the purpose of this study had very diverse and heterogenous Islamic education classroom environments. Some students in these classes were from households where religious instruction was not highly encouraged or appreciated. Negotiating expectations with regard to content, adherence to religious values, and differing worldviews created some tensions for Islamic education teachers, as they were required to navigate the sensitive topic of religion and religious instruction among students with differing views about the faith and its place in society. Teachers also alluded to how sometimes they were confronted with challenges by their students about topics, which may have contradicted information or messages they were receiving at home. Another challenge that teacher participants from private schools discussed was related to students that came from mixed religious backgrounds.

Teachers described how a number of their students came from mixed religious traditions, having one parent who was not Muslim. In some instances, parents of these students were not in favor of their children receiving religious instruction in their schools. However, as Islamic education was a required course for students who were classified as "Muslim," these students had to take Islamic education classes. Teachers often described difficult questions posed by students from mixed religious backgrounds and how managing differing worldviews created a number of challenges for them. Some teachers observed that a few of the parents of their students felt apprehension toward their children learning about Islam. Some of these parents felt that certain topics in the Islamic education program clashed with their values and beliefs. Despite the challenges associated with teaching Muslim students from non-religious families or students with parents from mixed religious traditions, teachers described how they tried to create judgment-free spaces in their classrooms to engage their students in meaningful conversations. Teachers empowered their students to voice their opinions, views, and concerns with regard to their religious beliefs and religious instruction even though they perceived these types of situations as challenging and uncomfortable.

Public school teachers described very different experiences in their Islamic education classes. Public schools in the UAE had more homogeneous student populations, with the majority of students being Muslim UAE nationals. However, teachers asserted the importance of their students learning about different cultures, as the UAE was composed of culturally and religiously diverse residents. In one instance described by a participant, her students partook in a Model United Nations forum. By participating in this event, students were able to interact with peers from different schools that were more culturally diverse. Through this process, the students were able to learn from the different viewpoints of the students attending this event. Furthermore, the participant's students were wearing the *hijab*, the Islamic head covering worn by many Muslim women, and were asked by the other attendees of the event about their *hijabs* and why they wore them. This exchange enabled students to share their thoughts and broadened their perspectives. The teacher participant felt that her students, as well as the students from other schools developed a greater sense of understanding of differences through this exchange. The teacher participant felt that these interactions between the students from different cultures and religious traditions attending this conference was an empowering experience. This event created opportunities for students to learn more about and garner an appreciation for other cultural and religious practices. Such introductory exchanges were positive entry points to further dialogue and discussions about tolerance and acceptance of differing world-views. Other participants also discussed how the Islamic education textbooks made efforts to discuss various religious traditions to promote inclusivity of differing religious perspectives. This was particularly important in the public school settings where a minority of students came from the Shiite Islamic tradition.

One participant described how the Islamic education textbooks at the grade 10 level discuss an important woman figure, Sukainah bint Alhussain, who is greatly venerated by Shiite Muslims. This participant felt that discussion of Sukainah was important and the curriculum developers who included her did so with a sense of wisdom. However, the participant observed that some students had objections to this lesson. She described how she would regularly be questioned by Sunni students as to why this figure in particular was selected to be discussed in their classes. Despite the students' objections to this topic, they still understood that such objections needed to be done in private because open criticism of this topic would be discriminatory. Nonetheless, the participant felt that through these discussions students were able to garner a better understanding and respect for religious differences. Though teacher participants described how they tried to create open spaces for dialogue in their classes, they still felt that students were vulnerable to misinformation.

The UAE like many other Muslim majority nations face a number of challenges when it comes to open sources of information through mass communications technologies. Through the internet, social media, and other technological devices, students are able to access information from essentially everywhere and anywhere. This creates countless opportunities to learn about various cultures, religions, and worldviews. However, it also opens up the doors for miseducation with regard to religious matters. This was a major concern discussed by a number of parents and teacher participants in both public and private schools. With regard to Islamic rulings, one teacher participant described how her students would ask her about rulings that they were not accustomed to concerning daily prayers and Muslim dress code. She would inform her students that some of these arise from legitimate differences of opinions within Islamic jurisprudence and that they are acceptable differences. The participant would try to explain how there was diversity in Islamic rulings and these differences should be respected; however, this did bring about tensions in her class. Another participant discussed how some students would dispute with her regarding the *hijab* and argued that the head veil was not an obligatory aspect of Muslim women's dress code. The participant welcomed these questions and concerns and tried to create a judgment-free space for her students to discuss these issues. She mentioned that she would try to challenge her students' views by referring to canonical religious texts and advised them to ensure that they took their knowledge from authenticated sources. In this instance, we see how the teacher participant was impressing Al-Zarnuji's notion of perseverance and mastery to her students. As the participant believed proper knowledge of Islamic tradition came from referencing authenticated resources and not simply accessing easily available information that may not be rigorously authenticated.

Ultimately, it was challenging for the teacher participant to straddle between what she felt were religious requirements and rulings and being open to differing views of students on the subject. Other teachers discussed concerns of how students could be exposed to extremist ideas through the internet, communications technologies, and social media. Though a number of these platforms are limited in the UAE through government regulations, teachers still felt it was an important area of concern. As such, participants felt it was essential to provide spaces for students to ask questions about these issues in their Islamic education classes to challenge extremist narratives even if these were difficult conversations to have. Having described the complexities and challenges associated with the structuring and teaching of Islamic education in the UAE, the chapter now discusses possible solutions and ways forward to develop and enhance this program.

FUTURE DIRECTIONS OF ISLAMIC EDUCATION IN THE UAE

From this exploration of Islamic education in UAE schools, there were a number of areas that participants identified as needing further development to increase their students' abilities to confidently engage in the global marketplace of ideas through an Islamic worldview. The interplay of various religions, cultures, and perspectives in the UAE necessitates that younger generations be prepared to confidently engage with them. The Islamic education curriculum is well placed to offer this, as religion forms the bed-rock of culture, values, and identity for many residents in the country.

Participants' responses indicated a strong need and emphasis toward professional development for teachers. For example, a number of the teacher participants described that there was an eagerness among students to learn about themes such as pluralism, multiculturalism, and tolerance. Islamic education teachers for the most part felt that their students were very receptive to these topics. However, a number of teachers felt they needed some type of professional development or additional training to address these issues in an appropriate manner. Though a number of these themes do come up in the Islamic education curriculum through the textbooks used by the teachers, these topics, like many others in the curriculum, are relatively new and traditionally have not been addressed in Islamic education textbooks. Professional development is something that is encouraged in schools across the UAE; however, practically speaking, most teachers were not able to benefit from this time that was allotted to them. Instead of having professional development built into teachers' schedules as a small apportioned amount of time over the span of a week, a more effective and useful approach would be to give larger chunks of time incrementally across the school year. As previously stated, teachers expressed how they needed at minimum half a day or more to learn useful and important skills and how to implement them in a classroom setting. This type of professional training would have more meaningful and lasting impacts for teachers. The timings that teachers felt would be most useful for professional development were during downtimes in the school year. Such times could be in the autumn before students return to school, at the end of the year when students finish exams, or right after mid-year testing and holidays. This approach places professional development in the hands of the schools' administrative team and does not place the burden on teachers who do not have ample opportunities to engage in professional development during their spare periods. Professional development needs to be practical, accessible, and relevant. A shift toward professional learning and the differentiation of professional growth opportunity was indicated by the participants. In order to come up with these professional development opportunities, participants felt that teachers needed to be consulted directly to ascertain their needs and to understand the challenges that they faced in the classroom. Another area that participants felt required specific attention was support for facilitating teacher specialization.

When teachers are required to teach five or six different grade levels, they become overburdened by lesson preparation. In these circumstances, teachers were often learning the curriculum as they were teaching it to their students. Concrete steps need to be taken to help reduce the lesson preparation burden. Some possible approaches could include creating lesson plan databases, facilitating and encouraging teacher collaborative work, and offering Islamic education resources and online learning support materials to teachers. By relieving some of the content burden for teachers, more opportunities would be gained for studying the grade-specific curricula and becoming grade-level specialists. When teachers have strong expertise in course content, they can invest their time in quality planning. They are better equipped to teach dynamic lessons, make efforts toward enrichment, create innovative lesson plans, and develop resources that can better facilitate a robust learning environment (Erickson, Lanning, & French 2017). Participants' comments suggested that teachers needed to become more specialized to effectively teach grade-specific Islamic education classes, as students become more engaged when teachers have stronger expert knowledge on content. Furthermore, participants felt that if teachers were making efforts to engage in enriching activities for their classes, they should be offered occasional release time to develop educational materials including course webpages, educational games, digital media, and other relevant digital learning tools. Another key area of improvement raised by participants was teacher retention and overcoming risk aversion to exercise more autonomy in their classes.

As teaching in the UAE is a profession with a high turnover rate, one of the greatest challenges for schools is retaining talented teaching staff. Measures should be taken to ensure that good teachers want to stay for the long term. Experienced teachers not only have a stronger experiential knowledge base, but can also provide mentorship to younger teachers who are still learning the profession (Palmer 1998). Additionally, if schools want their faculty to be innovative and be able to stimulate students' interest in Islamic education, teachers need to be less risk averse. Teachers need to feel a stronger sense of security if they are to try new and innovative practices in the classroom. Teaching needs to occur in a safe space where teachers are less concerned with being penalized for trying different teaching practices, and can expend more energy finding innovative ways to make Islamic education relevant and accessible to their students. Teachers will not feel afraid to try new approaches in their classes if they are assured that they will not be punished for trying new teaching methods and strategies that may or may not work. Finally, participants expressed that they needed greater access to resources for teaching the Islamic education program.

Aside from the Islamic education textbooks, teachers do not have access to sufficient resources to address multiculturalism, pluralism, tolerance, intolerance, and a number of other relevant and important issues that students are curious about. Many teachers have taken it upon themselves to develop resources and tools to teach these topics to their students. Given that some teachers have taken the initiative to develop these materials, it would be beneficial for novice teachers to have access to a collaborative online space where they could access resources that have been developed by their peers and colleagues. Such an open access platform could help Islamic education teachers supplement the existing resources that they have available to them through the Islamic education textbooks, which are important, but not sufficient on their own. In addition to having online platforms where teachers can share their resources, it would also be helpful if existing online resources were compiled in a centralized location as a resource list, where teachers could refer their students to when they have questions that they are unable to answer. A number of teachers discussed how their students are able to access unlimited resources through the internet, social media, and mass communication technologies. Some of this information may be useful and some may be contradictory to traditional Islamic views and teachings. As many students may not have the critical and analytical skills to decipher problematic content from authentic resources, teachers could help reduce some of these problems by providing their students with resource lists where they can find answers to their questions based on reliable sources.

CONCLUSION

Islamic education in UAE public and private schools forms an essential part of Muslim youth schooling. Muslim students in the UAE are required to take Islamic education classes every year of their formal education until they graduate from high school. Consequently, Islamic education curricula in the UAE forms an important aspect of daily Muslim youth lived experiences in the UAE. Islam is an integral part of the social and cultural identity of Muslim residents and Emiratis, as the state has branded itself as a country built on moderate Islamic values.

This study examined a number of challenges and complexities associated with teaching Islamic educational curricula in the UAE. Parent and teacher participants in this study described the importance of societal values and how they are reflected in the Islamic education curriculum. Furthermore, they described the complexities and dynamics of Islamic education in the UAE, which have brought about inefficiencies and challenges in teaching the program in a meaningful way.

Currently, there is little educational scholarship available on Islamic education curricula in the GCC in light of the challenges of modernity. This exploration of Islamic education provided insights on the gaps and opportunities in Islamic education curriculum development in the UAE and internationally. Furthermore, this study shed light on the complexity of Muslim youth cultures and religious instruction in the GCC and the pressures exerted on them in the context of globalization. As this qualitative analysis was an ethnographic study, the findings discussed were not meant to draw broad generalizations about UAE Islamic education teachers' experiences. Rather, by interviewing a smaller number of participants, this research was able to generate rich and in-depth data to provide meaningful insights on some of the lived realities of Islamic education in the UAE, as well as the challenges and complexities associated with it.

REFERENCES

Abu Dhabi University Knowledge Group. 2017. *Road to outstanding: a qualitative analysis of UAE school inspection reports.* White Paper, Abu Dhabi: Abu Dhabi University.

Al-Attas. 1979. "Preliminary thoughts on the nature of knowledge and the definition and aims of education." In *S.S. aims and objectives of Islamic education*, 19–45. Jeddah: King Abdulaziz University.

Alhashmi, Mariam, Naved Bakali, & Rama Baroud. 2020. "Tolerance in UAE Islamic education textbooks." *Religions* 11, no. 8: 377. https://doi.org/10.3390/rel11080377.

Alhashmi, Mariam, and Jase Moussa-Inaty. 2020. "Professional learning for Islamic education teachers in the UAE." *British Journal of Religious Education*, DOI: 10.1080/01416200.2020.1853046.

Al-Zarnuji, I. 2003. *Instruction of the student: The method of learning* (Von Grunebaum, G. E., & Abel, T. M., Trans.). New York: Starlatch Press.

Bakali, Naved, and Mariam Alhashmi. 2021. "Islamic education and youth culture: exploring the theme of tolerance in UAE Islamic education classrooms." In *Everyday youth cultures in the Gulf Peninsula: Changes and challenges*, by Emanuela Bescumi and Ildiko Kaposi, 201–216. London: Routledge.

Bakali, Naved, Mariam Alhashmi, and Nadeem Memon. 2018. *Islamic education in the United Arab Emirates: An assessment of the challenges, gaps, and opportunities.* Policy Report, Abu Dhabi: Tabah Foundation.

Chaudhry, Sujithra. 2016. "What makes UAE a role model of cohesion" *Gulf News: Society.* May 28. Accessed October 29, 2020. https://gulfnews.com/going-out/society/what-makes-uae-a-role-model-of-cohesion-1.1836341.

Elbih, Ronda. 2012. "Debates in the literature on Islamic schools." *Educational Studies* 48, no. 2: 156–173.

Erickson, H. Lynn, Lois Lanning, and Rachel French. 2017. *Concept-based curriculum and instruction for the thinking classroom.* Thousand Oaks: Corwin Press.

Erickson, H. Lynn. 2002. *Concept-based curriculum and instruction: Teaching beyond the facts.* Thousand Oaks: Corwin Press.

Government of the UAE. 2020. *Vision 2021 website.* January 20. Accessed October 15, 2020. https://www.vision2021.ae/en/uae-vision.

I Love Islam Books. 2020. *I Love Islam website.* Accessed February 10, 2020. www.iloveislambooks.com.

Ministry of Culture, Youth, and Community Development. 2009. *Ministry of Culture, Youth, and Community Development website*. Accessed September 6, 2013. https://mckd.gov.ae/sites/MCYCDVar/en-us/pages/faq.aspx.

Ornstein, Allan, and Francis Hunkins. 2009. *Curriculum: Foundations, principles, and issues, 5th edition*. Boston: Pearson.

Palmer, Parker. 1998. *The courage to teach: Exploring the inner landscape of a teacher's life*. San Francisco: Jossey-Bass.

UAE Ministry of Education. 2014. "The National Developed Document for the UAE Islamic Education Curriculum." *UAE Ministry of Education website*. Accessed December 20, 2017. https://www.moe.gov.ae/Arabic/Docs/Curriculum/Learning%20Standard/UAE%20Islamic%20Framework.pdf.

Zine, Jasmin. 2008. *Canadian Islamic schools: Unraveling the politics of faith, gender, knowledge and identity*. Toronto: University of Toronto Press.

Chapter 2

Developing a Reflexive Teaching Identity in a Cross-Cultural Teaching Context

The Experience of Islamic Studies Teachers in an International School in Qatar

Mohammed Adly Gamal

INTRODUCTION

International education has been seen by Gulf governments as an essential component of their aspiring views to shift from oil to a knowledge-based economy. The policies of internationalized education have led to a rapid growth of international schools where English is the medium of instruction and a transnational curriculum is taught. However, these schools are required to comply with the national regulations of GCC countries in which Arabic language and Islamic studies should be taught side by side with an international curriculum. As a result, there is an ongoing increase of Islamic studies teachers who join international schools. For this group of teachers, working in an international setting is a challenging task. In addition to linguistic barriers, Islamic studies teachers can face a dilemma between two philosophies of education. On the one hand, they should adhere to the Islamic educational traditions where audiocentrism is highly prized (Kalmbach 2020). Audiocentric teaching practices, such as memorization and recitation of Quran, are seen as an indispensable instrument to gain access to revealed knowledge. On the other hand, Islamic studies teachers are required to follow the pedagogical tenets of international schooling in which memorization is viewed at loggerheads with critical and analytical thinking skills. This belief is attributed to the centrality of ocularcentrism, which prioritizes sight over sound in Western traditions (Hirschkind 2006,

Tartaglia 2007). Additionally, since the age of enlightenment, educational discourse has viewed memorization as an antiquated practice because of its linkage to religious institutions (Carruthers 2008). As a result, Quran memorization has received much criticism and has been seen as inferior, compared with other teaching methods (Berglund and Gent 2018; Kalmbach 2020). These contested ideas may create a bewildering teaching space for the Islamic studies teachers who might face a dilemma between two conflicting pedagogical priorities.

This chapter explores how a group of Islamic studies teachers have navigated the terrain of international schooling where their traditional pedagogies might be unproductive to preserve the Islamic identity of their students. This group of teachers has attracted scant attention from the studies that examine the complexities of internationalized education across Gulf Cooperation Council (GCC) nations. This omission is coupled with the paucity of studies that draw the scholarly gaze of researchers to teachers within the literature of Islamic education (Memon 2011). I deploy the concept of teacher's identity as an analytic lens to discern the teachers' dispositions and their pedagogical decisions (Gee 2001). This study uses Archer's critical realist social theory of reflexivity (Archer 2003, 2012) to examine how Islamic studies teachers reflected upon their work in international schooling and how they acclimatized themselves to this new educational environment. In doing so, these teachers reconceptualized their role and rethought their pedagogical decisions.

The purpose of this study is threefold. First, as this volume analyzes the challenges that face teacher education in GCC countries, it is vital to recount the experience of working teachers to advise their prospective peers. Second, I seek to direct attention to Islamic studies teachers who have been omitted from the discussions over internationalized education in GCC countries and how internationalization has impacted them. Third, my chapter is intended to introduce the concept of teacher identity to the studies surrounding teacher education in GCC nations as this notion can reveal the concealed aspects of teachers' professional and personal lives (Day et al. 2006).

This chapter is based on a qualitative study conducted in an international school in Qatar. First, I will give a brief overview of the educational landscape in Qatar and the policies that created an environment conducive to the growth of international schooling. Furthermore, I will discuss the reasons behind the increasing popularity of international schools among parents in Qatar. Then, the concept of teacher identity will be articulated through the investigation of the literature. Afterwards, the theoretical framework and methodology of this study will be outlined. In the findings section, I will show how Islamic studies teachers have developed a reflexive identity by redefining their role and remolding their ideas about best pedagogical practices for teaching Islam.

Finally, the chapter concludes with some recommendations to improve teachers training programs in GCC institutions.

THE EDUCATIONAL LANDSCAPE OF QATAR AND
THE EMERGENCE OF INTERNATIONAL SCHOOLS

Before the public education system of Qatar was established, Quranic schools (al Kuttab) were the only form of schooling. The role of teachers (Mutawas) was to transmit the Qur'anic knowledge through memorization, in addition to Arabic literacy skills and simple arithmetic (Al-Kobaisi 1979). In 1952, Qatar had one primary school in which 240 students were enrolled and taught by six teachers. In 1980, the public education system of Qatar began to take shape as there were 141 schools across the state (Al-Maadheed 2012, Ammari 2004). By introducing the new education system, Islamic education became a subject in itself encompassed by the new curriculum.

Over recent decades, Qatar has pursued policies that seek to internationalize its education and to give a greater space to the English language within its curriculum (Barnawi 2017, Vora 2018). In 2001, Qatar consulted RAND, a global nonprofit American think tank, about possible reforms that can be made to its education system. One of the suggestions was to adopt English as a medium of instruction in public schools. Despite the fact that Qatar embraced this idea, this decision was shelved after a few years and Arabic now is the medium of instruction in the public schools (Mustafawi and Shaaban 2019). Another recommendation was to launch a voucher system, which partially covered the tuition fees of private and international schools for citizens of Qatar. The Qatari educational jurisdiction embraced this policy, leading to an unprecedented increase in international schools. In 2018, it has been reported that there are 462 international schools in Qatar, exceeding the 302 national schools (Qatar Ministry of Education 2018). The increasing popularity of international schooling is attributed to the perception that English, which is the medium of instruction in these schools, can equip students with the required skills to survive in a globalized labor market. Benmansour (2017) reports that the majority of the Qatari parents, who enroll their children in public and Arabic private schools, believe that being educated in a non-international school can hinder their children from securing a decent job in the future. The preference for international schools has also been voiced by Qatari students. For example, Graham et al. (2019) report that Qatari students believe that international schools can provide them with an invaluable learning experience as they can encounter people with a diversity of cultural backgrounds. However, parents and students expressed serious concerns about the linguistic and religious identities of Qatari society.

Many citizens see international schools and English as eroding factors for their national identity. These worries over the culture and heritage of Qatar are shared also by the government. This has been mirrored in Qatar vision 2030, in which the maintenance of Islamic values and cultural identity is accentuated. Accordingly, Qatar has taken a series of measures to minimize the corrosive effects of globalized education on its citizenry. One of them is to mandate international schools to teach Arabic language and Islamic studies in parallel with the transnational curriculum (Qatar Ministry of Education 2016). As a result, the teachers of these subjects have increased over the past decade in international schools.

ISLAMIC STUDIES TEACHERS
BETWEEN TWO PEDAGOGIES

The literature is replete with the critique of Islamic studies teachers' pedagogical practices as they fail to engage students in learning. For instance, Sahin (2013) reports that many students in the UK and Kuwait agree that "the provision of Islamic education in schools was simply boring" (7). Similarly, Abdallah (2018) indicates that students in Australian Islamic schools think that Islamic studies teachers lack a creative and engaging style of teaching. Furthermore, there is a tendency among Islamic studies teachers to privilege knowledge transmission over the other elements of Islamic education (Selçuk and Valk 2012 and Ucan 2019). Nevertheless, I argue that these prevalent teaching techniques are not Islamically authentic, and their roots go back to the monitorial schooling system which was brought to the Muslim world in the age of colonization (Kalmbach 2020, Sedra 2011, and Tschurenev 2008). In this respect, Memon and Alhashmi (2018) contend that the priority given to knowledge transmission in Islamic educational spaces is attributed to the "factory model" of schooling, which was prevalent in the nineteenth century. Due to this culture, Muslim educators have been preoccupied with the cognitive realm of Islamic education, overlooking other aspects.

In contrast to the aforementioned model of education, an Islamic authentic pedagogy, which is based on "Rahama" mercy and "Adab" ethics, views that the teacher's authority lies in their moral emulation of the Prophet Muhammad (PBUH) rather than their profound knowledge of Islam. Furthermore, children's agency in learning is respected as "the Qur'an takes seriously the reality of its first audience and utilizes a learner-centered strategy to teach its message" (Sahin 2013,180). Therefore, we should distinguish between two pedagogies within Islamic education. The first is referred to an "authentic" one, which I argue is derived from the Quran and prophetic traditions. Unfortunately, this authentic pedagogy is less common in the Muslim world. The second is referred to as an "inauthentic" pedagogy which, arguably, permeates all the majority of Islamic educational institutions. I argue that this inauthentic pedagogic model was introduced by an abrupt shift from Islamic education system to the public form in nineteenth-century Muslim world. However, further studies are needed to investigate the factors that contributed to the predominance of inauthentic pedagogies among Islamic studies teachers.

TEACHER IDENTITY

There has been a growing body of literature on teacher identity in educational studies. While this area of research has gained considerable attention from educationalists, opinions diverge greatly on the concept of teacher identity (Bukor 2015, Ballantyne and Grootenboer 2012). Beijaard et al. (2000) contend that teachers' pedagogical competences and their subject knowledge form crucial parts of their professional identity.

Al-Khatib and Lash (2017, 244) posit that the relationships with others in a particular context play a key role in defining the identity of the teacher. According to them, teacher identity "is the way one understands himself or herself in relation to others." Therefore, the role of contextual factors in constructing teacher identity cannot be overlooked. The remarkable shifts in teachers' identities can be ascribed to conflicting beliefs and practices between teachers and their contexts; additionally, the extent of the contrast between a teacher's culture and the ethos of a particular school can immensely impact the process of identity construction (Edwards and Edwards 2017). This is why the teachers in this study may have developed teaching identities distinct from those who worked in national schools.

TEACHER IDENTITY AND TAUGHT SUBJECTS

A number of studies have recognized the importance of the taught subject in shaping teachers' identities (Pennington and Richards 2016, Gayton 2016, Ballantyne and Grootenboer 2012). Thus, researchers have become increasingly interested in examining teaching identities with respect to subjects (e.g., Brown and McNamara 2011; Avraamidou 2016). However, it has been noted that the teaching identity of specific subjects has received little attention from educationalists. To illustrate, Sikes and Everington (2004) imply that few studies in educational research have sought to examine the work and life of religious education teachers. Everington (2016) argues that some areas of research about the teachers of religious education have not been explored.

Furthermore, O'Donoghue and Harford (2014) emphasize that the identity of the teachers who belong to a particular religion remains an unexplored area in educational research. This omission has been replicated within the research surrounding the role of the teacher in Islamic education. This is why more studies are required to capture how teachers of Islam, both in national and international schools, develop their teaching identities.

By deploying the concept of teacher identity within Islamic education, we can reveal teachers' views and dispositions toward teaching Islam in an ever-changing educational landscape of GCC nations. With its focus on the personal and professional realms of teaching, teaching identity can be a heuristic concept by which we can explore different roles of Islamic studies teachers. Being a role model and providing pastoral care are integral parts of teaching in Islamic traditions. Also, the educational programs of Islamic studies teachers need to introduce the notion of teacher identity as it gives future teachers a more nuanced understanding of their profession. According to Izadinia (2013,708), student teachers who embark early on their identity formation can "develop a deeper understanding of their future career, the roles they are going to shoulder and the objectives they want to fulfill."

THEORETICAL FRAMEWORK

This study draws on the theory of reflexivity which has been developed by the prominent critical realist Margaret Archer. Reflexivity is defined as "the regular exercise of the mental ability, shared by all normal people, to consider themselves in relation to their (social) contexts and vice versa" (Archer 2007, 4). The concept of reflexivity has gained wide currency within the sociological studies that explore identity formation (Adams 2006). The eminent sociologist Anthony Giddens (1992, 30) argues that "the self today is for everyone a reflexive project" (Giddens 1992, 30). It has been argued that this innovative concept can provide us with a lens through which we examine how individuals experience social changes in this modern globalized era (Adams 2006). According to May and Perry (2017, 4), reflexivity entails monitoring our traditional and habitual practices "as we meet unexpected circumstances and interact with other people who have different practices" (May and Perry 2017, 4). In this respect, Archer (2012) contends that people who experience "contextual discontinuity" have a propensity to show a higher degree of autonomous reflexivity. In other words, when individuals live in a milieu where sweeping sociocultural changes are taking place, they manifest a higher level of reflexivity.

I argue that Islamic studies teachers who work in international schools can be an excellent illustration of individuals who encounter "contextual discontinuity." The new educational landscape in GCC countries, wrought by internationalization and globalization, has posed many challenges for Islamic studies teachers who might wrestle between two educational discourses. Additionally, the receding status of the Arabic language and the dominance of European-inspired pedagogies and curricula can render Islamic studies teachers ill-equipped to instill Islamic values into children. As a result, these teachers need to negotiate and reconcile between conflicting demands. This cannot be achieved without reflective engagement with their teaching context. Guided by the theory of reflexivity, this study can show us the strategies utilized by Islamic studies teachers to meet the requirements of an international curriculum while clinging to the principles and pedagogies of Islamic education. Another theoretical benefit of Archer's (2007) theory of reflexivity is its capacity to help us to understand how contextual challenges in international schools can impact Islamic teachers' decisions and perceptions of their work.

This is why Ryan and Bourke argue that "it is crucial to include the element of reflexivity in any representation of professionalism to foreground the importance of understanding the ways in which teachers mediate their subjective and objective circumstances and make the decisions that they do" (2013, 414). Due to its theoretical capacity, the concept of reflexivity has been used by many scholars who have studied teachers' decisions and pedagogical practices (e.g., Hizli Alkan, Sinem, and Mark Priestley 2019; Willis et al. 2017). Others employed reflexivity to explore how teachers construct their professional identity (Westaway 2019).

RESEARCH METHODOLOGY

To examine how Islamic studies teachers negotiate their identities in international schooling, I restricted data collection to one international school based in the state of Qatar. I embraced the case study paradigm due to its capacity to give detailed analysis of the contextual conditions of the studied groups (Ridder 2017). According to Cohen et al., a case study can provide "a unique example of real people in real situations, enabling readers to understand ideas more clearly than simply by presenting them with abstract theories or principles" (2011, 289). Moreover, a case study approach can help researchers to scrutinize "the holistic and meaningful characteristics of real-life events— such as individual life cycles, small group behavior" (Yin 2013, 4). These advantages will allow me to see how Islamic studies teachers shape their identities in a milieu where their traditional ideas about teaching and learning are challenged. However, it might be argued that the findings of this case study, conducted in one school in Qatar, cannot be a general indication about

Islamic studies teachers' work in international schools in GCC countries. My argument is that my case study seeks to give what Thomas (2011) calls "exemplary knowledge," which aims to inform researchers and practitioners who face the same issues. In other words, the ambition of this study is to give some examples on how local teachers navigate international schools. Furthermore, it seeks to enlighten the would-be Islamic studies teachers about work in this form of schooling.

The data of this study were collected through semi-structured interviews with six Islamic studies teachers in 2018. The researched school is an IB school and has around 700 students from grade 6 to grade 12. The vast majority of students are Qatari who belong to affluent families. Apart from Arabic and Islamic studies departments, all teachers are native speakers of English from Australia, New Zealand, the UK, Canada, and the United States.

The preference for selecting this method is because "qualitative interviewing is particularly useful as a research method for accessing individuals' attitudes and values—things that cannot necessarily be observed or accommodated in a formal questionnaire" (Silverman 2015,114). As such, qualitative interviews allowed me to explore the multifaceted identities of teachers in this study. This method gave space to teachers to talk about their dispositions and their ways of adaptation while they were working in a school whose ethos were based on the values of global citizenship and international mindedness. In other words, interviews revealed how Islamic studies teacher exercised their reflexive thinking through mediation between two philosophies of education, the Islamic and the Western. My approach to interviewing was underpinned by Hollway and Jefferson's (2000) "free association narrative" method, in which participants' responses guide the researcher to subsequent questions that will be posed.

According to Hollway and Jefferson, this method can "secure access to a person's concerns which would probably not be visible using a more traditional method" (2000, 37). As such, this form of interviewing enables participants to reveal their feelings and thoughts about teaching Islam in an unrestricted fashion. Also, the free association interview method allowed me to capture the teachers' reflexivity as it was "exercised through people holding internal conversations" (Archer 2007, 63).

Interviews were conducted primarily in Arabic without the use of translation and the teachers were interviewed twice, with 65 minutes allocated for each interview. The participants represented a typical sample as they belonged to three Arab countries: Egypt, Jordan, and Palestine. It has been reported that the majority of Arabic and Islamic studies teachers in GCC states are citizens of less prosperous Arab countries (Ridge, Shami, and Kippels 2017). All the names of the participant teachers are pseudonyms.

FINDINGS

The data of this study were thematically analyzed. I opted for thematic analysis because it can provide a "rich and detailed, yet complex, account of the data" (Braun and Clarke 2006, 78). My thematic analysis was guided by the concept of reflexive identity as an analytic lens through which I explore how Islamic studies teachers reflected upon their roles in international schools. The data were themed and categorized according to teachers' reflections and views on their teaching practices in a new international milieu. The responses suggested that Islamic studies teachers rethought certain pedagogical techniques in order to keep their students attached to Islamic classes. The discussions below show the ways in which Islamic studies teachers tailored their teaching practices to achieve this goal, and how this entailed constructing a reflexive teaching identity.

Identity Agents Instead of Knowledge Transmitters

The interviewed teachers in this study believed that Islamic knowledge transmission should not be an end in itself, but a means by which they can preserve the Islamic identity of their students. For example, Ahmed, who newly joined international schools, stated that "within international schools, our main mission is to preserve the Islamic identity of our students. If the students would not learn their religion they will lose their religious identity." Another teacher, Mohammed, who has been teaching in international schools for twenty years, said, "Islamic Studies should not be defined by the epistemic realm of Islam but it should be seen as a moral message and identity construction."

Teaching for the sake of identity formation entails a spectrum of practices that are different from those that aim to transmit knowledge. For example, teachers of Islam who prioritize delivering religious knowledge tend to have rigid control on the learning process, as they think that they are authorized sources of knowledge (Selçuk and Valk 2012 and Abdalla 2018). This learning atmosphere has produced a hierarchical relationship between teachers and students in Islamic educational institutions (Kalmbach 2020). Conversely, education for identity preservation requires variant approaches. For instance, the interviewed teachers believed that safeguarding Islamic identity of their students necessitated building a less hierarchical social structure in the Islamic studies classroom. The quotation below from Mohammed demonstrates this view among the teachers in this study:

> The Islamic studies teacher in an international school should be caring and open-minded with his students and even in some cases less strict. . . . A strong

and friendly relationship should be established between Islamic studies teachers and students in an international setting.

These views accord well with the studies that indicate that socialization is an important tool to develop students' identities (Schachter and Rich 2011). Abdul Mabud (2018) suggests that Muslim teachers should understand the problems of their students and provide them with care if they are willing to serve as models of moral emulation. Also, there is a mutual relationship between showing empathy and religious identity. According to Riis and Woodhead (2010),

> The power of a religious community may be enhanced when it offers emotional resources that help life both inside and outside the religious community, but is diminished when it offers less emotional satisfaction than other spheres of social existence, or clashes unhelpfully with other emotional regimes. (169)

Therefore, socialization and emotional support are both integral parts of shaping a strong religious identity. Hood, Hill, and Spilka (2018) found that adolescents who show a tendency to adhere to their religious beliefs have caring and religious parents. Cohen-Malayev et al. 2014 mention that students who demonstrated a strong Jewish identity have attributed their sense of religious belonging to caring religious education teachers. It is no coincidence then to find the teachers in this study placed emphasis on their role as counselors of students rather than transmitters of Islamic knowledge. They believed their primary responsibility was to nurture their students emotionally to preserve their Islamic identity.

Seeking a Responsive Pedagogy in a New Teaching Setting

Working in a multicultural setting has enabled the studied teachers to reflect on their teaching practices. They think that a teacher-centered approach cannot engage students in meaningful learning that aims to retain the Islamic identity of new generations. One participant, Ali observed:

> Islamic studies teachers, who work in international schools, should adopt the new methods of teaching. Otherwise students will get easily bored as they are accustomed to the teaching methods of expatriate teachers who give students a greater space in the process of learning.

The participant teachers' sensitivity to the boredom of their students in Islamic studies classes resonates with a number of studies which reported how students are not engaged or interested in Islamic classes because of their teachers' approaches to pedagogy (Abdallah 2018, Sahin 2013, and Ucan 2019). Therefore, the interviewed teachers have expressed their view that traditional pedagogical practices should be rethought as they proved to be inefficient in our modern age. Furthermore, the interviewees demonstrated autonomous reflexivity by leveling criticism against their counterparts who still remain attached to conventional methods of teaching. For example, Mohammed criticized Islamic studies teachers who relied heavily on teacher-centered methods and rote learning. This was abundantly clear in the following quotes:

> Islamic Studies teachers tend to perceive learning as accumulation of Islamic knowledge, and they use heavily the teacher-centered method. If you want to work in an international school, you should be open-minded and progressive in your approach. We are living in a different world. . . . International curricula develop the autonomous personality of students, and they are endowed with critical thinking skills and an inquisitive mind. Therefore, we need a different approach.

The teachers held a belief that the overarching aim of Islamic teachers in internationalized schools was to preserve the Islamic identity of their students. This will not be attainable by creating a tedious learning environment inside Islamic studies classes. According to them, using rote learning exclusively might render other subjects more interesting and enjoyable compared with Islamic studies. Therefore, teaching Islam in an international school requires educators to embrace innovative methods of teaching if the purpose of the instruction is to reinforce students' commitment to their faith. The teachers' adherence to the new teaching culture can be seen as the reflexive adoption of projects (Archer 2007). The project of retaining the Islamic identity of students in international schools necessitates using a learner-centered approach. The teachers mentioned that Islamic education is based on the teachings of the Quran, which encourage believers to contemplate and think profoundly about the universe.

Reflection on Teaching the Quran Memorization

The teachers in this study reflected on the role of memorization and they believed that teachers who teach Islam in international settings need to achieve balance between the Islamic and Western educational views on this issue. For example, Salma, a female teacher who had been working in international schools for the past fifteen years, said:

> We are balanced in our teaching. We do not focus primarily on, and we do not overlook the memorization of the Quran. Unlike the Islamic Studies teachers in non-international schools, I think our teaching styles are not traditional.

According to the teachers, this balance can be achieved by studying the meanings of the Quranic verses before memorizing them. However, the teachers believed that international schools have reduced the proficiency of students in Arabic language. Consequently, it is an onerous task for the teachers to explain the meanings of the Quran before memorization. Despite this difficulty, the teachers have asserted that this approach was appropriate to teach the Quran in international schools, where students tend to devalue memorization. But when students memorize a comprehensible text, they will be engaged in Islamic studies classes. In addition to studying the interpretation of the Quran, the teachers employed some innovative strategies to overcome the monotonous routine of memorization classes. For example, they pointed to peer and self-assessment as a way in which students could enjoy the Quran classes. Additionally, teachers underlined the importance of technology in teaching Islamic studies.

This section has showed that Islamic studies teachers attempted to overcome "contextual discontinuity" by reflecting on their pedagogies and changing them to accommodate the students' needs. Archer (2007) assumes that when individuals work or live in a new cultural and social environment, they will encounter contextual challenges. To overcome them, they need to exercise reflexive monitoring of themselves and their projects in relation to new situations. This can be applicable to the teachers in this study. The Islamic studies teachers have realized that safeguarding the Islamic identity of their students required them to utilize the learner-centered approach. Additionally, the social relationship with students should be prioritized over knowledge transmission.

CONCLUSION

To conclude, I will draw on lessons from this case study to make some suggestions for more responsive teacher education and training programs through which future Islamic studies teachers can cope with the new educational scene of GCC nations.

The studied teachers indicated that teaching methods in international schools are different in various ways from those that are embraced in national institutions. This necessitates shifting to a new model of training programs, where teachers' learning should be contextualized, localized, and globalized (Cheng, Chow, and Mok 2004). It is, therefore, imperative to have a mandatory practicum component in international schools within the faculties of education across GCC states, which host the second largest number of these schools worldwide (Bunnell 2014). Training with veteran Islamic studies teachers in an international environment can assist student teachers to overcome the challenges of teaching Islamic studies in Western-based schools where certain Islamic pedagogical practices are questioned. Tanner and Davies (2009, 376) mention that "working alongside more experienced peers can foster and empower the learning of new professional skills."

Another recommendation is that reflexive engagement with teaching settings should be accentuated across the professional development of Islamic studies teachers and their training programs. This study concludes that reflexivity, which has been developed due to "contextual discontinuity," helped the teachers to make adjustments to their pedagogical practices. This has enabled them to be more responsive to their students' needs in a new teaching context. This dovetails well with the recent calls for a teacher education that reinforces reflective personal experience and shifts away from "a view of teacher knowledge as received and static" (Gallagher 2011, 143). What can be learned from the teachers in this study is that reflexivity is very important for novice and veteran Islamic studies teachers in GCC countries, where processes of acute global–local transition are taking place (Findlow 2006). In such an environment, "reflexivity is an essential element of teacher professionalism so teachers can mediate the diverse conditions within which they work" (Ryan and Bourke 2013, 411).

In addition to reflexivity, the professional identity of teachers, and how it can be constructed, should be embedded in teacher education programs. This stems from the fact that identity formation has been proven to be one of the essential ingredients for a successful teacher. There is growing recognition that teacher education needs to be informed by research on teaching identities (Izadinia 2013, Ruohotie-Lyhty 2018). It has been argued that teacher education and professional development programs should address all dimensions of teaching and go beyond the narrow focus on pedagogical practices and subject matter content (Jenlink 2014). This can be attainable through training programs that allow teachers to conceptualize a professional identity that drives "them to learn, develop, and sustain commitments to educational practice and to the profession" (Kaplan and Garner 2018, 71). Teacher education programs that fail to support student teachers to develop their professional identities have been criticized for not preparing them to meet the demands of a new challenging teaching context (Beauchamp and Thomas, 2009). Therefore, more studies are needed to shed light on the identity of Islamic studies teachers, and subsequently, these studies should contribute to establishing research-informed and innovative models of teacher training programs.

REFERENCES

Abdalla, Mohamad. 2018. "Islamic Studies in Islamic Schools: Evidence-Based Renewal." In *Islamic Schooling in the West Pathways to Renewal*, edited by

Mohamad Abdalla, Dylan Chown, and Muhammad Abdullah, 257–83. Cham, Switzerland: Springer International Publishing.

Abdul Mabud, Shaikh. 2018. "The Emergence of Islamic Schools: A Contextual Background." In *Islamic Schooling in the West Pathways to Renewal*, edited by Mohamad Abdalla, Dylan Chown, and Muhammad Abdullah, 11–33. Cham, Switzerland: Springer International Publishing.

Adams, Matthew. 2006. "Hybridizing Habitus and Reflexivity." *Sociology* 40 (3): 511–28. https://doi.org/10.1177/0038038506636672.

Al-Ammari, Jamal A. 2004. "Benefits and Barriers to Implementing Computer Use in Qatari Elementary Schools as Perceived by Female Teachers, an Exploratory Study." Phd Thesis, University of Ohio.

Al-Khatib, Amal J., and Martha J. Lash. 2017. "Professional Identity of an Early Childhood Black Teacher in a Predominantly White School: A Case Study." *Child Care in Practice* 23 (3): 242–57. https://doi.org/10.1080/13575279.2016.1188766.

Al-Kobaisi, Abdulla Juma. 1979. "The Development of Education in Qatar, 1950–1977 with an Analysis of Some Educational Problems." PhD Thesis, Durham University.

AL-Maadheed, Fatma. 2012. "Models of Bilingual Education in Majority Language Contexts: An Exploratory Study of Bilingual Programmes in Qatari Primary Schools." PhD Thesis, Oxford University, UK.

Archer, Margaret. 2003. *Structure, Agency, and the Internal Conversation.* Cambridge: Cambridge University Press.

———. 2007. *Making Our Way through the World: Human Reflexivity and Social Mobility.* Cambridge: Cambridge University Press.

———. 2012. *The Reflexive Imperative in Late Modernity.* Cambridge: Cambridge University Press.

Avraamidou, Lucy. 2016. *Studying Science Teacher Identity: Theoretical, Methodological and Empirical Explorations.* Rotterdam, The Netherlands: Sense Publishers.

Ballantyne, Julie, and Peter Grootenboer. 2012. "Exploring Relationships between Teacher Identities and Disciplinarity." *International Journal of Music Education* 30 (4): 368–81. https://doi.org/10.1177/0255761412459165.

Barnawi, Osman Z. 2017. *Neoliberalism and English Language Education Policies in the Arabian Gulf.* Routledge.

Beauchamp, Catherine, and Lynn Thomas. 2009. "Understanding Teacher Identity: An Overview of Issues in the Literature and Implications for Teacher Education." *Cambridge Journal of Education* 39 (2): 175–89. https://doi.org/10.1080/03057640902902252.

Beijaard, Douwe, Nico Verloop, and Jan D. Vermunt. 2000. "Teachers' Perceptions of Professional Identity: An Exploratory Study from a Personal Knowledge Perspective." *Teaching and Teacher Education* 16 (7): 749–64. https://doi.org/10.1016/s0742-051x(00)00023-8.

Benmansour, Nada Abdelkader. 2017. "Education in Qatar: The Complex Reality of Citizen Satisfaction a Research Published by the Social and Economic Survey Research Institute (SESRI)." Qatar University. Available online: https://qspace.

qu.edu.qa/bitstream/handle/10576/6383/Education%20in%20Qatar%20EN.pdf?s
equence=2&isAllowed=y (accessed on 15 October 2018).

Berglund, Jenny, and Bill Gent. 2018. "Memorization and Focus: Important Transferables between Supplementary Islamic Education and Mainstream Schooling." *Journal of Religious Education* 66 (2): 125–38. https://doi.org/10.1007/s40839-018-0060-1.

Braun, Virginia, and Victoria Clarke. 2006. "Using Thematic Analysis in Psychology." *Qualitative Research in Psychology* 3 (2): 77–101. https://doi.org/10.1191/147808 8706qp063oa.

Brown, Tony, and Olwen Mc Namara. 2011. *Becoming a Mathematics Teacher: Identity and Identifications*. Dordrecht: Springer.

Bukor, Emese. 2015. "Exploring Teacher Identity from a Holistic Perspective: Reconstructing and Reconnecting Personal and Professional Selves." *Teachers and Teaching* 21 (3): 305–27. https://doi.org/10.1080/13540602.2014.953818.

Bunnell, Tristan. 2016. *The Changing Landscape of International Schooling: Implications for Theory and Practice*. London: Routledge.

Carruthers, Mary J. 2008. *The Book of Memory: A Study of Memory in Medieval Culture*. Cambridge: Cambridge University Press.

Cheng, Yin Cheong, King Wai Chow, and Magdalena Mo Ching Mok. 2004. "Reform of Teacher Education amid Paradigm Shift in School Education." In *Reform of Teacher Education in the Asia-Pacific in the New Millennium*, edited by Yin Cheong Cheng, King Wai Chow, and Magdalena Mo Ching Mok. Dordrecht: Kluwer.

Cohen, Louis, Lawrence Manion, and Keith Morrison. 2011. *Research Methods in Education*. 7th ed. London: Routledge.

Cohen-Malayev, Maya, Elli P. Schachter, and Yisrael Rich. 2014. "Teachers and the Religious Socialization of Adolescents: Facilitation of Meaningful Religious Identity Formation Processes." *Journal of Adolescence* 37 (2): 205–14. https://doi.org/10.1016/j.adolescence.2013.12.004.

Day, Christopher, Alison Kington, Gordon Stobart, and Pam Sammons. 2006. "The Personal and Professional Selves of Teachers: Stable and Unstable Identities." *British Educational Research Journal* 32 (4): 601–16. https://doi.org/10.1080/0 1411920600775316.

Edwards, F. C. E., and R. J. Edwards. 2017. "A Story of Culture and Teaching: The Complexity of Teacher Identity Formation." *The Curriculum Journal* 28 (2): 190–211. https://doi.org/10.1080/09585176.2016.1232200.

Findlow, Sally. 2006. "Higher Education and Linguistic Dualism in the Arab Gulf." *British Journal of Sociology of Education* 27 (1): 19–36. https://doi.org/10.1080/0 1425690500376754.

Gallagher, Kay. 2011. "Becoming and Re-Becoming a Teacher in the Arabian Peninsula: Amal's Story of Hope." *Teacher Development* 15 (2): 141–55. https://doi.org/10.1080/13664530.2011.571491.

Gayton, Angela Mary. 2016. "Perceptions about the Dominance of English as a Global Language: Impact on Foreign-Language Teachers' Professional Identity." *Journal of Language, Identity & Education* 15 (4): 230–44. https://doi.org/10.1080/15348458.2016.1194209.

Giddens, Anthony. 1992. *The Transformation of Intimacy*. Cambridge: Polity Press.

Graham, Jan Marie, Mary Gene Saudelli, and Debbie Sheppard-LeMoine. 2019. "The Lived Experiences of Qatari Adolescents Attending International Secondary School." *Mental Health, Religion & Culture* 22 (4): 344–56. https://doi.org/10.1 080/13674676.2019.1593337.

Hirschkind, Charles. 2006. *The Ethical Soundscape: Cassette Sermons and Islamic Counterpublics*. New York: Columbia University Press.

Hizli Alkan, Sinem, and Mark Priestley. 2019. "Teacher Mediation of Curriculum Making: The Role of Reflexivity." *Journal of Curriculum Studies* 51 (5): 737–54. https://doi.org/10.1080/00220272.2019.1637943.

Hollway, Wendy, and Tony Jefferson. 2000. *Doing Qualitative Research Differently: Free Association, Narrative and the Interview Method*. 1st ed. London: Sage.

Hood, Ralph W., Peter C. Hill, and Bernard Spilka. 2018. *The Psychology of Religion: An Empirical Approach*. New York: The Guilford Press.

Izadinia, Mahsa. 2013. "A Review of Research on Student Teachers' Professional Identity." *British Educational Research Journal* 39 (4): 694–713. https://doi.org /10.1080/01411926.2012.679614.

Jenlink, Patrick M. 2014. *Teacher Identity and the Struggle for Recognition: Meeting the Challenges of a Diverse Society*. Lanham, MD: Rowman & Littlefield Education.

Kalmbach, Hilary. 2020. *Islamic Knowledge and the Making of Modern Egypt*. Cambridge University Press.

Kaplan, Avi, and Joanna K. Garner. 2018. "Teacher Identity and Motivation: The Dynamic Systems Model of Role Identity." In *Research on Teacher Identity Mapping Challenges and Innovations*, edited by Paul A. Schutz, Ji Hong, and Dionne Cross Francis. Cham: Springer.

May, Tim, and Beth Perry. 2017. *Reflexivity: The Essential Guide*. London: Sage.

Memon, Nadeem. 2011. "What Islamic School Teachers Want: Towards Developing an Islamic Teacher Education Programme." *British Journal of Religious Education* 33 (3): 285–98. https://doi.org/10.1080/01416200.2011.595912.

Memon, Nadeem A., and Mariam Alhashmi. 2018. "Islamic Pedagogy: Potential and Perspective." In *Islamic Schooling in the West Pathways to Renewal*, edited by Mohamad Abdalla, Dylan Chown, and Muhammad Abdullah, 169–94. Cham, Switzerland: Springer International Publishing.

Mustafawi, Eiman, and Kassim Shaaban. 2019. "Language Policies in Education in Qatar between 2003 and 2012: From Local to Global Then back to Local." *Language Policy* 18 (2): 209–42. https://doi.org/10.1007/s10993-018-9483-5.

O'Donoghue, Tom, and Judith Harford. 2014. "The Conception, Construction, and Maintenance of the Identity of Roman Catholic Female Religious Teachers: A Historical Case Study from Ireland." *Teachers and Teaching* 20 (4): 410–26. https ://doi.org/10.1080/13540602.2014.881638.

Ole Riis, and Linda Woodhead. 2010. *A Sociology of Religious Emotion*. Oxford: Oxford University Press.

Pennington, Martha C., and Jack C. Richards. 2016. "Teacher Identity in Language Teaching: Integrating Personal, Contextual, and Professional Factors." *RELC Journal* 47 (1): 5–23. https://doi.org/10.1177/0033688216631219.

Qatar Ministry of Education. 2016. "The Policy of Academic Monitoring of Private Schools." Available online: http://www.edu.gov.qa/En/ServicesCenter/PSO/S choolsRolesEnglish/PolticPrivateSchoolsEnglish.pdf (accessed on 7 December 2018).

Qatar Ministry of Education. 2018. "Statistical Bulletin of Education." Bulletin May 2018. Department of Educational Policy and Research Statistics Section. Available online: http://www.edu.gov.qa/Ar/structure/deputy/MonthlytStatistics Issues/Brochure%20ver2%20May%202018.pdf (accessed on 7 December 2018).

Ridder, Hans-Gerd. 2017. "The Theory Contribution of Case Study Research Designs." *Business Research* 10 (2): 281–305. https://doi.org/10.1007/s40685 -017-0045-z.

Ridge, Natasha, Soha Shami, and Susan Kippels. 2017. "Arab Migrant Teachers in the United Arab Emirates and Qatar Challenges and Opportunities." In *Arab Migrant Communities in the GCC*, edited by Zahra Babar, 39–63. New York: Oxford University Press.

Ruohotie-Lyhty, Maria. 2018. "Identity-Agency in Progress: Teachers Authoring Their Identities." In *Research on Teacher Identity Mapping Challenges and Innovations*, edited by Paul A. Schutz, Ji Hong, and Dionne Cross Francis. Cham: Springer.

Ryan, Mary, and Terri Bourke. 2013. "The Teacher as Reflexive Professional: Making Visible the Excluded Discourse in Teacher Standards." *Discourse: Studies in the Cultural Politics of Education* 34 (3): 411–23. https://doi.org/10.1080/0 1596306.2012.717193.

Sahin, Abdullah. 2013. *New Directions in Islamic Education: Pedagogy & Identity Formation*. Markfield: Kube Academic.

Schachter, Elli P., and Yisrael Rich. 2011. "Identity Education: A Conceptual Framework for Educational Researchers and Practitioners." *Educational Psychologist* 46 (4): 222–38. https://doi.org/10.1080/00461520.2011.614509.

Sedra, Paul. 2011. *From Mission to Modernity: Evangelicals, Reformers and Education in Nineteenth Century Egypt*. London and New York: I.B. Tauris & Co Ltd.

Selçuk, Mualla, and John Valk. 2012. "Knowing Self and Others: A Worldview Model for Religious Education in Turkey." *Religious Education* 107 (5): 443–54. https://doi.org/10.1080/00344087.2012.722473.

Sikes, Pat, and Judith Everington. 2004. "'RE Teachers Do Get Drunk You Know': Becoming a Religious Education Teacher in the Twenty-First Century." *Teachers and Teaching* 10 (1): 21–33. https://doi.org/10.1080/13540600320000170909.

Silverman, David. 2015. *Interpreting Qualitative Data*. 5th ed. London: Sage.

Talbani, Aziz. 1996. "Pedagogy, Power, and Discourse: Transformation of Islamic Education." *Comparative Education Review* 40 (1): 66–82. https://doi.org/10.1086 /447356.

Tanner, Howard, and Susan M. B. Davies. 2009. "How Engagement with Research Changes the Professional Practice of Teacher-Educators: A Case Study from the Welsh Education Research Network." *Journal of Education for Teaching* 35 (4): 373–89. https://doi.org/10.1080/02607470903220448.

Tartaglia, James. 2007. *Routledge Philosophy Guidebook to Rorty and the Mirror of Nature*. London: Routledge.

Thomas, Gary. 2011. "The Case: Generalisation, Theory and Phronesis in Case Study." *Oxford Review of Education* 37 (1): 21–35. https://doi.org/10.1080/030549 85.2010.521622.

Tschurenev, Jana. 2008. "Diffusing Useful Knowledge: The Monitorial System of Education in Madras, London and Bengal, 1789–1840." *Paedagogica Historica* 44 (3): 245–64. https://doi.org/10.1080/00309230802041526.

Ucan, Ayse Demirel. 2019. *Improving the Pedagogy of Islamic Religious Education in Secondary Schools: The Role of Critical Religious Education and Variation Theory*. New York: Routledge.

Ucan, Ayse Demirel, and Andrew Wright. 2018. "Improving the Pedagogy of Islamic Religious Education through an Application of Critical Religious Education, Variation Theory and the Learning Study Model." *British Journal of Religious Education* 41 (2): 202–17. https://doi.org/10.1080/01416200.2018.1484695.

Vora, Neha. 2018. *Teach for Arabia American Universities, Liberalism, and Transnational Qatar*. Stanford, CA: Stanford University Press.

Westaway, Lise. 2019. "The Role of Reflexivity in the Emergence and Expression of Teachers' Identities in Teaching Primary School Mathematics." *ZDM* 51 (3): 481–92. https://doi.org/10.1007/s11858-019-01042-y.

Willis, Jill, Leanne Crosswell, Chad Morrison, Andrew Gibson, and Mary Ryan. 2017. "Looking for Leadership: The Potential of Dialogic Reflexivity with Rural Early-Career Teachers." *Teachers and Teaching* 23 (7): 794–809. https://doi.org /10.1080/13540602.2017.1287695.

Yin, Robert K. 2013. *Case Study Research: Design and Methods*. 5th ed. London: Sage.

Chapter 3

Shifting Paradigms in Arabic Pedagogy and Policy in the UAE

Opportunities and Challenges for Teacher Education

Jessica Tsimprea Maluch and
Hanada Taha Thomure

INTRODUCTION

Similar to other countries in the Gulf region, the United Arab Emirates (UAE) education system has developed very swiftly. Established in 1972, the formal education system has seen waves of modernization and has experimented with various models. The Ministry of Education introduced several ambitious courses for rapid improvement. As the UAE is planning for a post-oil economy, vast attention has been directed to educating students and preparing them for a knowledge-based economy (UAE Government n.d.). As such, much attention and resources have been focused on disciplines like English language and science (UNDP 2014). This development has been largely at the expense of Arabic language. Until the past decade, Arabic as a language and how it is taught has received little attention by both researchers and policy makers.

However, Arabic language has become increasingly in the spotlight as a central concern with students' underperformance in international standardized assessments (Carroll, Al Kahwaji, and Litz 2017, 318; Mullis et al. 2017, OECD 2019). For example, the UAE participated in the International Reading Literacy Study (PIRLS) in 2011, as well as the 2016 cycles. While there was marked improvement from 2011 to 2016, close to half of the fourth graders, who were assessed in Arabic reading (49 percent), performed below the "low international" benchmark score. Similarly, in secondary school, the performance in the 2018 Program for International Student Assessment (PISA) shows a similar picture for 15-year-olds as the PIRLS in primary school. Overall, the UAE ranked forty-sixth out of seventy-nine participating countries and economies. Those who took the assessment in Arabic scored over 80 points lower in reading than those who took the assessment in English (OECD 2019), which can be interpreted as close to three years of school achievement (Hill, Bloom, Black, and Lipsey 2008). To address this, the UAE made strong Arabic language skills as one of the key objectives of the UAE Vision 2021 National Agenda (UAE Government n.d.).

To fulfill the Vision 2021 National Agenda and improve the quality of Arabic teaching and learning, the government of the UAE and the local governments of the seven emirates have supported over the years numerous policies and initiatives designed to have a positive effect on student achievement (Taha 2019). One such initiative is the development and implementation of the 2017 Arabic language standards (UAE Ministry of Education 2017). These standards call for a paradigm shift in the Arabic classroom from rote memorization of grammar to Arabic as a tool for higher order thinking and critical skills development. This new direction has many implications on the way educators teach Arabic and, therefore, how teachers must be trained to be effective Arabic educators. However, while there is increasing pressure for teachers to change their pedagogical practices, there is little ongoing support for pre-service and in-service professional development. Indeed, there are no federally funded Arabic language teacher preparation programs (ECAE, 2020).

In this chapter, we will address this new direction for Arabic language teaching and learning and some of the changes required for successful implementation. First, we will discuss the challenges of Arabic and how it has traditionally been taught. Thereafter, the chapter will describe the 2017 Arabic standards in further detail before presenting findings of professional development and training survey data from PISA 2018 and a classroom observation study by the authors assessing the effectiveness of the policy changes. The chapter will conclude by discussing possibilities for classroom practices and approaches to teacher education that align with this new direction for Arabic language instruction in the UAE.

LINGUISTIC CHARACTERISTICS OF ARABIC

Arabic as a language may pose several challenges for students. One challenge is that Arabic is diglossic (Aldannan 2010, Almoosa 2007)—defined as a language which has two distinct forms that are used simultaneously for different purposes (Ferguson 1959). Modern Standard Arabic (MSA), the formal language children learn in school and use in reading and writing, is noticeably different in its phonology, morphology, and syntax from the dialect form of Arabic, referred to as Spoken Arabic (SpA), which is the spoken language that is used in informal contexts (Mahfoudhi et al. 2011). In the Gulf region and specifically in the UAE, this is complicated by the wide use of English as the Lingua Franca in the greater community and in most public arenas. Many Arabic-speaking parents speak either SpA or English with their children (Malek 2015, Moukhallati and Al Amir, 2015), and many children speak broken Arabic or a language other than Arabic with their housemaids, nannies, and drivers (Tibi and McLeod 2014).

Beside the diglossic aspect of Arabic, another unique characteristic is its shallow and opaque orthography, as its script can be written with or without short vowels. When a text is written with short vowels, as is the case with all textbooks used in primary school, some religious texts and some children's books, the shallow orthography makes it relatively easy to derive the phonology and has been found to have a positive effect on reading comprehension (Abu-Rabia 1999, 2019, Taha & Azaizah-Seh, 2017). Children, when learning MSA in preschool and primary years, use texts and textbooks that are vowelized with diacritics or short vowels inserted on every letter to ease them into reading accurately, and then those short vowels are sporadically used starting around middle school. Some researchers have suggested that the addition of short vowels inhibits processing speed and fluency in early primary grades (Abadzi 2017).

As students enter formal schooling and despite overlap between SpA and Arabic (Feitelson, Goldstein, Iraqi, and Share 1993, Abu-Rabia 2000), children may face challenges in the skills necessary for strong language skills in MSA (Ayari 1996, Ibrahim and Aharon-Peretz 2005, Saiegh-Haddad & Everatt 2018). Both the diglossic and orthographic features of Arabic can create added challenges for language and reading development. However, if utilized well in Arabic language education, this diglossic feature may be an untapped resource that educators may utilize to improve language skills rather than viewing it as a weakness. Specifically, when diglossia is referenced explicitly in instruction regarding similarities between SpA and MSA in structure and vocabulary, it might support students' deeper understanding of the language and will allow them to see Arabic language in its entirety and how SpA and MSA are indeed intertwined. These challenges are exacerbated by the lack of proper Arabic teacher preparation and training that enables teachers to utilize students' background knowledge, as well as scaffold and support students' Arabic development. Rather, Arabic language has been taught in a rigid way, which focuses on accuracy, heavy content rather than fluency and long-term skills (Taha 2019).

ARABIC TEACHING AND LEARNING

Arabic pedagogy has traditionally focused on grammar, recitation, and memorizing syntactical and spelling rules (Faour 2012, Versteegh 2006). This is primarily due to the fact that as the language of Islam, Arabic is revered as a sacred language that needs to be preserved and protected in its pure and untainted classical form. This approach to Arabic teaching has changed very little over the years and has led to an overemphasis on memorized patterns and forms in classrooms that geared most of learning toward lower order thinking skills (Taha, 2019). Teachers have focused primarily on whatever content they find in the government-imposed textbooks to cover content, memorize verse and prose, labor over grammar, and memorize syntactical and spelling rules (Faour 2012). This traditional approach focused on Arabic primarily as an art form to be revered and accepted as is instead of a tool that can be used for discussion, problem-solving, invention, innovation, and communication. However, this approach has not proven to be efficient for language and literacy development. The 2018 PISA results indicate that UAE schools dedicate much more time to reading instruction compared to other countries with similar student performance (OECD 2019).

Furthermore, there is currently a lack of consensus of effective instructional practices to tackle the specific challenges of Arabic language and literacy development. Over the past decade, scholars across the region have made great strides in uncovering the unique aspects and components of Arabic language and literacy development (i.e., Mahfoudhi et al. 2011). While this is a vital first step, there is no evidence-based instructional strategies that have proved effective for teachers.

Several other steps have been taken to shift Arabic pedagogy toward one that focuses on higher order thinking skills. One such initiative is the introduction of school inspections for private schools in various Emirates in the UAE including Dubai, Abu Dhabi and more recently in Sharjah. For example, in Dubai, inspections are conducted on an annual basis by the Knowledge Human Development Authority (KHDA). Receiving an "outstanding" rating means that the school is doing exceptional work on a range of components including school culture, classroom environment, academic standards, curriculum delivery, safety procedures, provisions made for special needs students, and levels of achievement in every content area. The ratings are given for both attainment and progress and the scale used for these inspections is: outstanding, very good, good, acceptable, weak and very weak (KDHA n.d.). While seventeen schools were found to be outstanding in the 2018–2019 academic school year, there were no Arabic programs, for native or non-native Arabic learners within these schools that received "Outstanding." Only one school received a "Very Good" progress with the majority of Arabic programs receiving a "Good" or "Acceptable" rating. Furthermore, among the comments in the reports, Arabic was cited as a weakness among several of those schools in the final reports. The supposed weakness may stem from a variety of sources. It may be that there is a disjuncture or a misalignment between the methodology used in Arabic language teaching and learning in the classroom compared to other subjects and departments in the schools inspected. It also may be that teachers are not trained to implement student-centered methods to engage students.

THE NEW UAE STANDARDS-BASED APPROACH FOR ARABIC

In an effort to modernize and improve the teaching and learning of Arabic language in schools, a central initiative has been the development of the 2017 Arabic content standards by the Ministry of Education (MoE) in the UAE. These new standards may be the beginning of a call for a paradigm shift in how Arabic is taught in schools (Ministry of Education, 2017). The new standards-based curriculum, also designed and developed by the MoE, focuses on Arabic as a tool for learning and addresses the development of twenty-first-century skills within the framework of the Arabic language arts curriculum with a specific focus on communicative literacy development, critical thinking, and problem-solving skills. Developed in partnership with regional and international partners, these standards focus on higher order thinking and are divided into six areas of study: reading literacy, reading literary text, reading informational text, writing, listening, and speaking. There is a strong focus, as shown through the numerous learning outcomes, on literary texts, writing, and language throughout all grades with reading literacy strongly emphasized in the early grades. The standards are designed to support students' development not only in Arabic language arts but also in other disciplines they study in school that use Arabic as the medium of instruction.

The standards require that teachers introduce strategies for students to comprehend, analyze, and evaluate a variety of subjects as well as text types and genres (i.e., informational, literary, and poetic) and actively engage students to encourage them to become lifelong readers. Furthermore, the assessments, as a monitoring and evaluation tool of the new curriculum, focus on texts that are new to the reader as opposed to previous years where students were tested on the same texts they studied in class (Ministry of Education, 2017).

The new standards movement in the UAE calls for a new direction in the way Arabic is taught. In teaching according to the standards, Arabic teachers can no longer teach directly from the textbook and prioritize memorization of grammar rules and other more traditional techniques. As this is a relatively recent shift, there is a need to understand the extent to which this standards-based approach is being implemented in UAE classrooms and whether these changes are shifting the way teachers are teaching and students are learning.

TEACHER EDUCATION AND PROFESSIONAL DEVELOPMENT IN THE UAE

This new direction for Arabic teaching and learning has many implications for teacher education as there needs to be a shift in how teachers are prepared for the classroom. Teachers need suitable preparation and ongoing training to ensure quality and engaging instruction and strong learning outcomes (Darling-Hammond 2010, Taha-Thomure & Speaker, 2018). Teacher training programs have the dual goal to prepare and graduate teachers who both know their subject (i.e., in this case Arabic) and are able to implement effective pedagogy and methodology so that learning occurs (Taha 2017). Unfortunately, as Faour (2012) observes, many teachers in the Arab world do not have the content and pedagogical skills required to teach critical thinking, higher order thinking, reflection, or metacognition through student-centered learning. In the UAE, most teachers of Arabic have studied Arabic literature (Taha 2017). Many teachers have various degrees with little to no formal pedagogical training. The result of this is that teachers might be proficient in MSA but are not trained in language pedagogy.

Taha (2019) investigated the path to Arabic Education Teacher Preparation programs. With the UAE five federally funded higher education institutions and more than one hundred private higher education institutions (Nassir 2017), no federal institution of higher education offered an Arabic language teacher education program. Rather, education programs are offered with general pedagogy and possibly a course in Arabic or linguistics. Conversely, a few private institutions offer Arabic language teacher preparation programs, but these have been found to lack quality, rigor, and alignment with what modern programs of teacher preparation look like, all of which are needed for the paradigm shift the country is calling for (Taha 2019).

In an effort to improve educators' skills, the UAE Ministry of Education has introduced licensure for all teachers, including Arabic educators. As of 2017, it is mandatory for all teachers, including Arabic teachers, to be licensed within the first year in the classroom. Licensure includes passing two assessments: one in the specialization of the teacher and the other in pedagogy (UAE Government 2020). This is a step to ensure a certain level of competency for all teachers. However, while it ensures that educators in the field have the content knowledge and the skills necessary to implement the desired pedagogy in the classroom, there is no guarantee that any change will take place in the classroom, which is what is greatly needed.

UAE ARABIC TEACHERS' PERSPECTIVES OF THEIR TRAINING

To understand the current training experiences of Arabic teachers in the UAE, the authors analyzed data from the 2018 PISA. Along with student data, the PISA collects data from teachers and specifically language teachers about their qualifications, classroom practices, and satisfaction with professional educators. We were primarily interested in the qualifications and professional development opportunities of current Arabic teachers. The 2018 PISA sample surveyed 4,990 Arabic teachers about their education and ongoing training.

From this subsample, several trends appeared around Arabic teacher qualifications. Most Arabic teachers completed some teacher education or training program (86 percent) with most teachers reporting that they attended a standard teacher education or training program (74 percent) at an accredited educational institution. Far fewer reported attending an in-service teacher education program (17 percent), which allows teachers to be in the classroom while training for their license. One year after the introduction of teacher licensure, the clear majority of teachers have been or are in the process of obtaining some kind of teacher training. However, it is unclear if the mandate for licensure in the UAE has had any impact or if this was the status quo prior to 2017.

When asked about the content of their training, the sample of teachers responded that their training was distributed between reading literacy (35 percent), pedagogy of reading literacy (34 percent) and general pedagogical knowledge (31 percent). Similarly, almost all respondents reported that both Arabic as a language and the pedagogy of Arabic were areas of emphasis in their formal education.

Another topic of interest was the current professional development activities of Arabic teachers. Most teachers reported being required to attend professional development activities throughout the 2019–2020 academic year (75 percent). They also reported quite a variety of topics they attended. Table 3.1 shows the percentage of teachers who reported having the topics either included in their teacher education or their professional development over the course of the 2019–2020 academic year. This gives an indication as to which topics are being addressed in both teacher education and in-service professional development. Unsurprisingly, while much of teacher education is dedicated to content knowledge, pedagogy, and curriculum, professional development offers much more of a variety of subjects. Some of the more

Table 3.1 Arabic Teacher's Education and Professional Development Activities (in Percentages)

	Percentage Included in Teacher Education	Percentage Included in Professional Development Activities over the 2019–2020 Academic Year
Knowledge and understanding of my subject field	80	40
Pedagogical competencies in teaching my subject field	72	42
Knowledge of the curriculum	71	41
Student assessment practices	56	52
ICT (information and communication technology) skills for teaching	58	53
Student behavior and classroom management	61	50
School management and administration	29	35
Approaches to individualized learning	56	43
Teaching students with special needs	30	42
Teaching in a multicultural or multilingual setting	38	41
Teaching cross-curricular skills (e.g., problem-solving, learning-to-learn)	57	50
Student career guidance and counseling	38	38
Internal evaluation or self-evaluation of schools	31	44
Use of evaluation results	44	48
Parent-teacher cooperation	49	50
Second language teaching	24	24
Communicating with people from different cultures or countries	31	39
Teaching about equity and diversity	35	38

Source: Table created by authors using collected data.

frequent topics that Arabic teachers engage with are information and communication technology (ICT) skills, assessment practices, classroom management, cross-curricular skills, and parent-teacher cooperation. While all of these are vital topics for educators, what is surprising is that standards-based practices or student-centered learning are not among them. This data gives an indication of the type of professional development Arabic teachers are currently experiencing. However, it does not shed light on the quality and length of the professional development. Nor is the data able to show us to what extent skills and strategies acquired in those professional development sessions are getting transferred into the classroom.

It is a positive sign that during their teacher education many Arabic teachers reported engaging in activities linked to subject-specific pedagogical and content knowledge of Arabic. Furthermore, many teachers also reported having engaged in teacher education or professional development activities of a cross-curricular or multidisciplinary nature. Currently, most professional development workshops offered in the UAE are typically daylong seminars throughout the school year. Teachers attend professional development days in which they can select several different two-hour sessions on a variety of topics. While many of these sessions are interactive, there is often a mismatch between the topics being offered and the realities of the classroom and the actual needs of the teachers. Although, this indicates that these are topics that are being addressed in teacher training, it does not address the quality of training nor does it speak to the long-term transfer necessary to be fully integrated into the classroom.

OBSERVATIONS OF UAE ARABIC PRIMARY CLASSROOMS

To gain a more qualitative perspective into the pedagogical practices of Arabic language teachers, the first author in collaboration with several colleagues conducted a series of observations in primary Arabic classrooms in the UAE. This study was designed to shed light on the current pedagogical practices of Arabic teachers and to see if the many policy and structural changes to the education system since 2017 have had an impact on Arabic classroom practices. The observations discussed below were conducted as a case study in one private English medium school in the later part of 2019. The school population was overwhelmingly Arabic native speakers, who used SpA at home. The investigators observed nine classrooms from kindergarten through fifth grade and interviewed three teachers. While this remains a small sample, several reoccurring patterns of the primary Arabic classroom are worth discussing.

Preliminary analyses of the data show that two years after the introduction of the new Arabic standards, teachers at the schools did have their license from the MoE. However, we observed that the teachers still organized their classrooms in a traditional way. Most of the observed lessons were primarily focused on recitation and teaching of grammatical concepts. All observed classes in grades one through five were highly teacher-centered. It was observed that primary Arabic teachers focused on recitation and grammar for most of the lesson time. The textbook was the primary source of material for the classroom with only a few authentic sources available for use. The interactions in the classroom were mostly teacher-driven in a Question-Response-Evaluation format. Expressive production of Arabic language was minimal with students responding orally or in writing with single word or simple sentence responses. A positive sign was the increased amount of group work in the higher elementary grades. This encouraged students to practice their Arabic language skills, and students generally were mostly expected to be using MSA rather than dialects or English. When we interviewed the teachers, they mentioned that they were explicitly trying to incorporate more group work in the classroom.

To highlight, one class was centered around the theme of physical exercise. As typical for a lesson at the beginning of the unit, the new vocabulary was introduced. To engage students, the teacher brought in a soccer ball. This authentic artifact was used to engage students in the lesson and was, indeed, very effective. In a Question-Response-Evaluation format, the teacher probed the students for the vocabulary words required in the lesson. The teacher engaged in rich language and complex sentences in MSA. However, the students were only required to call out single words. This single word vocabulary was later reinforced with a worksheet, which also required a similar written response from students. The worksheet was completed in groups of four and answers were compared later in class. While it is important for students to be able to start from fundamental word-level vocabulary, this proved to be a reoccurring pattern throughout many observations. The teachers focused on the basic, low-level language skills and only intermittently challenged students to use their language in a more communicative way for higher order thinking.

NEW DIRECTIONS FOR ARABIC
TEACHER EDUCATION

Clearly, this paradigm shift toward standards-based instruction and teacher licensure in the UAE has important consequences for Arabic teacher education. However, based on the data presented above, there appears to be little change in what is happening in the classroom or in teacher training and professional development. To prioritize higher order thinking, like problem-solving, and frame Arabic as a tool, which is valuable to students, the general pedagogy must move to a more constructivist approach, implicitly fulfilling the priorities set by the standards. A constructivist approach can be defined as a theory of learning in which individuals build on what they know already using ideas and new knowledge in which they come in contact (Resnick 1989). A constructivist approach would shift the role of the student from being a passive participant to an active one in their learning and the role of the teacher from being the source of all knowledge to a facilitator that supports students in their quest for higher understanding, scaffolding new concepts with them (Atwell 1987).

Moving toward a more constructivist approach in Arabic language arts might have several implications. First, to make meaning of the new knowledge, students would develop higher order skills like critical thinking and problem-solving. Second, students may develop new perspectives toward Arabic language; seeing it as a tool to engage with texts of different genres and with authors who offer a whole range of new ideas and ways to use the language. While this approach may not be without critics, the shift does address the call to revise and modernize Arabic language teaching and learning to prepare students to participate in a knowledge society (UNPD 2014).

A constructivist approach would mean that Arabic teachers would utilize student-centered methods. A student-centered approach is not simply group work that the teacher assigns. Rather, it is where the focus of instruction shifts from the teacher to the student. The teacher becomes a facilitator and someone who scaffolds student learning through carefully planned learning experiences. One example of student-centered instruction is project-based learning (PBL). PBL can be defined as a method "in which students gain knowledge and skills by working for an extended period of time to investigate and respond to a complex question, problem, or challenge" (Knoll 1997, 59). PBL has not only been found to improve academic achievement (Geier et al., 2008) but also has been credited with increase in student engagement and motivation (Thomas, 2000). PBL often begins with the teacher asking a question and students devising their own direction to solve the question (Thomas, 2000). Through PBL in an Arabic language arts classroom, students employ Arabic language to engage in complex reasoning and problem-solving skills. Organized around a central theme, the teacher can reinforce and expand students content knowledge of Arabic vocabulary as well as grammar and mechanics (Knoll 1997, 59). The PBL method would emphasize Arabic as a tool for written and oral communication that has everyday value.

Another method that has been found to be very effective in other language arts classrooms is the workshop approach. Pioneered by Lucy Calkin (1994), the workshop approach starting in upper primary grades allows for extensive time of task for students' independent reading and writing. The workshop approach divides the classroom instruction into sections, where in the first part of the class the teacher gives a mini lesson focusing on one aspect of language (i.e., sentence structure). Then students engage in individual writing or reading. The advantage of this method in a language arts classroom is that it allows teachers to have explicit teaching time as well as develops students' autonomy in the writing and reading process (Calkin 2006). Another important outcome is that students have ample opportunities to practice different types of writing and working their way through the writing process. In a reading workshop, students are exposed to a vast quantity of texts. In the 2018 PISA teacher questionnaire, teachers reported that the longest text that they used was only a few pages. Students need to be able to develop the skills, stamina, and grit to handle longer texts. To increase student fluency, students need to be extensively and repeatedly exposed to texts of varying lengths and genres. The workshop approach allows for this, once students are able to read fluently, while also enabling teachers to focus on specific aspects of mechanics as well as individualized learning by utilizing mini lessons in the classroom.

RECOMMENDATIONS FOR POLICY MAKERS

Not only must teachers reevaluate how they are conducting their classes, but policy makers can also support this shift in several ways. The most important aspect is improving the quality of teacher preparation and teacher training programs. It is well documented that educators who have deep understanding and knowledge of their discipline and can implement effective pedagogy are the key to student success (Darling-Hammond 2000, Faour 2012, Taha 2017). While this combination of content and pedagogical knowledge is required in the licensure process, it is also imperative for teacher preparation and training programs to offer and ensure that their graduates have both. Currently in the UAE, preservice educators can be prepared through a formal education program that focuses on either general pedagogy or on Arabic Literature, which focuses on the understanding of deeper topics in literature with heavy emphasis on literary critique and classical prose and verse. There are no federally funded Arabic language teacher preparation programs (ECAE, 2020). The establishment of such programs would provide an opportunity to set a high standard of training with modern and effective preparation for teachers.

It is not only important to have a strong preparation system for teachers prior to entering the classroom, but teachers who are already in the classroom must have the chance to develop and refresh their skills for the classroom. This is especially true of all teachers currently in the field using the new UAE Arabic content standards. As discussed above, Arabic teachers are currently attending professional development on a variety of topics but the professional development model being utilized does not guarantee long-term transfer of skills. A more effective model might be to have a continuous, bottom-up approach (Villegas-Reimers 2003). In this approach, schools, departments, and teachers are active stakeholders in deciding the focus of the program of professional development creating stronger teacher buy in. Most importantly, professional development needs to occur over a sustained duration (Darling-Hammond, Hyler, and Gardner 2017). Professional development which takes place over a sustained duration allows for learning that is both rigorous and cumulative. Furthermore, it gives teachers the opportunity to apply what they have learned in professional development with ongoing support in an iterative process, which is more likely to lead to sustained change.

Policy makers can also support the development of an evidence-based set of "best practices" in the Arabic classroom similar to the Reading Panel's (2000) in the United States. The Reading Panel, consisting of a group of experts in the field of reading and education, was brought together by the US government to assess the effectiveness of different reading approaches in English language arts (National Reading Panel 2000). This group made great headway in determining "best practices" on how to implement effective literacy and reading instruction in the United States. An Arabic language equivalent would require both energy and resources but would enable teacher education and professional development programs to have a strong research and evidenced-based repertoire of "best practices" to train teachers for the Arabic language classroom.

CONCLUSION

In this chapter, we have attempted to highlight the current transformation in Arabic teaching and learning and its effects on teacher education in the UAE. Through many initiatives, the UAE government has tried to modernize and transition Arabic from a traditional focus on recitation and grammar to Arabic as a tool for communication and higher order thinking. This shift is strongly emphasized through the development of the 2017 Arabic language standards. However, despite this new direction for Arabic language arts, it is unclear if the standards approach has had any impact on classroom practices. Preliminary research shows that there has been little effect. A vital next step is to provide ongoing support for teachers in the implementation of these standards to help them transform their classrooms. This can be most effectively achieved through reevaluating and redesigning Arabic teacher education and professional development practices. This type of support will ensure that teachers not only understand but can implement twenty-first-century learning competencies in their classrooms and can help students to acquire them through the use of extensive reading of authentic Arabic texts of varying genres. This will also ensure that modern theories of language learning and development, as well as current methods, might be implemented in the classroom. Giving teachers the skills and the sustained support to develop those skills will transform the Arabic classroom. It is through this change that students will be prepared for the knowledge economy and for a future that depends on its youth having the needed literacy skills.

REFERENCES

Abadzi, Helen. 2017. "Improving Arab students' academic achievement: The crucial role of rapid reading and grammar mastery in the early grades." *Sheikh Saud bin Saqr Al Qasimi Foundation for Policy Research* 20. https://doi.org/10.18502/aqf.0047.

Abu-Rabia, Salim. 1999. "The effect of Arabic vowels on the reading comprehension of second- and sixth-grade native Arab children." *Journal of Psycholinguistic Research* 28, no. 1: 93–101. https://doi.org/10.1023/A:1023291620997.

Abu-Rabia, Salim. 2000. "Effects of exposure to literary Arabic on reading comprehension in a diglossia situation." *Reading and writing* 13, no. 1–2: 147–157.

AlDanan, Abdullah. 2010. *The theory of teaching MSA through natural practice: Application, assessment and dissemination.* Damascus-Syria: AlBasha'er Publishing House.

AlMousa, Nihad. 2007. *Arabic language in the modern era: Constant values and changing values.* Amman: AlShurouq Publishing House.

Atwell, Nancie. 1987. *In the middle: Writing, reading, and learning with adolescents.* Portsmouth: Heinemann Educational Books.

Ayari, Salah. 1996. "Diglossia and illiteracy in the Arab world." *Language, Culture and Curriculum* 9, no. 3: 243–253. https://doi.org/10.1080/07908319609525233.

Blumenfeld, Phyllis C., Ronald W. Marx, Joseph S. Krajcik, Barry Fishman, Elliot Soloway, and Juanita Clay Chambers. 2008. "Standardized test outcomes for students engaged in inquiry based science curricula in the context of urban reform." *Journal of Research in Science Teaching: The Official Journal of the National Association for Research in Science Teaching* 45, no. 8: 922–939.

Calkins, Lucy. M. 1994. *The art of teaching writing.* Portsmouth: Heinemann.

Calkins, Lucy. 2006. *A Guide to the Writing Workshop, Grades 3-5.* Portsmouth: First Hand.

Carroll, Kevin S., Bashar Al Kahwaji, and David Litz. 2017. "Triglossia and promoting Arabic literacy in the United Arab Emirates." *Language, Culture and Curriculum* 30, no. 3: 317–332.

Darling-Hammond, Linda. 2010. *Evaluating teacher effectiveness: How teacher performance assessments can measure and improve teaching. Center for American Progress.* Washington DC: Center for American Progress.

Darling-Hammond, Linda, Maria E. Hyler, and Madelyn Gardner. 2017. *Effective teacher professional development.* Washington DC: Learning Policy Institute.

Emirates College for Advanced Education. 2020. http:// www.ecae.ac.ae.

Eunice Kennedy Shriver National Institute of Child Health and Human Development. 2000. *Report of the national reading panel: Teaching children to read: Reports of the subgroups (00-4754).* Washington, DC: U.S. Government Printing Office.

Faour, Muhammad. 2012. *The Arab world's education report card: School climate and citizenship skills.* Washington, DC: Carnegie Endowment for International Peace.

Feitelson, Dina, Zahava Goldstein, Jihad Iraqi, and David L. Share. 1993. "Effects of listening to story reading on aspects of literacy acquisition in a diglossic situation." *Reading Research Quarterly* 28, no. 1: 71–79.

Ferguson, Charles A. 1959. Diglossia. *Word* 15, no. 2: 325–340.

Hill, Carolyn J., Howard S. Bloom, Alison Rebeck Black, and Mark W. Lipsey. "Empirical benchmarks for interpreting effect sizes in research." *Child Development Perspectives* 2, no. 3 (2008): 172–177.

Ibrahim, Raphiq, and Judith Aharon-Peretz. 2005. "Is literary Arabic a second language for native Arab speakers? Evidence from semantic priming study." *Journal of Psycholinguistic Research* 34, no. 1: 51–70. https://doi.org/10.1007/s10936-005-3631-8.

Knoll, Michael. 1997. "The project method: Its vocational education origin and international development." *Journal of Industrial Teacher Education* 34: 59–80.

Knowledge and Human Development Authority. 2020. *School inspection reports.* https://www.khda.gov.ae/en/DSIB/Reports?isSearched=1.

Mahfoudhi, Abdessatar, John Everatt, and Gad Elbeheri, 2011. Introduction to the special on literacy in Arabic. *Reading and Writing* 24, no. 9: 1011–1018.

Malek, Caline. 2015. "Arab children snubbing Arabic." *The National.* Education, October 12, 2015.

Moukhallati, Dana, and Salam Al Amir. 2015. "Sheikh Mohammed bin Rashid's reading initiative 'to enrich children's imagination.'" *The National.* Education, September 17, 2015.

Mullis, Ina. V. S., Michael O. Martin, Pierre Foy, and Martin Hooper. 2017. *PIRLS 2016 International Results in Reading.* http://timssandpirls.bc.edu/pirls2016/international-results/.

Nassir, Sarwat. 2017. "New ratings system for UAE universities." *Khaleej Times.* UAE, November 20, 2020. https://www.khaleejtimes.com/nation/new-ratings-system-for-uae-universities-education-quality.

OECD. 2019. *PISA 2018 Results (Volume I): What Students Know and Can Do.* https://doi.org/10.1787/5f07c754-en.

PIRLS. 2016. *International results in reading: PIRLS 2016 countries.* http://timssandpirls.bc.edu/pirls2016/international-results/pirls/about-pirls-2016/pirls-2016-countries/.

PISA. 2018. *Program for International Student Assessment (PISA).* https://www.oecd.org/pisa/.

Resnick, Lauren. B. 1989. "Introduction." In *Knowing, learning, and instruction,* edited by Lauren. B. Resnick, 1–24. Hillsdale, NJ: Lawrence Erlbaum.

Saiegh-Haddad, Elinor, and John Everatt. 2018. "Early literacy education in Arabic." In *The Routledge international handbook of early literacy education,* edited by Natalia Kucirkova, Catherine Snow, Vibeke Grover, and Catherone McBride-Chang, 185–199. London: Routledge. https://doi.org/10.4324/9781315766027-17.

Shousha, Farouk. (2014). ElSaid Badawi: A one of a kind scholar. *AlAhram Newspaper.* http://www.ahram.org.eg/NewsPrint/271563.aspx.

Taha, Hanada. 2017. "Arabic language teacher education." In *Applied linguistics in the Middle East and North Africa,* edited by Atta Gebril, 269–287. Amsterdam: John Benjamins Publishing Company.

Taha, Haitham, and Hanan Azaizahshe. 2017. Visual word recognition and vowelization in Arabic: New evidence from lexical decision task performances. *Cognitive Process* 18: 521–527. https://doi.org/10.1007/s10339-017-0830-9.

Taha, Haitham, and Taha Hanada. (2020). "Morpho-orthographic preferences among typical and poor native Arab readers." *Writing Systems Research*. DOI10.1080/17 586801.2020.1805394.

Taha, Hanada, and Richard B. Speaker. 2018. "Arabic language arts standards: Revolution or disruption?" *Research in Comparative and International Education* 13, no. 1: 1–19.

Thomas, John W. (2000). *A review of research on project-based learning*. San Rafael, CA: The Autodesk Foundation.

Thomure, Hanada Taha. 2019. "Arabic language education in the UAE: Choosing the right drivers." In *Education in the United Arab Emirates*, edited by Kay Gallagher, 75–93. Singapore: Springer.

Tibi, Sana, and Lorraine McLeod. 2014. "The Development of young children's Arabic language and literacy in the United Arab Emirates." In *Handbook of Arabic Literacy*, edited by Elinor Saiegh-Haddad and Malatesha R. Joshi, 303–321. Dordrecht: Springer. https://doi.org/10.1007/978-94-017-8545-7_14.

UAE Government. 2020. *Vision 2021*. https://www.vision2021.ae/en.

UAE Government. 2020. *Qualifications to be a teacher*. https://u.ae/en/information-and-services/education/school-education-k-12/joining-k-12-education/qualifications-to-be-a-teacher.

UAE Ministry of Education. 2017. *The general framework for curriculum standards 2017 Arabic language*. https://www.moe.gov.ae/En/ImportantLinks/Curriculum AndAssessment/Pages/GeneralStandards.aspx.

UNDP. 2014. *The Arab knowledge report for 2014: Youth and the nationalization of knowledge*. https://www.knowledge4all.com/uploads/files/AKR2014UAE/en/AK R2014_UAE_Full_En.pdf.

Versteegh, Kees. 2006. "History of Arabic language teaching." In *Handbook for Arabic language teaching professionals in the 21st century*, edited by Kassem Wahba, Zeinab A. Taha, and Liz England, 3–12. UK: Routledge.

Villegas-Reimers, Eleonora. 2003. *Teacher professional development: An international review of the literature*. Paris: International Institute for Educational Planning.

Part II

PEDAGOGICAL APPROACHES AND PRAXIS IN TEACHER EDUCATION

Chapter 4

Teachers' Preparedness for Inclusive Education in Oman

Exploring the Role of Teachers' Agency for Inclusive Practices and Professional Skills

Mahmoud Mohamed Emam and
Ali Hussain Al-Bulushi

INTRODUCTION

Implementing and generating educational reform in schools is largely contingent on teachers' active engagement and involvement. Teachers' continuous learning and professional development are considered key determinants of how teachers adapt to and accept change in pedagogical practice and educational policy. The creation and implementation of new educational ideas in schools provide teachers with opportunities for engagement and collaborative learning. Therefore, the idea of teachers as active agents of school change and development has become central to both educational policy and practice. Alternatively, an argument of the lack of agency and taking the initiative to lead educational change has come to the forefront of the discourse on school development in the educational systems across the globe in general and in Oman in particular (Bakkenes, Vermunt, and Wubbels 2010, Pyhältö, Pietarinen, and Soini 2014).

The Sultanate of Oman is one of the Arab states of Gulf Cooperation Council (GCC), which is a regional intergovernmental political and economic union consisting of all Arab states overlooking the Arabian Gulf. GCC countries include, in addition to Oman, the Kingdom of Saudi Arabia, Bahrain, Kuwait, Qatar, and United Arab Emirates. It borders Yemen in the south, the United Arab Emirates in the northwest, and Kingdom of Saudi Arabia in the west. Although the educational system in Oman is a centralized

57

system, it encourages teachers to be autonomous professionals in implementing national educational initiatives in their school contexts. Thus, any educational reform that brings about change in pedagogical practice in Oman is implemented by teachers and school leaders. Little is known, however, on how Omani teachers respond to initiatives that involve change in policy and practice (Emam 2016). The current chapter explores how teachers perceive their agency with regard to inclusive education (IE) policy and practice. To do so, we first describe IE in Oman in terms of both policy and practice by reviewing policy mandates and empirical research. Second, we report some preliminary findings from a research project that examines associations between teachers' agency for inclusive practices (TAIP), professional skills, and support in school context.

INCLUSIVE EDUCATION IN OMAN: A SYNERGY OF POLICY AND PRACTICE

IE represents a large-scale school reform in Oman that has posed several challenges since it was first introduced in 2002. The challenges have been mainly connected with the profound multilevel changes required to occur in the Omani comprehensive school system. IE is based on the Ministry of Education (MoE) mandate which was issued in 2007, emphasizing the rights of all students with special educational needs (SEN) for receiving their education in public schools and have access to the general curriculum. The core aim of this mandate was to support pupils with SEN to learn and reach their full potential in a least restrictive environment. The IE initiative in Oman was motivated by several factors. First, Oman responded officially to the international rights-based discourse on IE, which was advocated by international organizations and propagated by world declarations such as the UNESCO World Declaration on Education for All (EFA) in 1990, the Salamanca Statement and Framework for Action on Special Needs Education in 1994, and the Convention on the Rights of Persons with Disabilities that was adopted in 2006.

The international documents, which were officially endorsed by the Omani government, informed the recent development of IE practices in schools in Oman. Furthermore, IE in Oman was reinforced through the issuance of royal decrees and the passing of judicial acts aimed primarily to the enhancement of the quality of life for people with disabilities and their families. The Omani Children with Disabilities Care and Rehabilitation Act (OCDCR) which was first issued in 1996 and reauthorized in 2008 has set the stage for structural and organizational changes in the Omani educational system, as well as the social welfare scheme for families of children with disabilities. According to Article 24 of the 2008 Act, all students with disabilities are eligible for admission in public schools and should be provided with quality educational services within an inclusive school context that supports their needs. The MoE has translated the royal decrees and officially acts into the educational agenda by granting access to public schools to different categories of children with disabilities, including students with learning disabilities (LD), students with intellectual disabilities, students with physical disabilities, students with emotional and behavioral difficulties, and students with sensory impairments. In 2015, the MoE responded to the societal calls for providing IE services to students with autism spectrum disorders (ASD). The call came as part of the National Scheme for Children with ASD that was based on a joint initiative between Oman and United Nations International Children's Emergency Fund (UNICEF). The plan was aimed primarily at changing the landscape of the educational provision for students with ASD who used to receive rehabilitation care in specialized centers operated under the supervision of the Ministry of Social Development. Long before these legislative initiatives came into effect, children with disabilities in general (e.g., learners with visual and/ or hearing impairment) used to receive their education in separate special schools or in specialized social centers. They were, however, offered educational services in self-contained classrooms in public schools and spent plenty of time and performed extracurricular activities with typically developing peers. Two decades ago, the majority of children with disabilities received their education in care centers called Al-Amal. Several families, however, have benefited from the legislative acts and policy mandates and have had their children transitioned to public schools. Students with LD represent the largest category of students with disabilities benefiting from inclusive practices and a formal system of support in school contexts. The MoE established the LD program in all cycle 1 (i.e., equivalent to primary education in other contexts) schools in Oman, which include grades 1 to 4. The program aimed at providing students with disabilities evidence-based educational practices in a resource room as a pull-out program, but without decreasing the amount of learning engagement time in the regular classroom. The resource room is led by specialized teachers who have qualifications or intensive training in teaching students with LD. A specially designed endorsement program in the form of a one-year diploma was developed in joint initiative between Sultan Qaboos University and the MoE to prepare teachers to work effectively with students with LD. The program had been running for over 10 years from 2004 to 2016 and was then replaced by a master program in LD.

The aforementioned IE policy and practice changes have been combined with similar efforts at the research level. In 2012, Sultan Qaboos University funded a large-scale project that aimed at developing a national framework for identifying students with LD and provided them with evidence-based instructional intervention (Emam and Kazem 2015). The project, which continued for three years resulted in developing evidence-based diagnostic instruments that were grounded in empirically supported models including the aptitude-achievement discrepancy model, the cognitive deficit model, and the response to intervention model. The project involved training teachers across Oman on using the diagnostic instruments and intervention materials to support students with LD in schools. Additionally, the number of research articles which examined inclusive practices and explored the quality of educational services to students with disabilities in Oman has increased over the last decade. A number of research studies written in English and published in indexed peer-reviewed journals examined IE practices in Oman. Emam (2016) conducted a qualitative inquiry by interviewing twenty-five school leaders to examine the barriers and challenges that face IE in Oman. The barriers included teachers' lack of the necessary competencies for inclusive pedagogies such as adaptation of instructional and assessment strategies, lack of resources, and weak inclusive culture in schools. The study concluded that there was a dichotomy that could best describe IE in Oman, namely a distinction between IE as theoretically embraced versus as practically implemented. Informed by the qualitative enquiry, Emam proposed a three-level prism-shaped framework for action to enhance IE practices in Oman schools. The framework placed teachers at the core fundamental level in order to build the capacity of IE practitioners in Oman. In a recent study, Emam and Al-Mahdy (2020a) explored the construct of teachers' efficacy for inclusive practices among general educators and to what extent it was influenced by gender and years of teaching. The study surveyed 287 teachers from both genders in cycles 1 and 2 schools in Oman and found that teachers with more years of teaching experience and female teachers generally reported higher levels of efficacy for inclusive practices, particularly in using inclusive instruction and in collaborating with other teachers to support students with SEN.

TEACHER AGENCY AND IE:
THE SEARCH FOR A DEFINITE MATCH

Although school reforms in Oman in general and in relation to inclusive practices in particular are based on centralized decisions at the MoE, the implementation of inclusive practices is constructed and negotiated by different stakeholders at different levels in a reciprocal manner. The demands associated with inclusive pedagogies require teachers to collaborate, adapt, and adopt those reforms. However, the reforms could also be ignored or at least inadequately addressed by teachers and schools because the response of teachers depends largely on their involvement in the educational changes. Despite the strides that Oman has taken toward creating a model of best IE practice, there is still a problematic gap between policy and practice (Emam 2016). This is exemplified in the lack of school culture that supports IE, the lack of collaboration between teachers and other staff, and the fragmented pedagogies that are implemented in the regular classroom to support diverse learners (Florian and Linklater 2010, Gaad 2010). Recently, a number of scholars have argued that general constructs and variables, which have been examined in schooling contexts, may need to be revisited and investigated in relation to IE, such as efficacy for inclusive practices and inclusive school climate (Ahsan, Sharma, and Deppeler 2012, Emam and Al-Mahdy 2020b, Emam and Al-Mahdy 2020a, Park et al. 2016, Sharma and Nuttal 2016), and agency for inclusive practices (Li and Ruppar 2020, Wang, Mu, and Zhang 2017).

Pyhältö, Pietarinen, and Soini (2014) posit that a single behavioral attribute such as self-efficacy, motivation, or attitude cannot solely explain teachers' engagement with educational changes and school reform-related practice. It seems that other integrative concepts such as professional agency are important to examine teachers' engagement in educational change, response to new educational initiatives, and commitment to school reform. Research on teacher agency was primarily informed by research on human and professional agency in general (Bandura 2018, Priestley et al. 2012, Priestley, Biesta, and Robinson 2016). In particular, the study of teacher agency was mainly influenced by the sociocultural perspective on human agency as a "temporally embedded process of social engagement" (Emirbayer and Mische 1998, 963). Emirbayer and Mische (1998) argued that human agency implies a dynamic combination of "iterational," "projective," and "practical evaluative" elements, which reflect the interplay between learning from past experiences, having an orientation toward alternative possibilities in the future, and engaging the past and the future at the current time.

Teacher agency has been recently examined in various international contexts in relation to social justice, and IE (Pantić 2017, Pantić and Florian 2015). The main premise in connecting teacher agency and IE is that teachers are viewed as having a significant role in transforming educational settings to cater for students with SEN. Agency for inclusive practices was primarily envisioned by special educators, who were seen as active decision-makers and school change contributors (Li and Ruppar 2020, 2). Generally, scholars posit that TAIP can help narrow the gap between policy and practice in IE (Emam 2016, Waitoller and Artiles 2013). Research on agency for IE is limited. In a recent review, Li and Ruppar (2020) located only nine empirical research studies which examined TAIP. Of the nine studies five were grounded in qualitative enquiry, two used quantitative methods, and two employed mixed method approach to examine TAIP. The nine studies were all conducted in non-Arabic-speaking countries. In their review, Li and Ruppar (2020) found that 78 percent of the research studies examined TAIP from a sociocultural perspective which conceptualizes teacher agency as a temporally embedded process of social engagement, and as an outcome of an intentional interaction between teachers and school context. Wang, Mu, and Zhang (2017), for example, suggested that the search for successful IE practices requires agentic teachers. They also proposed that TAIP needs to be examined in more depth in relation to other school and teacher-related variables. Alternatively, 22 percent of the reviewed studies examined teacher agency from a social cognitive perspective which conceptualizes TAIP as an individual and collective capacity to create inclusive school climate by sharing knowledge, skills, and collaboration among school teachers (Lyons, Thompson, and Timmons 2016). Based on their review, Li and Ruppar (2020) proposed a conceptual framework for TAIP which includes five core elements:

1. inclusive teacher identity
2. professional competence
3. inclusive professional philosophy
4. autonomy
5. reflectivity

Thus, in the current chapter, we argue that agency for inclusive practices could imply a reciprocally interdependent relationship between the individual's capacity and choices to serve students with SEN and the contextual opportunities, resources, and challenges that may permit or curb such capacity. This conceptualization is based on the sociocultural perspective of human agency as a temporally embedded process of social engagement and as employed in Wang et al.'s study (Wang, Mu, and Zhang 2017). We report some preliminary data on the association between TAIP, teachers' professional skills, and school support. The aim of the empirical data reported in the current chapter is threefold: (1) to examine the association between TAIP and teachers' professional skills; (2) to investigate the impact and moderating effects of gender, teachers' years of teaching, and teachers' experience of teaching students with SEN on TAIP, teachers' professional skills and school support; and (3) to examine the mediating effects of school support in the association between TAIP and teachers' professional skills.

METHODOLOGY

The data which we report in the current chapter is part of a lager research project about the preparedness of general educators in the Sultanate of Oman for transforming public elementary schools to inclusive schools, which would cater for the diverse needs of students with disabilities. The data for the pilot study was collected from teachers in elementary schools in Muscat, the capital and largest city of the Sultanate of Oman. In general, the elementary educational system in Oman is comprised of cycle 1 and grades 5 and 6 from cycle 2 schools. The Ministry of education granted the research team access to schools after discussing the research project. The research was also approved by the College of Education research committee and was given institutionalized ethical clearance in the area of human research. The research study uses a cross-sectional design to examine the associations between TAIP, professional skills, professional experience, and school support.

PARTICIPANTS

Convenience sampling was employed to recruit teachers to participate in the pilot study. An online survey using Google Forms was designed and included comprehensive information on the research study goals. The use of Google Forms ensured the confidentiality of the teachers' responses. The Google Form URL was shared with teachers in schools through the Technical Office at the MoE, which is responsible for coordinating research studies. We also sent the survey link to teachers through formal teacher WhatsApp groups. The use of Google Forms was appropriate for data collection particularly as the COVID-19 pandemic limited the opportunities for approaching teachers using other methods. During data collection, schools were adopting remote education modalities and online learning. Only 133 teachers submitted their responses. The number was sufficient for a pilot study. All schools had a learning disability resource room (LDRR), which provided special education services to students referred for LD. This implies that teachers had previous exposure to working with students with SEN. Participants included both males (34, 26 percent) and females (97, 74 percent). All had a minimum of a bachelor degree in education. Age of the participating teachers ranged from 26 to 46. Participants' teaching experience varied widely from less than one year (coded as 0) to fifteen years. Participants' year of experience teaching students with SEN ranged from less than one year (coded as 0) to seven years.

INSTRUMENTS

Single Item Measures

Teachers' previous and current professional experiences were measured by a set of single-indicator variables, including years of teaching experience and years of experience teaching students with SEN.

Multiple Item Measures

We measured teacher agency and professional skills by using the teacher agency and professional skills subscales of the Teacher Professional Competence Scale (TPCS) (Mu et al. 2015). The TPCS is comprised of four subscales, including teacher agency, professional skills, teacher knowledge, and teacher attitude. SPSS-26 was used to perform the internal consistency reliability test on the sample of the current study, and AMOS-26 was used to perform Confirmatory Factor Analysis (CFA) in order to test the construct validity of the measurement. We translated the two subscales of teacher agency and professional skills to Arabic using the back translation method (Sperber 2004). The teacher agency subscale includes six items which examine teacher's engagement and proactivity to seek support of their efforts to teach students with SEN (e.g., I use resource rooms to help students with disabilities) (Cronbach's $\alpha = 0.874$). The professional skills subscale includes eight items and explores teachers' knowledge of how to cater for the needs of students with disabilities in a regular classroom (e.g., I am able to adjust teaching objectives and requirements according to the characteristics of students with disabilities) (Cronbach's $\alpha = 0.822$). CFA was performed to construct a two-factor measurement model with eight indicators loaded on professional skills and six indicators loaded on teacher agency. The model fit reasonably well, with NFI, RFI, IFI, TLI, and CFI equal to 0.954, 0.0.949, 0.0.964, 0.947, and 0.952 respectively, RMSEA = 0.062, and ($\chi^2/76 = 2.66$, $p < 0.001$). Results from Cronbach's α test and CFA are indicative of the high reliability and validity of the measurement.

Teacher Support

We measured quality of the overall support that teachers receive from schools by using the Teacher Support Scale (TSS) (Wang et al. 2015). We translated the TSS to Arabic using the back translation method (Sperber 2004). The TSS assesses the multifaceted support which teachers receive to teach students with SEN, including specialist, peer, physical, cultural, and institutional support. The specialist support scale has four items and explores the specialized support that is provided to students with SEN in class through special educators or learning disability teachers (e.g., Special education professionals regularly come to my class to provide service [e.g., health care and language therapy] [Cronbach's $\alpha = 0.862$]). The peer support scale has two items that describe the quality of interactions between the teacher and his/her colleagues to helps students with SEN reach their optimal learning level (e.g., Other subject teachers actively communicate with me about the conditions of students with special needs) (Cronbach's $\alpha = 0.815$). The physical support scale includes eight items and examines the size and function of the classroom, as well as assistive and material resources for teaching students with SEN in regular classrooms (e.g., The classroom has enough space for me to conduct teaching activities that address students' special needs) (Cronbach's $\alpha = 0.838$). The cultural support scale consists of six items and is about the values and dispositions, which create an environmental friendliness for teaching students with SEN in regular classroom (e.g., My class has a fair, sharing, and collaborative culture) (Cronbach's $\alpha = 0.880$). The institutional support scale is comprised of six items, which assess the support the teacher receives at the organization (e.g., My school encourages teachers to design diverse, flexible approaches to assess the performance of students with disabilities) (Cronbach's $\alpha = 0.891$). CFA was performed to construct a five-factor measurement model with eight indicators loaded on physical support, four indicators loaded on specialist support, two indicators loaded on peer support, six indicators loaded on institutional support, and six indicators loaded on cultural support. The model fit reasonably well, with NFI, RFI, IFI, TLI, and CFI equal to 0.0.938, 0.927, 0.0.948, 0.0.945, and 0.940 respectively, RMSEA = 0.074 and ($\chi^2/289 = 2.35$, $p < 0.001$). Results from Cronbach's α test and CFA are indicative of the high reliability and validity of the measurement.

DATA ANALYSIS AND RESULTS

To answer the first research question, we used SPSS-26 to perform regression analysis. To answer the second, third, and fourth research questions, we used SPSS-26 with Process Analysis Add-on (Hayes 2013) to detect moderation and mediation effects. In the sections to follow, we report our quantitative data analysis in relation to the research questions.

Question One: Relationship between TAIP and Their Professional Skills

We used simple linear regression to analyze the relationship between TAIP (independent variable) and professional skills (dependent variable). The model fits well (F [1, 129] = 116.46, $p < 0.001$), with 47.47 percent of the variance of professional skills explained by TAIP. TAIP had a significant contribution to professional skills (b = 0.94, $\beta = 0.689$ $p < 0.001$). More agentic teachers tend to be more skillful in implementing inclusive teaching practices.

Question Two: The Effects of Gender, Teaching Experience, and Prior Experience of Teaching Students with SEN on TAIP, Professional Skills, Physical Support, Specialist Support, Peer Support, Cultural Support, and Institutional Support

A three-way multivariate analysis of variance (three-way MANOVA) was applied to evaluate the possible effects of the gender, teaching experience, and prior experience of teaching students with SEN on TAIP, professional skills, physical support, specialist support, peer support, cultural support, and institutional support. First, we used Box's test of equality of covariance matrices. For the variables TAIP and professional skills, there was equality of covariance matrices F (36, 1929.85(= 1.27, p > 0.05); for the variables physical support, specialist support, peer support, cultural support, and institutional support, there was equality of covariance matrices F (90, 3639.23) = 1.15, p > 0.05). Second, we performed a three-way MANOVA. As shown in table 4.1, there are no significant effects (all p values > 0.05) of gender, teaching experience, and prior experience of teaching students with SEN on TAIP, professional skills, physical support, specialist support, peer support, cultural support and institutional support.

Question Three: The Relationship between TAIP and Professional Skills Moderated by Teachers' Years of Experience and Prior Experience of Teaching Students with SEN

We used process analysis to detect possible moderators of the relationship between TAIP and professional skills. Years of experience, teaching students with SEN (see the aforementioned single-indicator variables) were treated as moderators. The moderation model fit well (F [5, 125] = 24.26, p > 0.001), and the moderation effect was not significant for years of experience (F [1, 125] = 0.13, p > 0.05). In addition, moderation effect was not significant for teaching students with disabilities (F [1, 125] = 2.12, p > 0.05).

Question Four: The Relationship between TAIP and Professional Skills Mediated by School Support

We used process analysis to examine the mediation effect of school support on the relationship between TAIP and professional skills. Physical support, specialist support, peer support, institutional support, and cultural support were treated as five mediators. The relationships between TAIP and the five

Table 4.1 The Results of Three-Way Multivariate Analysis of Variance (Three-Way MANOVA)

Variables	Effect	Pillai's Trace	F	Hypothesis df	Error df	P Value
Professional skills	Intercept	0.89	398.13	2	98	0.000***
Teacher agency	Gender	0.01	0.39	2	98	0.681
	Teaching experience	0.04	0.42	10	198	0.937
	Teaching students with disabilities	0.08	1.08	8	198	0.380
	Gender * Teaching experience	0.03	0.26	10	198	0.988
	Gender * Teaching students with disabilities	0.03	0.47	6	198	0.829
	Teaching experience * Teaching students with disabilities	0.11	0.66	18	198	0.850
	Gender * Teaching experience * Teaching students with disabilities	0.03	0.45	6	198	0.842
Physical support	Intercept	0.88	144.58	5	95	0.000***
Specialist support	Gender	0.07	1.36	5	95	0.245
Peer support	Teaching experience	0.33	1.39	25	495	0.103
Cultural support	Teaching students with disabilities	0.28	1.49	20	392	0.082
Institutional support	Gender * Teaching experience	0.36	1.42	25	495	0.087
	Gender * Teaching students with disabilities	0.15	1.02	15	291	0.434
	Teaching experience * Teaching students with disabilities	0.31	1.27	45	495	0.119
	Gender * Teaching experience * Teaching students with disabilities	0.19	1.65	15	291	0.061

Notes: *** $p < 0.001$.
Source: Table created by authors using collected data.

mediators and those between the five mediators and professional skills were all significant (see table 4.2), which fulfill the statistical requirement for mediation analysis. The five mediators were added to the model simultaneously. The model goodness of fit was statistically acceptable (F [6, 124] = 26.93, p < 0.001), with 56.58 percent of the variance of professional skills jointly explained by TAIP and school support (the five mediators). Only the institutional support, cultural support, and specialist support mediators were found to be significant (see table 4.3). The total effect of TAIP on professional skills (β = 0.689, p < 0.001) consisted of two parts: the direct effect of TAIP on professional skills (β = 0.277, p < 0.001) and the indirect effect of TAIP on professional skills through the mediators (β = 0.412, p < 0.001). In brief, the five forms of school support significantly and partially mediated the relationship between TAIP and professional skills.

DISCUSSION

In the current chapter we reviewed research on teacher agency in relation to IE. We described the historical development of IE in Oman and reported some preliminary results on the effect of TAIP, professional skills, and school support as key factors in advancing IE practices. Our main goal was to underscore the importance of general educators agency for inclusive practices as an essential component for creating a model of best practices in IE across the country. It is argued that when teachers are agentic, they seek various available supports within the school context and target their own personal professional development even though resources may be scarce. We collected data to answer four research questions, which found that Omani general educators who intentionally seek resources and provide assistance within and beyond the school context perceived themselves as skillful and competent in teaching students with SEN. This finding was in line with previous research, which showed that teacher agency was a significant element of teacher professionalism (Biesta, Priestley, and Robinson 2015, Lipponen and Kumpulainen 2011, Priestley, Biesta, and Robinson 2013, Rogers and Wetzel 2013). Even though teacher agency and teacher professionalism are argued to be multidimensional constructs, our preliminary data showed that Omani general educators' TAIP was reflected in their active engagement in seeking support, which, in turn, had an impact on their professional skills.

The second research question found no possible significant effects of gender, teaching experience, and prior experience of teaching students with SEN on TAIP, professional skills, physical support, specialist support, peer support, cultural support, and institutional support. Our hypothesis was not supported. This could be attributed partially to the relatively small size of our

Table 4.2 Pearson Correlation Coefficients between Professional Skills, Teacher Agency and Physical Support, Specialist Support, Peer Support, Cultural Support, and Institutional Support

Variables		Physical Support	Specialist Support	Peer Support	Cultural Support	Institutional Support
Professional skills	Pearson Correlation	0.507	0.218	0.250	0.288	0.302
	P value	0.000***	0.012*	0.004**	0.001**	0.000***
Teacher agency	Pearson Correlation	0.610	0.485	0.566	0.593	0.525
	P value	0.000***	0.000***	0.000***	0.000***	0.000***

Notes: *** p < 0.001, **p < 0.01, *p < 0.05.
Source: Table created by authors using collected data.

Table 4.3   Mediation Effect of School Support

Mediator	Effect (β)	Sobel test (Z)	P Value
Institutional support	0.182	2.893	0.004**
Cultural support	0.076	2.057	0.040*
Peer support	0.006	0.265	0.791
Specialist support	0.077	2.139	0.032*
Physical support	0.071	1.151	0.250

Notes: **p < 0.01, *p < 0.05, β = standardized effect.
Source: Table created by authors using collected data.

sample. However, another reason could be that teacher agency, professional skills and receiving school support are not really influenced in the regular school context. Qualitative research on teacher agency provided anecdotal evidence that, regardless of gender, teaching experience or other demographic variables, three mechanisms determine to some extent the success of bringing change and reform to school practices. These mechanisms include peer learning, patterned social interaction, and shared instructional understandings, aims and practices (Bridwell-Mitchell 2015, Bridwell-Mitchell and Sherer 2017, Ganon-Shilon and Schechter 2019, Martin and Carter 2015, Philpott and Oates 2017).

In the third question, however, we examined the data more deeply by examining the moderation effect of general educators' years of teaching experience and their prior experience in teaching students with SEN on the association between TAIP and professional skills. Our research question was based on the argument that teachers' previous experiences may have an impact on their current and future pedagogical performance teaching SEN learners. We hypothesized that previous experience in teaching students with SEN and the number of teaching experiences in general may moderate the relationship between TAIP and professional skills. Our data showed no moderation effect of both variables. This, however, does not imply that both variables are not important for teacher agency. In particular, we may argue that prior exposure to teaching students with SEN is implicitly accrued but may not come to the forefront of teachers' selective attention until a challenging situation arises. Also, it could be argued that years of experience and prior experience of teaching students with SEN are necessarily manifested in professional skills but they may form a personal resource and may grow over years to shape an unwritten code of serving students with SEN in and beyond school borders.

The fourth research question evaluated the mediational effect of school support in the association between TAIP and professional skills. Our findings showed that, of the five school support mediators, institutional support, cultural support, and specialist support were found significant. These findings resonated with the three distinctive elements of teacher agency, namely cultural aspects associated with values and discourse on IE, the structural element which involves roles and relationships, and the school physical environment. Recently, Emam and Al-Mahdy (2020b) argued that inclusive school climate is necessary for teachers to engage actively with students with SEN, collaborate with other teachers and school staff to support students with SEN, and to prioritize the learning academic outcomes of students with SEN. An adequate inclusive school climate comprises three main dimensions: teacher prosocial motivation toward IE, inclusive school leadership, and academic excellence. Based on our findings, it could be argued that agentic teachers for inclusive practices are likely to engage with students with SEN by identifying, seeking, securing, and creating support even though the school may be a resource-scarce context. They evaluate the conflict between shortage of support and the needs of students with SEN within the classroom. They count on their agency in compensating for the gap between the type and quality of resources they request and what is actually available on hand. Teacher agency examines all types of support available whether associated with values and dispositions, or with organizational and structural aspects of school, or connected with the powerful collegial relationships with colleagues. This finding was corroborated by previous research studies (Emam and Al-Mahdy 2020a, Priestley et al. 2012, Datnow 2012, Emam 2016). There is research evidence that agentic teachers tend to collaborate with each other (Schweisfurth 2006), and that teacher agency is connected with principal support for novice teachers. Furthermore, our finding may imply that TAIP may help create an adequate ecology for IE. Support-seeking behavior is recognized as a significant catalyst for successful inclusive practices (Wang, Mu, and Zhang 2017, Consortium 2001), and professional skills development (Tomlinson 2001).

CONCLUSION AND FUTURE RESEARCH

We attempted to describe how IE in Oman has developed in the last two decades and how it was informed by the global discourse on the rights of students with disabilities for equal opportunities in schools. Additionally, the chapter provided an enquiry into the construct of teacher agency as a significant factor that could describe how teachers can enact practice and engage with policy in the area of IE. TAIP has emerged recently as a concept to emphasize the role of teachers as the most influential factor on school improvement in implementing inclusive practices. Omani general educators who deliberately seek resources and collaborate with others within and beyond their schools' context perceive themselves as skillful and competent in teaching students with SEN. Our inquiry mainly examined the association between TAIP, professional skills, and five dimensions of school support. Based on searching various scientific databases, we may claim that this is the first inquiry of TAIP in an Arab context. Our preliminary investigation and findings, therefore, need to be replicated and extended to other Arabic-speaking countries. Overall, we found no significant effects of gender, teaching experience, and prior experience of teaching students with SEN on TAIP, professional skills, and the five school support mediators.

The contribution of our enquiry is timely as Oman, informed by international discourse on IE, is making strides toward transforming public schools to inclusive schools. We are currently collecting more data from different Arabic-speaking countries which have grappled with the implementation of IE in schools. The findings that we reported in this chapter are, therefore, inconclusive and further investigations may provide a more in-depth understanding of how TAIP may be associated with a successful model of IE. Further investigations may consider collecting qualitative data in order to provide more insight into quantitative findings, particularly as the initial empirical investigations of teacher agency was based on qualitative enquiry. Future studies may examine TAIP in relation to school leadership, school policies, and school reform agendas, and the curricular and instructional aspects.

REFERENCES

Ahsan, M. T., U. Sharma, and J. M. Deppeler. 2012. "Exploring pre-service teachers' perceived teaching-efficacy, attitudes and concerns about inclusive education in Bangladesh." *International Journal of Whole Schooling* 8 (2):1–20.

Bakkenes, I., J. D. Vermunt, and T. Wubbels. 2010. "Teacher learning in the context of educational innovation: Learning activities and learning outcomes of experienced teachers." *Learning and Instruction* 20:533–548.

Bandura, A. 2018. "Toward a psychology of human agency: Pathways and reflections, toward a psychology of human agency: Pathways and reflections." *Perspectives on Psychological Science* 13 (2):130–136.

Biesta, G., M. Priestley, and S. Robinson. 2015. "The role of beliefs in teacher agency." *Teachers and teaching* 21 (6):624–640.

Bridwell-Mitchell, E. N. 2015. "Theorizing teacher agency and reform: How institutionalized instructional practices change and persist." *Sociology of Education* 88 (2):140–159.

Bridwell-Mitchell, E. N., and D. G. Sherer. 2017. "Institutional complexity and policy implementation: How underlying logics drive teacher interpretations of reform." *Educational Evaluation and Policy Analysis* 39 (2):223–247.

Consortium, Interstate New Teacher Assessment and Support. 2001. *Model standards for licensing general and special education teachers of students with disabilities: A resource for state dialogue.* Washington, DC: Council of Chief State School Officers.

Datnow, A. 2012. "Teacher agency in educational reform: Lessons from social networks research." *American Journal of Education* 119 (1):193–201.

Emam, M. 2016. "Management of inclusive education in Oman: A framework for Action." *Support for Learning* 31 (4):296–312.

Emam, M., and Y. F. H. Al-Mahdy. 2020a. "Teachers' efficacy for inclusive practices in the Sultanate of Oman: Effect of gender and teaching experience." *School Psychology International* 41 (2):170–192.

Emam, M. M., and Y. F. H. Al-Mahdy. 2020b. "Building School Capacity for Inclusive Education in the Sultanate of Oman: A Construct Validation of the Inclusive School Climate Scale." *Leadership and Policy in Schools* 1–16.

Emam, M. M., and A. M. Kazem. 2015. "Teachers' perceptions of the concomitance of emotional behavioural difficulties and learning disabilities in children referred for learning disabilities in Oman." *Emotional and Behavioural Difficulties* 20 (3):302–316.

Emirbayer, M., and A. Mische. 1998. "What is agency?" *American Journal of Sociology* 103 (4):962–1023.

Florian, L., and H. Linklater. 2010. "Preparing teachers for inclusive education: using inclusive pedagogy to enhance teaching and learning for all." *Cambridge journal of education* 40 (4):369–386.

Gaad, E. 2010. *Inclusive education in the Middle East.* Vol. 41. London: Routledge.

Ganon-Shilon, S., and C. Schechter. 2019. "School principals' sense-making of their leadership role during reform implementation." *International Journal of Leadership in Education* 22 (3):279–300.

Hayes, A. F. 2013. *Introduction to mediation, moderation, and conditional process analysis: A regression-based approach.* New York: The Guilford Press.

Li, L., and A. Ruppar. 2020. "Conceptualizing Teacher Agency for Inclusive Education: A Systematic and International Review." *Teacher Education and Special Education* 0888406420926976.

Lipponen, L., and K. Kumpulainen. 2011. "Acting as accountable authors: Creating interactional spaces for agency work in teacher education." *Teaching and Teacher Education* 27 (5):812–819.

Lyons, W. E., S. A. Thompson, and V. Timmons. 2016. "We are inclusive." *International Journal of Inclusive Education,* 20 (8):889–907.

Martin, J., and L. Carter. 2015. "Preservice teacher agency concerning education for sustainability (EfS): A discursive psychological approach." *Journal of Research in Science Teaching* 52 (4):560–573.

Mu, G. M., Y. Wang, Z. Wang, Y. Feng, M. Deng, and S. Liang. 2015. "An Enquiry into the Professional Competence of Inclusive Education Teachers in Beijing: Attitudes, Knowledge, Skills, and Agency." *International Journal of Disability, Development and Education,* 62 (6):571–589. DOI: 10.1080/1034912X.2015.1077934.

Pantić, N. 2017. "An exploratory study of teacher agency for social justice." *Teaching and Teacher Education* 66:219–230.

Pantić, N., and L. Florian. 2015. "Developing teachers as agents of inclusion and social justice." *Education Inquiry* 6 (3):333–351.

Park, M. H., D. M. Dimitrov, A. Das, and M. Gichuru. 2016. "The teacher efficacy for inclusive practices (TEIP) scale: Dimensionality and factor structure." *Journal of Research in Special Educational Needs* 16 (1):2–12.

Philpott, C., and C. Oates. 2017. "Teacher agency and professional learning communities; what can Learning Rounds in Scotland teach us?" *Professional Development in Education* 43 (3):318–333.

Priestley, M., G. Biesta, and S. Robinson. 2013. "Teachers as agents of change: Teacher agency and emerging models of curriculum." In M. Priestley, & G. Biesta (Eds.), *Reinventing the curriculum: New trends in curriculum policy and practice.* London: Bloomsbury Academic.

Priestley, M., G. Biesta, and S. Robinson. 2016. *Teacher agency: An ecological approach.* London: Bloomsbury Academic.

Priestley, M., R. Edwards, A. Priestley, and K. Miller. 2012. "Teacher agency in curriculum making: Agents of change and spaces for maneuver." *Curriculum Inquiry* 42(2): 191–214.

Pyhältö, K., J. Pietarinen, and T. Soini. 2014. "Comprehensive school teachers' professional agency in large-scale educational change." *Journal of Educational Change* 15 (3):303–325.

Rogers, R., and M. M. Wetzel. 2013. "Studying agency in literacy teacher education: A layered approach to positive discourse analysis." *Critical Inquiry in Language Studies* 10 (1):62–92.

Schweisfurth, M. 2006. "Education for global citizenship: Teacher agency and curricular structure in Ontario schools." *Educational Review* 58 (1):41–50.

Sharma, U., and A. Nuttal. 2016. "The impact of training on pre-service teacher attitudes, concerns, and efficacy towards inclusion." *Asia-Pacific Journal of teacher education* 44 (2):142–155.

Sperber, A. D. 2004. "Translation and validation of study instruments for cross-cultural research." *Gastroenterology* 126:S124–S128.

Tomlinson, C. A. 2001. *How to differentiate instruction in mixed-ability classrooms.* Alexandria, VA: ASCD.

Waitoller, F. R., and A. J. Artiles. 2013. "A decade of professional development research for inclusive education: A critical review and notes for a research program." *Review of Educational Research* 83 (3):319–356.

Wang, Y., G. M. Mu, Z. Wang, M. Deng, L. Cheng, and H. Wang. 2015. "Multidimensional classroom support to inclusive education teachers in Beijing, China." *International Journal of Disability, Development and Education* 62 (6): 644e659.

Wang, Y., G. M. Mu, and L. Zhang. 2017. "Chinese inclusive education teachers' agency within temporal-relational contexts." *Teaching and Teacher Education* 61:115–123.

Chapter 5

Special Education and Teacher Training in Abu Dhabi

Reality and Prospects

Ahmed Hassan Hemdan, Maria Efstratopoulou, and Ashraf Moustafa

Education is like a lantern, which lights up your way in a dark alley.

—Sheikh Zayed Bin Sultan Al Nahyan
(late president of the UAE)

OVERVIEW OF THE SPECIAL NEEDS EDUCATIONAL SYSTEM IN THE UAE

The United Arab Emirates' (UAE) interest in educating students with disabilities (SWD) in general education schools first arose in 2006 through a federal law, which was mandated in 2009 and ratified by the UAE government. Later, it was amended to better protect the educational rights of SWD. In addition, the government signed the optional protocol with the United Nations (UN), which initiated the implementation of various effective inclusive practices, to ensure equal opportunities for all. Inclusive philosophies led to an increase of educating SWD in regular education classrooms or at least the regular school environment, which, in turn, required the development of teacher training/ education programs to prepare future teachers to work effectively with SWD within mainstream settings (Alghazo, Dodeen and Algaryouti 2003, 515– 552). However, the efficacy of the overall inclusive education management in the UAE has been questioned by several researchers, since both the country itself and its educational laws and initiatives are fairly new. Moreover, as Gaad and Almotairi (2013) state, one of the most significant factors that prohibit successful inclusion of SWD in the UAE mainstream schools is the lack of proper teacher/staff training and knowledge around the area of special educational needs (SEN). Although Gaad (2004) found that teaching children with special needs is considered a stressful job, there has been an increasing interest in delivering services to the students with special needs and including them within the regular setting of schools (Sartawi, Gaad, Alghazo and Tibi 2005). The UAE Ministry of Education (MoE) is in charge of special education organizational structures and is responsible for overseeing all the preuniversity education in the UAE.

Education has been one of the highest priorities in the UAE since it became a country in 1971 under the leadership of the late Sheikh Zayed Bin Sultan Al Nahyan. Before the discovery of oil in the UAE, traditional occupations included date palm cultivation, fishing, and pearl diving. With oil came dramatic changes to the lifestyle and social structure of the Emirates. Infrastructure development, such as the construction of roads, hospitals, and schools, brought a stream of foreign workers into the UAE, which is now home to over 200 nationalities (SMCCU 2006, cited in Aldabas 2020). The country has made some amazing accomplishments in its infrastructure, social, and economic development over the past half-century. The Emirates are populated by a diversity of cultural groups.

The education system of the UAE is relatively new. In 1952, there were few formal schools in the country. In the 1960s and 1970s, a school building program expanded the education system. The current public UAE educational system was established in the 1970s and includes four stages: kindergarten for 4–5-year-olds, primary schools for 6–11-year-olds, the preparatory stage for 12–14-year-olds and secondary schools for 15–17-year-olds. In 1971, 64 schools served 28,000 students and the government-financed education abroad for those who wished to continue beyond secondary school. In 2006–2007, approximately 650,000 students were enrolled at 1,256 public and private schools. In the 2013–2014 academic year, approximately 910,000 students were enrolled at 1,174 public and private schools. Now, education at the primary and secondary level is universal (Embassy of the United Arab Emirates Cultural Division).

Many private schools, which are funded by nongovernment sources, provide education for the children of the UAE's large expatriate population. The MoE oversees school operations and provides funding for government schools. In 2006, 37 percent of the total budget for the country was allocated for education (both public and higher education). Over time, funding for public education has increased. For example, during the period 1994–2003, there was a financial increase of 95 percent for education (Education budget allocation 2006, cited in Benkohila, Elhoweris and Efthymiou 2020).

This chapter examines the training needs of preservice and in-service educators in the UAE, with regard to their efficacy in teaching children with SEN in inclusive settings. More precisely, acknowledging the scarcity of research in this field and the questioned management and implementation of inclusive education practices in the UAE, we conducted an inquiry in order to gather information about the perspectives, SEN training experiences, and needs and attitudes toward inclusive education of preservice and in-service teachers in the UAE. Through the use of interviews and group discussion with two groups of SEN teachers and graduate SEN students, valuable information was gathered regarding possible modifications and suggestions for improvements in teachers' training and professional development programs, as well as for reforming several aspects of the overall organization, management, and implementation of the inclusive education system in the UAE.

INCLUSION OF SEN STUDENTS IN UAE REGULAR SCHOOLS

During the last ten years, the UAE has instituted several important initiatives to ensure successful inclusive education; for example, the UAE joined the United Nations Human Rights Council in 2010 and followed the basic principles of the Convention on the Rights of Persons with Disabilities (CRPD) and Articles 23 and 28 of the Convention on the Rights of the Child (CRC). These included the creation of a barrier-free academic environment, provision of sufficient support to allow SWD to develop their full potential (i.e., personality, talents, mental and physical abilities), provision of health care and rehabilitation services, a recreation of opportunities, and preparation for future employment (AlObeidli 2008, PhD diss.). At the same time, the MoE, in collaboration with the UAE Ministry of Social Affairs (MOSA), released a guidebook named "School for All" or "General Rules for the Provision of Special Education Programs and Services." Inclusive Education, in this guidebook, is defined by the UAE Minister of Education as follows: "Inclusive Education means that all students in a school, regardless of their strengths and weaknesses in any area, become part of the school community" (Hassan 2008, quoted in Anati and Ain 2012). It also includes specific sections about the country's view toward inclusion and several rules concerning SEN. Similarly, other GCC countries recently adopted the "inclusion movement," by integrating SWD in all levels of general education, including higher education (HE). Examples of such initiatives across the UAE include the "Dubai Disability Strategy 2020," which aimed to achieve equal rights and services for people with special educational needs and disabilities (SEND) by 2020; the Services for Educational Development,

Research and Awareness for Inclusion (SEDRA) foundation (SEDRA 2016, cited in AlObeidli 2018), which emphasized equality in five main aspects of human life (i.e., education, health care, employment, social protection, and universal accessibility); the "National Project for SEND people" (Abu Dhabi e-Government Gateway 2017; the National 2017, cited in AlObeidli 2018); and the "National Strategy for Empowering People with Disabilities," which mainly focused on the need for close communication between all parties involved, to successfully implement inclusive and special education (Khaleej Times 2017, cited in AlObeidli 2018). However, several studies have revealed a low degree of readiness among teachers in mainstream educational settings (in all levels of education, i.e., preschool, primary, secondary, and postsecondary) for the practice of inclusion, which is indicative of problems in the development and implementation of well-organized preservice (undergraduate and postgraduate) and in-service training programs for teachers/educators working with SEN students (Sartawi et al. 2003; Anati & Ain 2012; Hamaidi, et al. 2012; Eren 2014; Hourani and Litz 2018, cited in Moore, 2020, PhD diss.).

CHALLENGES OF TEACHING: PRESERVICE AND IN-SERVICE TRAINING OF TEACHERS IN ABU DHABI

It is important to note that the quality of teaching is paramount in comparison to the amount of teaching and the time spent on teaching SEN. Quality teaching does not only imply that time is spent on teaching; rather it includes the efficient use of time and resources, providing feedback, directing students, and encouraging them to learn. It also entails teaching in small groups, teaching students individually, and integrating students into the learning process (Sitronik and Kimball 1994). In addition, teachers' attitudes toward the inclusion of children with disabilities in mainstream schools have a significant impact on shaping their perceptions and knowledge, which in turn influences what they gain from the experience and teaching practices (White 2000, cited in King 2004).

Evidence from school improvement literature consistently highlights that effective principal and teacher leaders exercise an influence on a school's capacity to improve upon the achievement of students drawing on systematic, in-house, and sustainable professional development (Harris 2002). While the quality of teaching most strongly influences levels of student motivation and achievement, it has been demonstrated that the quality and levels of leadership matter in determining the motivation of teachers and the quality of teaching in the classroom (Fullan 2001). As the limitations of individual leadership have become increasingly evident through recent research (Arif and Gaad,

2008; AlMahdi and Bukamal, 2019), collective or teacher leadership, consisting of teachers who lead within and beyond the classroom, contribute to a community of teacher-learners and leaders, influence others toward improved educational practice (Katzenmeyer and Moller 2009, 17), and has become increasingly well established. The charismatic teacher leader may achieve school improvement and student achievement and be a role model for students and other teachers.

Several studies have acknowledged the need for providing better training to educators, teachers, and academic members for working with SEN, especially when it comes to differentiation and modification methods designed to allow SWD to fully access the curriculum and improve their learning outcomes to the maximum (Gaad and Almotairi 2013). Gaad and Almotairi also claim that to ensure a better practice of inclusion in HE of the UAE, institutions need to provide a better implementation of Individual Education Plans (IEPs) for monitoring included SWD's progress, proper funding to better support inclusive practices and availability of specialized personnel (e.g., psychologists, speech therapists, special needs educators) in HE institutions of UAE.

It is noteworthy that the professional development of in-service special education teachers in Abu Dhabi is important to ensure a high level of quality and efficiency in their profession. The officials in Abu Dhabi are keen to have teachers' professional development as a top priority. One of the most important professional development practices in the field of special education is the field trips in which in-service teachers communicate with preservice teachers and they exchange knowledge, skills, and training programs. Another existing policy in Abu Dhabi is that in-service teachers have some time of cooperation through establishing professional learning communities regarding issues around the school or district levels, as well as issues related to disability. There is an annual professional development week dedicated to each disability (e.g., a week for professional development for speech therapists, and a week for teachers of students with vision impairment, learning disabilities, and autism), in which there are specialized workshops where recent knowledge in diagnosis and intervention programs for each disability are introduced.

Teachers in the UAE come from diverse backgrounds, as regards their qualifications and contexts of experience. Accordingly, their training differs significantly. Teachers are required to attend about thirty hours of professional development every year. The Abu Dhabi Department of Education and Knowledge (ADEK) and MoE offer some teacher training programs delivered throughout the school year. The importance of professional development is a top priority in the federal budget of the country. Therefore, the education authorities in the country delineate specific standards for both teachers' employment and the type and quality of professional development training programs. These educational authorities include: ADEK, which is responsible for supervising governmental and private schools in Abu Dhabi, and Dubai Knowledge and Human Development Authority (KHDA), which supervises private schools in Dubai, and the MoE (which supervises governmental and private schools in the Northern Emirates and governmental schools in Dubai). As a result, teacher standards vary across different emirates. Hence, the three aforementioned authorities try new systems to teacher licensure systems which consists of the same set of criteria on the national level. These new systems require that teachers pass a test and present a portfolio that includes evidence of teaching in the country (Pennington 2016). This reform is the result of ongoing discussions for several years and will be implemented in 2021. The focus now is on ensuring the existence of a national framework of teacher admission standards. These changes are aimed at raising the efficiency and quality of in-service teachers. A lot of teachers will need to uplift their education levels to meet the new standards.

Over the past ten years, the College of Education at the United Arab Emirates University (UAEU) has been undergoing major changes in restructuring its programs. Standards have been integrated into the restructuring of all programs to better qualify future teachers to effectively educate students with and without disabilities (Sartawi, Gaad, Alghazo and Tibi 2005). In addition, according to Tennant, Al Jafari, and Woolsey (2017), teacher preparation colleges in the Emirate of Abu Dhabi are trying to provide their graduate students with the knowledge, skills, and attitudes required to overcome issues related to inclusive education. Tennant et al. (2017) continue that if a more focused collaboration between the MoE, ADEK, Zayed Higher Organization (ZHO), and teacher education institutions is achieved, the inclusion process may soon synchronize and the current barriers in educating children with disabilities will be reduced. An earlier study carried out by Anati and Ain (2012) in twenty-six mainstream public and private primary and secondary schools of the UAE, stresses the need for more qualified special education professionals, proper SEN training of all teachers, financial support for inclusion purposes, special equipment, resources and tools in mainstream educational environments.

Exploring the implementation of inclusion in several private schools within Abu Dhabi, the study of Moore (2020) revealed that general education teachers' attitudes toward inclusion were "neutral" but also highlighted the issue of professional training as the main contributing factor in relation to levels of inclusion acceptance. The study points out the need for a "pro-inclusion culture," which should initially develop in teachers of lower educational levels (e.g., preschool, primary, and secondary) of public and private schools in the UAE and which will eventually lead to a successful inclusive policy in the HE level. Hence, according to Moore, it is the general education teachers' change of attitude toward inclusion that will truly make the difference. However, as Hourani and Litz 2018; Tant and Watelain 2016; and Eren 2014 (cited in Moore 2020) point out, this change of attitude can only take place through the teachers' involvement and contribution to the planning and achievement of objectives, development of IEPs for SWD, teaching/educational purposes, and self-assessment procedures (i.e., through the development of their training skills).

A straightforward involvement of general education teachers in formulating objectives for SWD, as Alborno (2017) claims, provides them with a clear definition of their role and responsibilities concerning inclusive education practices and a clearer position toward the families of their students. Hence, only proper training and true involvement of teachers can lead to the real implementation of inclusive education. In their study of 211 general and special education teachers in the UAE, Elhoweris and Alsheikn (2010, 37–48) also found that teachers had only a moderate level of awareness with regard to testing modifications for SWD. The need for training teachers in organizational planning for better management of their busy classrooms has also been identified in the study of Arif and Gaad (2008).

In a similar study, Hamaidi, Homidi, and Reyes (2012, 94–101) found that, although the general attitudes of early childhood educators in the UAE, Jordan, and the United States toward social and emotional aspects of inclusive education were positive, it seemed that, when it came to practice, there was a "gap" between theory and the actual practices. This gap has been attributed to a number of factors, two of the most important being the economic/financial resources factor and the teacher training factor. The significance of teachers' knowledge, training, and experience in teaching SEN students, is clearly reflected upon Efthymiou and Kington's (2018, 18) statement: "The greatest influence on the educational and social outcomes of these students is the behaviour and practices of the classroom teacher."

The overall findings suggest the need for offering teachers better organizational planning skills, action-research training programs for simulating real-life field experiences, and more effective staff training programs to strengthen their skills in relation to assessment procedures, IEP development, and behavior modification methods, through the use of case studies and real-life examples (Arif and Gaad 2008).

Considering the above, a major problem is that, despite their limited training skills, mainstream schoolteachers are expected to successfully meet the needs of all their students, including those with special needs. More specifically, teachers are not only expected to deliver their knowledge, usually in crowded classrooms along with a shortage of qualified and/or auxiliary staff, but they are also involved in important decision-making procedures, such as students' future placements (Anati and Ain 2012). In addition, they are often required to alter the curriculum, plan and modify their own teaching approaches and/or exam papers.

RATIONALE FOR THE STUDY

Taking into account the fact that the efficacy of the overall management of inclusive education in the UAE has been questioned and given the scarcity of research in the field of inclusion as a practice and in the area of effective teaching in the UAE, especially concerning teacher training, the purpose of the current study was to examine teachers' and students' perspectives in relation to training skills efficacy. The importance of the study, therefore, stems from the need to determine the skills that constitute effective instruction that teachers find difficult to implement and, therefore, consider them when designing curriculum for preservice teachers. Assessing teachers' beliefs about how they view their own performance is an important step in planning the reform of the education system. The information gathered from teachers could help in making decisions as to what modifications are important in pre-service and in-service training programs. In addition, the assessment of graduate students' views regarding both quantity and quality of knowledge and skills they received during their special education studies can shed light on the advantages and possible limitations of preservice training currently available at UAEU and can lead to modifications in the relevant course structures.

METHODOLOGY

The purpose of the present study was to shed more light on teachers' perspectives in relation to inclusive education practices in the UAE, especially with regard to their own preservice and in-service special education training skills. More specifically, two focus groups of SEN teachers and SEN students of the UAEU were interviewed about their views and experiences on teacher training. The first focus group consisted of fifteen SEN teachers (eight males and seven females), while their years of teaching experience ranged between five and seventeen years. The second focus group consisted of six female graduate students, four of which specialized in sensory impairments, one in gifted and talented children and one in children with mild and moderate learning difficulties (see tables 5.1 and 5.2 for the demographic characteristics of the two focus groups). Valuable information was gathered in relation to both groups' overall views of inclusive education, teacher training needs, and suggestions for better ways of preservice and in-service training in order to support SEN students in inclusive settings.

Table 5.1   Characteristics of Participants (Teachers in Abu Dhabi)

Participants' Codes	Gender	Working Experience (Years)	Specialization
Teacher (1)	Male	13	SEN teacher
Teacher (2)	Male	10	SEN teacher
Teacher (3)	Male	15	SEN teacher
Teacher (4)	Male	17	SEN teacher
Teacher (5)	Female	5	SEN teacher
Teacher (6)	Female	5	SEN teacher
Teacher (7)	Male	5	SEN teacher
Teacher (8)	Female	8	SEN teacher
Teacher (9)	Male	11	SEN teacher
Teacher (10)	Male	7	SEN teacher
Teacher (11)	Female	9	SEN teacher
Teacher (12)	Female	5	SEN teacher
Teacher (13)	Female	15	SEN teacher
Teacher (14)	Female	8	SEN teacher
Teacher (15)	Male	10	SEN teacher

Source: Table created by authors using collected data.

Table 5.2   Characteristics of Participants (SEN Graduated Students)

Participants' Codes	Gender	Specialization
Student (1)	Female	Sensory impairment
Student (2)	Female	Sensory impairment
Student (3)	Female	Sensory impairment
Student (4)	Female	Sensory impairment
Student (5)	Female	Gifted and talented
Student (6)	Female	Mild and moderate

Source: Table created by authors using collected data.

More specifically, to investigate teachers' and students' perspectives and ideas on teacher training in the UAE, a qualitative study was designed and the following data collection methods were used:

1) Focus groups: researchers held focus group interviews with teachers in schools and graduated students in special education from UAEU.
2) Group discussion: participants were engaged in both formal and informal dialogue with the researchers about aspects of teachers' training and their professional development. During this phase, participants were encouraged to interact by sharing their own views and experiences.

The main subjects discussed during the interviews with the teachers were:

a) The training they have already received during their studies.
b) Extra seminars/training they have attended to complement their knowledge, skills and experience in special education and the participation of
   parents in these training sessions.
c) Finally, they were asked to make suggestions for further training needed,
   to feel competent in successfully supporting their students to reach their
   full potentials in schools.

In addition, a group discussion with the six special education students
revealed valuable information regarding their training experiences gained
during their study period at the UAEU. The main themes explored in this
discussion with the students were the availability of training courses or seminars and the level of training experience throughout their studies. Finally, all
participants were informed about the purpose of the study and were reassured
concerning the anonymity of the data and ethical considerations for privacy
and personal data issues.

INTERVIEWS WITH TEACHER PARTICIPANTS

Semi-structured group interviews with teachers revealed problems with the
workload (e.g., altering the curriculum, writing formal reports, constructing IEPs for their students, completing assessment forms, and cooperating
with parents and other professionals), lack of coherence and unsuitability of
the current teachers concerning the nature of the students they teach. It also
became clear that training was needed to help teachers and teacher assistants
to cope and deal with very young and sometimes demanding children. These
limitations became clear through Asma's (SEN teacher) comments, after
observing a special education classroom:

> I have noticed that there is a desperate need for proper training. Though the
> working is good and everything is fine, there is a need for effective Individual
> Educational Plans (IEPs). At the moment, the children learn as typical main-
> stream students, and the individual learning needs of the children with special
> educational needs are not met.

Asma continued:

> For example, I have observed a child in my classroom with mild to moderate
> learning disability who also has visual impairments. However, I do not feel able
> to meet that particular child's individual needs. In fact, I am not trained to work
> on individual needs of SEN students.

Although most teachers recognized the significance of being trained to develop IEPs, the teachers admit that they have not received such training so far. They have been using a model designed by staff at the university, but they feel it does not relate to students' needs and does not have enough flexibility to suggest/alter plans.

Regarding professional development of teachers, participants were asked what type of professional development training in special education they have recently (the last two or three years) received and which professional body (university, organization, institution, etc.) provided this certification or training? All participants replied that they had received their certification and/or training through the MoE of the UAE. Two participants stated that their courses were provided through the MoE, Department of Education and Knowledge, Jordan Centre of Excellence. For example, Salema (SEN teacher) answered:

> I received much training in the field of specialization, including accurate diagnosis of people of determination, childish autism scale, and diagnosis of learning difficulties, attention deficit and hyperactivity, Princess Tharwat's College Scales for learning difficulties, individual educational plan, and preparation of educational programs and means for people of determination.

With regard to the practical utility of their training (i.e., to what extent they made use of this training in their career), teachers were asked to answer the following question: To what extent did you make use of this training in your career? Was this training effective in your career? All participants answered that the training they received was helpful and effective in their teaching and they all agreed on the importance of receiving this type of extra training. A representative reply is that of Abdul (SEN Teacher):

> This training benefited me in identifying the diagnosis and accurate assessment of all cases that I work with. They also contributed to the success of the individual educational plan with different cases because they are based on scientific and educational foundations and according to the needs of each student with special needs.

When participants were asked about parents' participation in the training, how beneficial was this interaction for the child, and /or the professionals in their role, most of them agreed on the importance of engaging parents in the training procedure, especially in cases with severe disabilities, as well as for the improvement of the parents' skills development. For example, Mona (SEN teacher) stated:

The presence of parents and their attendance to training, professional development and workshops are important, especially in cases of autism and very severe
cases, to identify their most important features and methods of treatment and
interim intervention to improve the performance level.

Salema added:

> From my point of view parents need a set of workshops of their own in terms of
> ways on how to deal with their children with special needs as well as on meth-
> ods of communication, early detection and provision of their needs.

Finally, we asked teachers to share their ideas and suggestions on future
training or workshops that they wished to attend in their field. All participants
agreed on the great importance of continuous training and professional development in the field of special education. The particular areas on which they
mostly focused were the following: assessment in education; diagnostic and
evaluation methods; use of technology in teaching; inclusion strategies; and
training on how to use assessment tools and scales for specific disorders to
evaluate the effectiveness of interventions. For example, the reply of Mariam
(SEN teacher) to this question was as follows:

> One of the most important proposals is to give the special education teacher
> authority to make recognized diagnoses and to increase training on diagnostic/
> evaluation methods and inclusion mechanisms for the disabled in schools.

DISCUSSION WITH STUDENTS

When student participants were asked what types of training and professional development they received during their undergraduate studies in
special education in UAEU and if they benefited from them, all of them
answered that the training they received helped them stabilize mostly
theoretical aspects of knowledge with minor practical applications. In addition, all participants stressed that the training was usually not relevant to
their areas of specialization. For example, Aysha (graduate student) stated:
"Our training mainly included cases of children with mild learning disabilities or autism, but none with sensory impairment, which is our area of
specialization."

Other students specializing in sensory impairments also argued that they
had the chance to take part in a two-month workshop (with a certificate of
attendance) about the practical applications of Braille and sign language.
However, although, in relation to theoretical knowledge, the workshop was

helpful, once again, its practical application in schools involved other areas of disability. For example, Reem (graduate student) stated:

> As for field experiences, which we had a subject, we were sent to schools to see cases. For me, I am a student of sensory disabilities, but they did not have sensory cases. We used to go to the Al Foah centre, but we learned about the rest of the cases such as Down syndrome and Autism and this is it.

Two students (namely, Fatima and Hanna) claimed that the extra experience they needed was gained through personal efforts (e.g., participation in external, distance learning courses and/or teaching provided by other regional universities, such as Edraak and Zayed University). The rest of the students claimed that such workshops offered by external sources were difficult to access since they were not synchronized with the UAEU course schedule (i.e., they coincided with their main courses). With regard to the content of the courses offered in their program, most students argued that the knowledge offered in specific areas (e.g., sign language) was restricted only to an introductory level. Jamila (graduate student) observed: "Most of the courses were provided only as an introduction, just like sign language. The rest you should, as a student, research about it. All these introductions are not enough for some students."

In addition, although students participated in several conferences offered by the university, they reported that there was only 5 percent coverage of subject areas of interest. Moreover, although the university organized several workshops in which SEN teachers shared their knowledge, experiences, and various innovative practices, students felt that, even though these added to their knowledge, for the most part they targeted different fields of special education. Amal (graduate student) states:

> There were conferences in other fields of SEN. For example, the previous course in our college had a forum for people with autism, it involved practices concerning autism and it had workshops after the main lectures. This added to our information, but in another field of special education.

Overall, students reported that they rarely felt that they were practicing their specialization when attending seminars, workshops, or conferences. Rather, students stated that issues of availability and frequency of such courses provided within UAEU were also a barrier to their attendance. A representative reply regarding the above issue was provided by Jamila:

> The courses in the university are considered according to their availability; if they are available and I like them and I have an opportunity to join. . . . But if we talk about the courses outside the university, I try, for example, every month to enroll in a distance course from the existing courses.

Regarding the benefits from virtual classes that have become more prevalent during the COVID-19 pandemic, preservice teachers mentioned difficulties with applying teaching strategies and with teaching basic skills to their students. They also stated that the "distance" barrier made it difficult for them to build trusting relationships with new SEN students. Concerning parental involvement in training seminars, all students were positive; however, they added that a disadvantage of these seminars was that, usually, they were not free of charge. Ultimately, all students clearly expressed a need for experiences that were more practical and a more balanced curriculum in terms of theory and practical application of knowledge. According to Aysha:

> Practical training is very important. The practical application course was a nice addition, but it was just one course, one day a week. This means that only next year students will have the opportunity to enter the field of work again. However, the skills we acquire through practical experiences provide us with self-confidence.

RECOMMENDATIONS FOR IMPROVEMENT

Summarizing the recommendations made by participants with regard to improvement and/or restructuring of the preservice training provided, students made the following suggestions:

- There is a need for more practical applications and real-life experiences with SEN students from the first year of studies to gain self-confidence in teaching and supporting students with SEN.
- There needs to be more opportunities to work with SWD that match their specializations.
- There needs to be more emphasis on learning teaching strategies and methods according to their particular area of specialization instead of general SEN strategies, which cannot be easily applied to other fields of expertise.
- Attempts should be made to organize "clubs," on a standard basis, in which specific subjects will be taught (sign language, Braille, etc.) and students will have the opportunity to choose the ones they wish to attend to acquire extra training.

CONCLUSION

The new teacher employment standards mandate that in-service teachers maintain appropriate professional development to continue their full-time status. As such, the use of new licensure requirements represents a good step toward the continuous improvement of in-service teachers' support. Although some professional development workshops offered to in-service special education teachers in Abu Dhabi were successful, some teachers had concerns on workshops and assigned tasks. Those teachers pointed out that such workshops were repetitive, they contained repeated training materials, or they were conducted by unqualified trainers, and some of these workshops were too general in nature.

In-service special education teachers reported that the most effective professional development programs were related to the knowledge and skills related to the field of special education and their impact on teaching and the quality of working with students with special needs. The teachers also reported that they needed, and would benefit from, training options that were more specialized and that were more related to the special cases that they regularly encounter in the resource rooms or special education classrooms. Accordingly, policy makers in special education should prepare a list of professional development training options from which special education teachers can choose and allow them to find the professional development opportunities that meet their needs.

In this framework, ADEK offered some training workshops that were available throughout the year to provide full support to assistants (shadow teachers) in inclusive classrooms in Abu Dhabi schools. ADEK also invited all current and new assistants (a total of 114) to attend the workshops that were prepared especially to qualify them to work with students with SEN, brief them with their roles and responsibilities toward the students, and illuminating special education teachers with the strategies used to deal with various disabilities. The assistants in the classrooms function as a mediator between the teachers and the lesson objectives and plays a pivotal role in planning and preparing activities and individual resources for each student with SEN.

The content offered in professional development workshops should be more practical and hands-on rather than theory-based. Teachers need more specialized courses related to specific categories of disabilities (e.g., visual impairment, hearing impairment, learning disabilities). In Abu Dhabi schools, the teachers received training workshops in which they had a training kit. Teacher participants, however, reported that the kit focused mainly on the policies of dealing with students with special needs with few case studies. They had concerns about trainers who were not well specialized in the assigned topic.

Another important outlet for in-service special education teachers is to encourage them to pursue post-baccalaureate degrees such as diplomas, masters, and doctoral degrees. There are several graduate programs offered at the major universities in Abu Dhabi such as UAEU, Al Ain University, Zayed University, Abu Dhabi University, and Higher Colleges of Technology. Furthermore, local in-service teacher training programs encourage structured forms of collaboration that aim to develop inclusive practices. This kind of collaboration is still lacking in the region among different professionals and leaders in inclusive education (Khochen-Bagshaw 2019). On the research level, there needs to be more studies that examine in-service and preservice special education teachers' professional development training needs. Research in this area is scarce and there are unmet needs to address teachers' concerns in this regard.

Special education teachers should be trained within an existing framework of clear standards for them to absorb theory and practice of special education. As such, training must be carried out by specialists in special education who are carefully selected so that they have both theoretical background and field experience, keeping in mind the state-of-art changes and advances in the field.

REFERENCES

Alborno, Nadera E. 2017. "The 'yes . . . but' Dilemma: Implementing Inclusive Education in Emirati Primary Schools." *British Journal of Special Education* 44, no. 1: 26–45. https://doi.org/10.1111/1467-8578.12157.

Aldabas, Rashed. 2020. "Special Education Teachers' Perceptions of Their Preparedness to Teach Students With Severe Disabilities in Inclusive Classrooms: A Saudi Arabian Perspective Original Research." *SAGE Open* (July–September): 1–14. https://doi.org/10.1177/2158 244020950657.

Alghazo, Emad M., Dodeen Hamzah and Algaryouti Ibrahim A. 2003. "Attitudes of Pre-Service Teachers towards Persons with Disabilities: Predictions for the Success of Inclusion." *College Student Journal* 37: 515–552. https://www.semanticscholar .org/paper/Attitudes-of-Pre-Service-Teachers-towards-Persons-Alghazo-Dodeen /06901dbe406de12f86664c49693f2408 1f8b3b11.

AlMahdi, Osama and Bukamal Hanin. 2019. "Pre-Service Teachers' Attitudes toward Inclusive Education during Their Studies in Bahrain Teachers College." *SAGE Open*: 1–14. https://doi.org/10.1177/2158244019865772.

AlObeidli, Nooreya. 2018. "The Effectiveness of Existing Policies and Procedures in the Admission of Students with SEND in the UAE Higher Education." PhD diss., British University of Dubai.

Anati, Nisreen, and Ain, Al. 2012. "Including Students with Disabilities in UAE Schools: A Descriptive Study." *International Journal of Special Education* 27, no. 2: 75–85. https://www.researchgate.net /publication/285994640.

Arif, Mohammed, and Gaad, Eman. 2008. "Special Needs Education in the United Arab Emirates (UAE): A Systems Perspective." *Journal of Research in Special Educational Needs* 8: 111–117. https://doi.org/10.1111/j.1471-3802.2008.00108.x.

Benkohila, Amel, Elhoweris, Hala, and Efthymiou, Efthymia. 2020. "Faculty Attitudes and Knowledge Regarding Inclusion and Accommodations of Special Educational Needs and Disabilities Students: A United Arab Emirates Case Study." *Psycho-Educational Research Reviews* 9, no. 2: 100–111. https://www.journals .lapub.co.uk/index.php/perr/article/view/1458.

Efthymiou, Efthymia and, Kington, Alison. 2017. "The Development of Inclusive Learning Relationships in Mainstream Settings: A Multimodal Perspective." *Cogent Education* 4, no. 1: 1–21. https://doi.org/10.1080/2331186X.2017.13 04015.

Elhoweris, Hala and, Alsheikh, Negmeldin. 2010. "UAE Teachers' Awareness & Perceptions of Testing Modifications." *Exceptionality Education International* 20, no. 1: 37–48. https://doi.org/10.5206/eei.v20i1.7656.

Fullan, Michael. 2001. *Leading in a Culture of Change*. New York: Jossey Bass.

Gaad, Eman and, Almotairi, Mishal. 2013. "Inclusion of Student with Special Needs within Higher Education in UAE: Issues and Challenges." *Journal of International Education Research* (JIER) 9, no. 4: 287–292. https://doi.org/10.19030/jier.v9i4 .8080.

Gaad, Eman. 2004. "Cross-cultural perspective on the effect of cultural attitudes towards inclusion of children with intellectual disabilities." *International Journal of Inclusive Education* 8, no. 3: 313–328.

Hamaidi, Diala, Homidi, Moayyad and, Reyes, Luis, V. 2012. "International Views of Inclusive Education: A Comparative Study of Early Childhood Educator's Perceptions in Jordan, United Arab Emirates, and the United States of America." *International Journal of Special Education* 27, no. 2: 94–101. https://files.eric.ed .gov/fulltext/EJ982864.pdf.

Harris, Alma. 2002. "Effective Leadership in Schools Facing Challenging Contexts." *School Leadership & Management* 22, no. 1: 15–26. https://doi.org/10.1080 /1363243022014 3024a.

Katzenmeyer, Marilyn H. and, Moller, Gayle V. 2009. *Awakening the Sleeping Giant: Helping Teachers Develop as Leaders*. Third edition. California, USA: Corwin Press Inc. Thousand Oaks.

Kechichian, Joseph A. 2000. *Iran, Iraq, and the Arab Gulf States*. New York: Palgrave Macmillan.

Khochen-Bagshaw, Maha. 2019. "An Exploration into the Phenomena of Dropping Out of School Education in Algeria, Causes and Interventions Strategies." Algiers: British Council Algeria. https://www.researchgate.net/publication/342530397.

King, Sharondrea R. 2004. "Pre-Service Teachers' Perception and Knowledge of Multicultural Education." PhD diss., University of South Florida.

Moore, Karla Marie. "Private Education Teachers in Abu Dhabi, UAE and their Acceptance of the Inclusion of Students with Disabilities." PhD diss., Northcentral University, 2020.

Pennington, Roberta. 2016. "UAE-Wide Teacher Licensing Scheme to Begin in 2017, Minister Says." *The National*. 2016, May 1. https://www.thenationalnews.com/ uae/uae-wide-teacher-licensing-scheme-to-begin-in-2017-minister-says-1.196240.

Sartawi, Abdel, Aziz M., Gaad, Eman, Alghazo, Emad M. and Tibi, Sanna T. 2005. "Restructured Special Education Program: Standards and Accreditation." *Special Education Academy Journal* 7: 201–226.

Sirotnik, Keneth A., and Kimball, Kathy. 1994. "The unspecial place of special education in programs that prepare school administrators." *Journal of School Leadership* 4, no. 6: 598–630. https://doi.org/10.1177/105268469400400602.

Tennant, Lilly, Al Jafari, Hanadi, and Woolsey, M. Lynn. 2017. "Special Needs Center Facilitating Inclusive Education in the Emirate of Abu Dhabi." *International Journal of Advanced Research* 5, no. 4: 25–32. www.journalijar.com.

Chapter 6

The Triple Helix of Teacher Quality after the Pandemic

A Case Study from Bahrain

Lucy Bailey

INTRODUCTION

The 2020 COVID-19 pandemic led to widespread school closures across the world, in many countries for extended periods of time. Students, teachers, school leaders, and parents scrambled to find ways in which learning could continue as economies suddenly closed. The pandemic highlighted and exacerbated educational inequalities, such as the digital divide between households of differing incomes (Harris and Jones 2020). In this chapter, I consider the impact of the pandemic not only in the short term but also in terms of the disruptive possibilities it introduces to teacher and leadership education in the countries of the Gulf Cooperation Council (GCC).

As COVID-19 infections spread westwards in the early months of 2020, the GCC countries closed their schools and universities, and tried to continue learning using virtual formats. The pandemic led to a fall in the price of oil, a key commodity in all the GCC economies, leading to increased pressure on the public purse at the same time as investment was needed to meet the challenges of online education. In this chapter, by examining the case study of the Kingdom of Bahrain, I will argue that the pandemic heightened challenges already faced by GCC education systems and stymied their economic ability to overcome these difficulties, but new opportunities arose.

I begin by examining the challenges faced by education systems in the GCC before the COVID-19 pandemic. Then, the impact of the pandemic on education is detailed, with specific attention paid to the case study of Bahrain. It is suggested that the role of the teacher has been thrown into question by these changes, and consequently should provide an impetus for revision of teacher education. Thereafter, the chapter considers in detail the disruptive effect of the pandemic on three aspects of education: teacher leadership, teacher recruitment, and teacher education. In each case, possibilities for positive outcomes as a result of this disruption are identified.

BEFORE THE PANDEMIC:
KEY CHALLENGES FOR EDUCATION IN THE GCC

Although extensive measures have been taken to reform the education systems of the GCC countries over the past quarter century, there have remained concerns about teacher quality and the education children receive. International comparative data suggests that students from GCC education systems fall significantly below the Organization for Economic Cooperation and Development (OECD) average on a range of learning outcomes (Schleicher 2020). For example, both the Trends in International Mathematics and Science Study (TIMSS) and the Program for International Student Assessment (PISA) global comparative data show that GCC countries fall below OECD averages. OECD data also show that students from GCC countries fall significantly below OECD average of having a growth mindset.

El-Saharty et al. (2020), in a report on human capital for the World Bank, point to additional problems with the education systems of the GCC countries before the pandemic. They note that low levels of basic proficiency among schoolchildren, when compared with other high-income countries, include a particularly sharp underachievement among boys. They suggest that the skills fostered by education do not match those needed by the labor market, and note that there has been an historical reliance on public sector employment, where wages are high and employment is guaranteed. In addition, they identify other worrying aspects of basic education including high rates of teacher absenteeism and tardiness; a greater emphasis on gaining credentials than acquiring skills; a focus on rote memorization rather than critical thinking; and highly centralized education decision-making. They note a wide divergence between private and public schooling in student achievement.

Several researchers have drawn attention to problems with recruiting and training quality teachers for government schools in the region. Gallagher's (2019) discussion of teacher recruitment, preparation and development in the UAE, explains how an original reliance on teachers from the Arab region, many of whom had no practicum training and were trained largely in content knowledge, was replaced by a reliance on recruiting Western educators from the early 2000s onwards. More recently, nation-building has been sought by means of training Emirati teachers, though this has not been without difficulties. For example, it has been hard to secure practicum experiences with mentor teachers who practice suitable student-centered approaches, as there remain many unqualified or low-qualified teachers in Emirati schools. There also remains a lack of male candidates in teacher education programs in the Emirates.

These concerns about teacher quality are echoed by Wiseman and Al-Bakr (2013), who seek to evaluate the impact of teacher education programs by asking whether there is a connection between teacher certification and student achievement. They find a weak overall correlation across the GCC between teacher certification and student achievement on TIMSS; however, a more detailed examination shows that there is only a positive correlation for Qatari maths teachers and Dubai science teachers. In all other GCC contexts, the correlation between teacher certification and student achievement on TIMSS scores is either statistically insignificant or weak. In other words, teacher training in maths and science does not seem to be effective in improving student attainment. Put simply, other factors—such as socioeconomic background or education spending—seem to be more important than teacher education in raising student results in the region. They argue that designing teacher education to focus more effectively on key skills such as pedagogy, motivation and student engagement should be a priority for policy makers across the GCC.

A range of efforts were made before the pandemic to address shortcomings in teacher preparation. Although the GCC states have resisted unthinking acceptance of Western norms and expectations for education, there has equally been a readiness to engage in extensive policy borrowing, and they have relied heavily on borrowed models of teacher quality (Wiseman, Davidson and Brereton 2017). Romanovski and Alkhabeet (2020) note the trend toward seeking CAEP accreditation of teacher preparation courses in the GCC. However, they argue that CAEP accreditation comes from an American perspective and assumes that common standards for teacher education can be replicated unproblematically in diverse parts of the world. Moreover, it assumes that teacher education outcomes can be measured, and focuses attention on the measurable. Romanovski and Alkhabeet (2020) suggest that CAEP accreditation pays scant attention to the values and traditions that underpin various aspects of schooling in the region and does not consider how the epistemology of teacher education in the region may be culturally rooted, with religion playing a central role. Consequently, they conclude that CAEP accreditation threatens a "McDonaldization" of international systems of teacher preparation, with little or no regard for cultural differences in teacher education, language and Indigenous forms of knowledge. In pointing to these very real dangers, they overlook the ways in which CAEP accreditation may nevertheless serve as a useful catalyst for reform.

Other attempts to raise educational standards in the region have focused on the need to reform school leadership. Research into school leadership before the pandemic suggests a reliance on highly centralized decision-making (Al-Harthi and Al-Mahdy 2017; Stephenson, Dada and Harold 2012), resulting in inflexible schooling systems. Although there is a dearth of empirical studies into school leadership in the region (Hammad, Samier and Mohammed 2020), there was emerging evidence of shifts in styles of school leadership in the years preceding the pandemic. For example, data from Oman suggest that while hierarchy with control resting firmly with the principal has been the traditional approach, the Ministry of Education has endorsed more distributed leadership approaches, which have been slowly gaining ground (Al-Harthi and Al-Mahdy 2017). In the UAE, Stephenson, Dada, and Harold (2012) identified small pockets of emerging teacher leadership, slowly eroding hierarchical and centralized decision-making. In Saudi Arabia, Algarni and Male (2014) argued that the school system was slowly becoming more open to flexibility and autonomy to replace the concentration of power in the person of the principal. Although these trends were promising, Bailey et al. (2019) argue that the existing frameworks for conceptualizing school leadership have been imported from Western contexts and do not speak of the cultural specificities of the region. They argue that these differences explain why strategies for school turnaround originating in Western contexts are of limited or no use in GCC countries.

Other solutions to the concerns raised above have focused on teacher recruitment and training. El Sarharty et al. (2020) identify possible solutions for addressing these issues with education in the countries of the GCC, including improving teacher training so that teachers can support low achievers, empowering teachers and school leaders, and making sure that high-quality candidates enter the teaching profession. They suggest that "rigorous selection into the education profession, appropriate incentives for good performance, and the necessary authority to teach and manage effectively" (Saharty et al. 2020, 31) will help difficulties in attracting high-quality recruits.

Having identified these issues with education in GCC countries, and observed that teacher quality is at the heart of the issue, the remainder of this chapter will consider how the COVID-19 pandemic has impacted three key means to raise teacher quality—school leadership, teacher recruitment, and teacher training. I do this by first considering the immediate impact of the crisis on the case study country of Bahrain.

THE COVID-19 CRISIS IN BAHRAIN EDUCATION

In the Kingdom of Bahrain, all schools were closed on February 25, 2020. The government began streaming live classes from March 17, using both

Microsoft Teams and television broadcasts. In addition, activities and resources were prepared by teachers and made available on the nation's EduNet portal (which was launched in 2015), and the school year was completed without any return to physical classes. In July, Prince Salman bin Hamad Al Khalifa, the crown prince and first deputy prime minister, announced that all parents should be given the choice during the next academic year to continue with fully remote classes or to attend school once institutions reopened. Private schools were able to reopen in September 2020, although many students chose to continue their studies remotely. Government schools remained closed until October 25, when they partially reopened. Students were then offered a choice of online or hybrid learning, with students in school for two days a week. All students in school were expected to wear face masks and observe physical distancing. As with the private schools, many parents continued to keep their children studying online. Some teachers therefore had classes with small numbers of students; other teachers were assigned to work entirely with online learners. Initial media reports suggest very few students were physically present in school, with some schools reporting as few as twenty-five students in attendance (Al Sherbini 2020).

In Bahrain, all initial teacher education for government schools is conducted at the Bahrain Teachers College (BTC), which is part of the University of Bahrain. The BTC also offers leadership training to leaders of government schools. All teaching at the university moved online on February 25, 2020, including all levels of teacher and leadership education. Classes remained online for the remainder of the academic year. Students were given a choice between pass/fail or graded assessments for that semester. In September 2020, it was announced that the academic year 2020–2021 at the University of Bahrain would be entirely online, excepting practicum experiences. Online proctoring software was purchased by the university, and it was announced that assessments would be graded for all students during this semester.

During the spring of 2020, teacher practicums in schools were replaced by the use of video, both conducting observations and for the recording of mock teaching. It was recognized that some student teachers were under increased pressure, as they were asked to care for younger siblings who were out of school. This situation was leveraged advantageously by asking students to video themselves teaching younger relatives, where possible, as part of the revised practicum requirements. A practicum conducted from outside of school continued to be used for the Year One practicum experience in the autumn semester. Students in Year Three of the Bachelors program, who had already had one altered practicum, were able to return to schools once they reopened. The Ministry of Education agreed that they could all be supervised by teachers offering face-to-face teaching. Students studying for the Post-Graduate Diploma in Education (PGDE), which provides on-the-job initial teacher training, were by this stage running classes in schools. Circumstances meant that both these types of trainees could only teach two days a week, but they were able to observe online classes and classes taught to other age groups during the remaining three days. Trainees were also encouraged to observe those teachers whose responsibilities were for running online class-rooms, as well as to observe live classes in schools. With classrooms having fewer than ten learners, trainees did not gain the experience of managing large classes, nor were they permitted to use pair work, group work or dis-tribute resources. Classrooms were strictly socially distanced, removing the possibility of kinesthetic approaches to learning.

COVID-19 AND EDUCATION ACROSS THE GCC

Evidence is still emerging of the impact of similar changes to education and teacher training across other GCC countries, but initial reports from across the region have highlighted a number of concerns. One initial effect of moving online was to widen inequalities in schooling, with struggling children likely to fall further behind (El-Saharty et al. 2020). Additionally, a preceding lack of comfort with, and commitment to, educational technolo-gies and online learning hampered some GCC countries' ability to transition smoothly to online learning (Alhouti, 2020). Online learning requires self-motivation and independent learning, but these are some of the very skills that Arab education systems have hitherto failed to foster in students (Al Lily et al. 2020). Drawing on a study, which examines research from the MENA region, Al Lily et al. (2020) argue that there was a disconnect between crisis distance education and some aspects of Arab learning; many families live in large, intergenerational households, and there could be difficulties with many children requiring digital devices and internet access simultaneously. More positively, Al Lily et al. (2020) suggest that for some young Arab women, distance education facilitated fuller participation in education, as they were more comfortable using the written chat in online classrooms than speak-ing up in face-to-face classrooms. Meanwhile, while the GCC countries had previously been seeking to expand their market economies, the pandemic has accelerated the move away from a dependence on oil and an oil-financed public sector, leading to sharpened interest in developing student soft skills needed for employment in the private sector (Coutts et al. 2020).

COVID-19 has been educationally disruptive, introducing a schism between the way that things have always been done and the way that things can or should be done henceforth, a point at which norms are brought into doubt. In a study of the educational responses to the pandemic in Bahrain, Iraq, and Russia, Coutts et al. (2020) identify three trends in education that have been heightened by the pandemic—the use of technology; issues around quality and inclusion; and the need to pay attention to employability skills. Building on their work, I suggest that it has introduced opportunities to transform home-school relationships; move schooling away from rote memorization; and stimulate investment in educational technologies and the training teachers need to use such technologies effectively. Its economic impact may spur efforts to bridge the mismatch between learning outcomes and the needs of the labor market. The very different experiences that children have had educationally during school closures could lead to a heightened awareness of the need for differentiation.

To date, this potential for change has not been fully realized. For example, Al Lily et al. (2020) note that in some Arab countries teachers have been expected to complete numerous forms related to their distance teaching; therefore, although the technology has the potential to reduce bureaucracy, it has, in some instances, increased it. Indeed, in some countries such as Kuwait, learning has been paused because of technological difficulties (Alhouti 2020). Nevertheless, in the following section, I consider the opportunities offered by the pandemic for more far-reaching changes to teacher quality.

THE TRIPLE HELIX OF TEACHER QUALITY: SCHOOL LEADERSHIP, TEACHER RECRUITMENT, AND TEACHER PREPARATION

In this section, I examine how teacher quality may be impacted by the pandemic by looking at the key issues of school leadership, teacher recruitment, and teacher preparation. I also acknowledge the threats the pandemic poses to improving teacher quality in each of these ways. Throughout, it is suggested that these three together constitute a triple helix of teacher quality.

School Leadership

School leadership is central to school turnaround (Bailey et al 2019), and the pandemic has fundamentally altered the nature of leadership of schools, in the GCC and elsewhere. The VUCA acronym was developed in the 1980s to capture the leadership challenges of volatility, uncertainty, complexity, and ambiguity to which agile businesses must be able to respond. However, the pandemic has made these a reality for many school leaders in unprecedented ways (Myung and Kimner 2020).

There is an emerging literature charting the impact of the pandemic on school leaders worldwide. Much of this work is speculative and anecdotal, rather than empirical in nature. Harris and Jones (2020) identify some of the ways in which the pandemic impacted school leaders: the loss of informal opportunities to build social relationships, rapidly changing regulations, uncertain staffing, and a lack of precedents or relevant research. They make seven claims about how school leadership has changed as a result of the pandemic:

1. School leadership is undergoing radical, and possibly permanent, change.
2. School leadership preparation no longer matches current challenges.
3. Self-care by leaders is needed so they can continue to support their community.
4. Technology is increasingly salient, but needs to support, rather than dominate, pedagogy.
5. Crisis and change management has become a central skill of a school leader.
6. Parent and community links have become more important.
7. Distributed leadership is necessary to manage the increased pressures on school leaders.

Fernandez and Shaw (2020) use the metaphor of the "allostatic" leader to describe the ideal leader of academic institutions during COVID-19, an observation that applies no less to schools. Allostasis refers to the ways in which an organism achieves stability through adaptive change. They identify three leadership best practices to achieve this:

1. Servant leadership, in which others' needs are placed above those of the leader themselves.
2. Distributed leadership, to facilitate timely and responsive decision-making.
3. Communication, through clear, frequent, and varied means.

However, Fernandez and Shaw's work is rooted in research about approaches to leadership that have worked well in previous crises rather than specifically based on the context of national lockdown during a pandemic.

In summary, the pandemic has created a rupture in leadership practices, increased pressures to adopt distributed leadership practices, and changed school leaders' relationships with other stakeholders in the school community. All schools have had to change their division of responsibilities between parents and teachers during a period when teachers are reliant on parents and guardians to support online instruction. There is a consequent mismatch between the training that these school leaders received earlier in their careers, and the needs of school leadership today.

These changes have created an impetus for leader and teacher development to deal with the current crisis. Such short-term goals need to be complemented by longer-term strategies to build up teacher quality. A collaborative approach to surviving the crisis may enable leaders to see the value in distributed approaches to leadership in the longer term. The awareness that training is acutely needed to cope with the extraordinary circumstances may be used to build up a habit of continuous leadership and teacher development. In such ways, the effects of the pandemic may be leveraged for sustained change. This is the first strand of the triple helix to develop quality teachers in the region.

Teacher Recruitment

The second strand of this helix is effective teacher recruitment. This is a highly complex issue in the region, which has relied on large numbers of nonnational teachers alongside in-country teacher education (Gallagher 2019), and with many countries having large private education sectors with different recruitment challenges to those of the public sector; however, the primary focus in this chapter is on teacher recruitment for in-country teacher education. There was a long-standing concern in the region prior to the pandemic about how to recruit an adequate supply of high-quality applicants into teacher education programs. For example, Gallagher (2019) identifies several barriers to recruitment of higher quality national teachers in the UAE, including the low status given to teaching (particularly for men) and its poor remuneration relative to other professions. Both these barriers may have been lessened by the indirect consequences of the pandemic.

COVID-19 has rendered teaching a more attractive profession for several reasons. It has raised the status of teachers by repositioning them as essential workers (Hill, Rosehart, St Helene and Sadhra 2020). In addition, after parents have struggled to teach even their own children during school closures, there may now be an increased awareness of both the importance and complexity of teachers' work (Hill, Rosehart, St Helene and Sadhra 2020); as Hargreaves and Fullan (2020) point out, prior to the pandemic, most people relied on their recollections from childhood for their understanding of what teachers do. Now, teachers have been profiled in the media as energetic problem-solvers, feeding the local community or delivering materials to students in imaginative ways (Hargreaves and Fullan 2020). While there were some initial concerns about health risks while teaching, due to the contact with large numbers of young people, to date strict government measures in the GCC countries to socially distance schools have quietened such fears.

Shutdowns of national economies and the fall in the price of oil (Arezki, Fan and Nguyen 2020) may have inadvertently rendered teaching more attractive in comparison to other professions. Salary cuts and lay-offs in the private sector have highlighted the economic security offered by a career in teaching. An increase in applications to teacher training programs has already been reported in some countries such as the UK (BBC News 2020).

Looking ahead, the changes wrought by the pandemic may precipitate a more flexible approach to teacher recruitment, shifting the balance between in-country and overseas teacher recruitment. Thinking radically, once institutions are comfortable with remote teaching and learning, the need to persuade teachers physically to relocate is reduced; an online teacher can deliver their material from anywhere in the world. In other words, the flexible approaches necessitated by the pandemic may facilitate the recruitment of high-quality teachers from anywhere in the world, and enable them to support gaps in the domestic teaching workforce. This may complement any remaining gaps in domestic teacher recruitment.

In summary, there is reason to be cautiously optimistic about the impact of the pandemic on recruitment into teacher education. In the following section, we consider how the pandemic has impacted the teacher education these recruits receive.

Teacher Education

The third strand in the helix of teacher quality is teacher education. The pandemic has had an enormous immediate impact on teacher education, jeopardizing its quality in multiple ways, some of the most salient being that it has focused teacher educators' attention on technical aspects of delivery; it has impacted effective teacher practicums; and it has impeded effective forms of teacher assessment, both formative and summative. While such immediate challenges have absorbed the attention of many teacher educators in the short term (Kidd and Murray 2020), in a collation of changed teacher education practices globally, Ellis, Steadman, and Mao (2020) argue that the effect has been widescale innovation. The pandemic also raises two more fundamental, long-term questions for teacher education: What skills and dispositions do teachers require for a post-pandemic future, and how can these be acquired through reformed teacher education? These two issues will need to guide any revisions made to teacher education programs across the GCC countries. We shall examine each of these questions in turn.

In considering what skills and dispositions educators need for the future, it is important to note how the pandemic has problematized the role of the teacher. COVID-19 has been pedagogically disruptive. It has heightened an awareness of the multifaceted nature of a teacher's role in the classroom; in so doing, it has demonstrated that technology can never replace human interaction for learning, but it has also accelerated the introduction of technology into different aspects of teaching. For example, there has been a rapid increase in the use of apps and games, as well as technologies for communicating with parents and students. Broader aspects of the teachers' role have also been re-evaluated. Hill, Rosehart, St Helene, and Sadhra (2020) note that themes such as well-being, connection, and supporting diverse learners have become more salient. In addition, it is increasingly apparent that school students will need different skills and dispositions for the post-pandemic world, such as an ability to deal with VUCA themselves (Hadar et al 2020); schools need to develop greater resilience in students, for example, to face this uncertain world. Teachers will need to find ways to develop this in their students.

Conversely, the pandemic may inhibit some conceptualizations of teaching, and lead people to fall back on familiar approaches in uncertain times. In the GCC countries, the recent move toward collaborative, student-centered learning may be regressed by the pandemic; social distancing is easier in a traditional teacher-centered format in which individualized learners are cocooned from their peers, and maintaining collaborative learning in this format requires creativity and persistence. The potential of technology to overcome these difficulties may not be fully realized because of concerns about equity, online safety, and the physical health of students engaged in sedentary online study. However, despite these real risks, there is reason to be cautiously optimistic about the impact of the pandemic on teaching strategies. Whereas Gallagher's (2019) work in the UAE pointed to the psychocognitive difficulty of persuading students who have themselves graduated from a didactic system to internalize student-centered approaches to their classrooms, one result of social distancing and virtual learning is that student teachers and new recruits can no longer approach their classrooms with the expectation of behaving in the way that teachers have always done. This may facilitate the move toward new teaching strategies as they are continually aware that they are constructing a new normal for schools.

So, to turn to our second question, how can teacher education meet this need for new approaches to teaching? I suggest that such a fundamental disruption in how things are being done in schools could precipitate a move toward a different model of teacher education (Darling-Hammond and Hyler 2020). In the past, the GCC has often turned to imported policies for improving teacher education (Wiseman, Davidson and Brereton 2017), with insufficient attention to culturally rooted epistemologies of teacher education (Romanovski and Alkhabeet 2020). With teacher education globally now in a flux, more reciprocal approaches to program revisions may now be possible. Conversations about the future direction of teacher training are now, paradoxically, easier than before, as COVID-19 has facilitated the development of collaborative networks, ranging from neighborhood support to international professional exchanges (Azorin 2020). In place of traveling to international conferences to discuss ideas on an annual basis, or enjoying rare visits by a consultant, teacher trainers are now at ease with ongoing virtual collaboration with colleagues from across the region. Although dialogue is currently stymied by the intense pressures on faculty during these extraordinary circumstances, in the longer term the pandemic has fostered the skills needed to energize and democratize collaborative international networks.

The impact of these opportunities will vary according to the needs in different cultural and national contexts. Hill, Rosehart, St. Helene, and Sadhra (2020) argue the pandemic has highlighted the importance of teacher education addressing social inequalities, attending to child mental health, addressing colonialism, and attending to humans' relationship with the natural world. In other words, it has enabled reflection on the nature and purpose of teacher education and how it intersects with the wider social issues faced in their Canadian context. From an Irish perspective, Murray et al. (2020) call for a re-centering on care in teaching training, arguing that the shift to online learning has been the catalyst for deeper thinking about supportive educator-student relationships. Here in the GCC countries, the pandemic has highlighted other possibilities for change in teacher education, in how teaching practice is conceptualized, key components of the practicum, attitudes to the integration of technology, and in diverse and broad forms of assessment. With the pandemic problematizing the nature and purpose of teaching, this offers an unparalleled opportunity to revitalize teacher education, so that it becomes better able to deliver the quality teaching workforce that GCC economies need to emerge from the brutal effects of this health emergency.

CASE STUDY:
THE TRIPLE HELIX DURING THE
PANDEMIC IN BAHRAIN

Attention to the elements of this triple helix has already impacted on the work of BTC. Here, we took a decision in September 2020 to refocus our leadership center on supporting school leaders with the reopening of schools. We began with a training needs analysis, in which school leaders identified the training needs of themselves and their teachers to equip them for the new normal. The decision was made to create a toolkit for schools, to share examples of best leadership practice, and to run training workshops on the revised quality assurance framework that had been developed for schools during these extraordinary circumstances. The work of our leadership center was revitalized by the demands of the pandemic.

Teacher recruitment in the kingdom has also benefited from the pandemic. It is notable that applications to join BTC increased significantly during the 2020 recruitment cycle. Bahrain has long been dependent on importing many of its teachers, so this has been an impactful change.

However, the greatest impact has been the different effects on our teacher education program. Over a decade before the pandemic, Ure, Gough, and Newton (2009) identified four distinct models of teacher professional learning:

1. The Partnership or Collaborative Learning Model, in which the student teacher, school teachers and academics are seen as engaged in learning together through collaboration.
2. The Reflective Model, in which the purpose of the practicum is to develop the student teacher's ability to engage in reflective practice.
3. The Academically Taught or Clinical Model, in which the university and partner school must work closely together to offer the student teacher extensive clinical practice.
4. The Pedagogical Content Knowledge Model, in which the key focus of teacher education is to understand how teachers organize and adapt subject matter for the purpose of instruction.

In practice, these models have influenced different elements of the initial teacher training programs at BTC. Students are expected to write daily reflections on their teaching practice (Model 2). There has been an emphasis on learning and applying a large number of psychological theories, which students are expected to apply during their teaching practice (Model 3). There has been an emphasis on teaching of subject knowledge, with disciplinary identity being the organizing feature of the college (Model 4). Overall, while there is no clear institutional vision about the nature of teacher professional learning—and I am not suggesting that a homogeneous approach is necessary—the most salient exception has been any embrace of Model 1 in the structure of our training programs. There has been no shared sense of learning together with practitioners in schools.

There are early indications that the schism between how things used to be and how they are now that has been affected by the pandemic may change this. Intensive dialogue has taken place between the college and the Bahrain Ministry of Education to ensure students can resume their teaching practicum in a safe and effective manner, and this has necessitated reflection on the fundamental purpose and components of the practicum. Student teachers now undertaking teaching practice are exploring together with their mentors in schools and their supervisors at BTC how to create effective socially distanced teaching strategies.

By disrupting ways in which teacher education is done, the pandemic has also opened up possibilities for further change in the post-pandemic world. First, other aspects of the practicum have been impacted. Grudnoff (2011) identified a number of ways in which research participants felt that a conventional practicum ill-prepared them for their first job. First, during a conventional practicum, classroom rules and routines have already been established, while their first challenge as a new teacher is to establish these. Second, a traditional practicum has been focused on what happened inside the classroom, whereas a teacher's role involves much more than this, ranging from administration to meetings to a number of out-of-class responsibilities. In both these ways, the pandemic has forced us to look anew at the teaching practicum. During the autumn 2020 semester in Bahrain, students and teachers worked together to devise socially distanced routines. Moreover, given the small (and unpredictable) number of children in schools, student teachers were encouraged to collaborate with teachers outside of the classroom, especially those working with students online.

A second consideration for further change is how the pandemic has accelerated the use of technology in teacher education. Although the literature has suggested for many years that effective use of educational technologies can enhance practicum experiences (English and Duncan-Howell 2008; Cheong 2010; Wright 2010), it has hitherto scarcely been used at BTC. As a result of the pandemic, there is now increased emphasis on using virtual platforms for student exchange of reflections. Additionally, the use of videos in practicums has been greatly increased in various national contexts (e.g., Kalloo, Mitchell and Kamalodeen [2020], reporting on Trinidad and Tobago), a trend that has also been adopted in Bahrain.

Third, the pandemic has necessitated revisions to assessment of teacher education (Kalloo, Mitchell and Kamalodeen 2020). As discussed above, El-Saharty et al. (2020) identified an emphasis on rote memorization as one of the impediments to education systems in the GCC countries meeting the skills needed by labor markets. Similarly, at BTC, there was extensive reliance on examination assessments, and within those a preponderance of multiple choice questions, prior to the pandemic. During the lockdown, it was recognized that it would be impossible to proceed with exams as normal. In place of these, a range of alternative assessments was suggested, and many faculty opted to use assignments in place of examinations; other courses gave students the choice between a graded examination or an ungraded piece of coursework. For these examinations, faculty were forced to assume that every exam was de facto open book. As a result, many faculty incorporated more questions involving higher order thinking skills that would inhibit cheating. The option of ungraded assignments enabled faculty who were more conversant with writing examinations to experiment with non-examination assessment. In such ways, COVID-19 has disrupted existing assessment practices, and thereby has opened up possibilities for focus on assessing more diverse skills and dispositions in post-pandemic teacher training.

CONCLUSION

This chapter has examined the impact of the COVID-19 pandemic on educational leadership, teacher recruitment, and teacher education in the Kingdom of Bahrain to identify some of the threats and opportunities the pandemic poses for raising teacher quality in the GCC countries. The chapter began by identifying concerns about learning outcomes (El-Saharty et al. 2020; Schleicher 2020) and teacher quality (Wiseman and Al-Bakr 2013) in the GCC countries before the pandemic, noting long-standing concerns about teacher recruitment (Gallagher 2019) and about centralized and hierarchical approaches to school leadership (Algarni and Male 2014; Stephenson, Dada and Harold 2012). It then charted the immediate changes wrought on schooling in Bahrain by the lockdown. It thereafter considered some of the longer-term possibilities opened up by such change.

The pandemic has forced significant immediate changes on teacher education in the countries of the GCC. It has transformed the expectations placed upon school leaders and interrupted teacher recruitment processes. Each of these three strands of the triple helix guaranteeing teacher quality is at risk of unraveling as a result of the pandemic and I have charted some of the threats that exist; however, my focus has been on stressing the possibilities for more positive change. The pandemic has dislocated, disrupted, and interrupted, but the resulting fissures have opened up new possibilities and forced diverse change. The role of the teacher is being reconceptualized, the status given to the teaching profession is growing, and the leadership of schools is experiencing seismic change. There is now an historic opportunity to reconstruct teacher education (Ellis, Steadman and Mao 2020), and to ensure that it better meets the need for a quality teaching workforce across the countries of the GCC.

REFERENCES

Al Lily, Abdulrahman E., Abdelrahim F. Ismail, Fathi M. Abunasser, and Rafdan H.A. Alqahtani. 2020. "Distance education as a response to pandemics: Coronavirus and Arab culture." *Technology in Society* 63, 101317. https://doi.org/10.1016/j.techsoc.2020.101317.

Al Sherbini, Ramadan. 2020. "Covid-19: Low turnout of students at Bahrain schools." *Gulf News,* November 1, 2020. https://gulfnews.com/world/gulf/bahrain/covid-19-low-turnout-of-students-at-bahrain-schools-1.74974113.

Algarni, Fatehyah and Trevor Male. 2014. "Leadership in Saudi Arabian public schools: Time for devolution?" *International Studies in Educational Administration (Commonwealth Council for Educational Administration and Management [CCEAM])* 42, no. 3: 45–59.

Al-Harthi, Aisha S. A., and Yasser F. H. Al-Mahdy. 2017. "Distributed leadership and school effectiveness in Egypt and Oman: An exploratory study." *International Journal of Educational Management* 31, no. 6: 801–813.

Alhouti, Ibrahim. 2020. "Education during the pandemic: The case of Kuwait." *Journal of Professional Capital and Community* 5, nos. 3/4: 213–225.

Arezki, Rabah, Rachel Y. Fan, and Ha Nguyen. 2020. "Coping with a dual shock: A perspective from the Middle East and North Africa." In *COVID-19 in Developing Economies*, edited by Simeon Djankov and Ugo Panizza, 69–85. London: CEPR Press.

Azorín, Cecilia. 2020. "Beyond COVID-19 supernova. Is another education coming?" *Journal of Professional Capital and Community*. Ahead of print, https://doi.org/10.1108/JPCC-05-2020-0019.

Bailey, Lucy, Ted Purinton, Osama Al-Mahdi, and Hala Al Khalifa, 2021. "Conceptualizing school leadership in the Gulf Cooperation Council (GCC) cultures: Demarcating challenges for research." *Educational Management Administration and Leadership*, 49, no.1: 93–111.

BBC News, 2020. "Coronavirus: 'Teacher training application rise' during lockdown." *BBC News*, July 27th 2020. https://www.bbc.com/news/uk-wales-53498342.

Cheong, Donguk. 2010. "The effects of practice teaching sessions in second life on the change in pre-service teachers' teaching efficacy." *Computers and Education* 55 no. 2: 868–880.

Coutts, Christine E.N., Mohamed Buheji, Dunya Ahmed, Talal Abdulkareem, Budhoor Buheji, Sajeda Eidan, and Nikolay Perepelkin. 2020. "Emergency remote education in Bahrain, Iraq, and Russia during the COVID-19 pandemic: A comparative case study." *Human Systems Management*, (Preprint): 1–21.

Darling-Hammond, Linda, and Maria E. Hyler. 2020. "Preparing educators for the time of COVID . . . and beyond." *European Journal of Teacher Education* 43, no. 4: 457–465.

Ellis, Viv, Sarah Steadman, and Qiming Mao. 2020. "'Come to a screeching halt': Can change in teacher education during the COVID-19 pandemic be seen as innovation?" *European Journal of Teacher Education* 43, no. 4: 559–572.

El-Saharty, Sameh, Igor Kheyfets, Christopher H. Herbst, and Mohamed I. Ajwad. 2020. *Fostering Human Capital in the Gulf Cooperation Council Countries*. Washington, DC: World Bank Group. https://openknowledge.worldbank.org/bitstream/handle/10986/33946/9781464815829.pdf?sequence=2.

English, Rebecca, and Jennifer Duncan-Howell. 2008. "Facebook© goes to college: Using social networking tools to support students undertaking teaching practicum." *Journal of Online Learning and Teaching* 4, no. 4: 596–601.

Gallagher, Kay. 2019. "Challenges and Opportunities in Sourcing, Preparing and Developing a Teaching Force for the UAE." In *Education in the United Arab Emirates* edited by Kay Gallagher, 127–145. Singapore: Springer.

Grudnoff, Lexie 2011. "Rethinking the practicum: Limitations and possibilities." *Asia-Pacific Journal of Teacher Education* 39, no. 3: 223–234.

Hadar, Linor L., Oren Ergas, Bracha Alpert, and Tamar Ariav 2020. "Rethinking teacher education in a VUCA world: Student teachers' social-emotional competencies during the Covid-19 crisis." *European Journal of Teacher Education* 43, no. 4: 573–586.

Hammad, Waheed, Eugenie A. Samier, and Azzam Mohammed. 2020. "Mapping the field of educational leadership and management in the Arabian Gulf region: A systematic review of Arabic research literature." *Educational Management Administration and Leadership,* 1–20. https://doi.org/10.1177/1741143220937308.

Hargreaves, Andy, and Michael Fullan 2020. "Professional capital after the pandemic: Revisiting and revising classic understandings of teachers' work." *Journal of Professional Capital and Community* 5, no. 3–4: 327–336.

Harris, Alma, and Michelle Jones. 2020. "COVID 19–school leadership in disruptive times." *School Leadership and Management* 40, no. 4: 243–247.

Hill, Cher, Paula Rosehart, Janice St. Helene, and Sarine Sadhra. 2020. "What kind of educator does the world need today? Reimagining teacher education in post-pandemic Canada." *Journal of Education for Teaching* 46, no. 4: 565–575.

Kalloo, Rowena C., Beular Mitchell, and Vimala J. Kamalodeen. 2020. "Responding to the COVID-19 pandemic in Trinidad and Tobago: Challenges and opportunities for teacher education." *Journal of Education for Teaching* 46, no. 4: 452–462.

Kidd, Warren, and Jean Murray. 2020. "The Covid-19 pandemic and its effects on teacher education in England: How teacher educators moved practicum learning online." *European Journal of Teacher Education* 43, no. 4: 542–558.

Murray, Cliona, Manuela Heinz, Ian Munday, Elaine Keane, Niamh Flynn, Cornelia Connolly, Tony Hall and Gerry MacRuairc. 2020. "Reconceptualising relatedness in education in 'distanced' times." *European Journal of Teacher Education* 43, no. 4: 488–502.

Myung, Jeannie, and Hayin Kimner. 2020. *Continuous Improvement in Schools in the COVID-19 Context: A Summary Brief.* Policy Analysis for California Education. https://edpolicyinca.org/sites/default/files/2020-09/pb_myung_sep2020.pdf.

Romanowski, Michael H., and Hadeel Alkhateeb. 2020. "The McDonaldization of CAEP accreditation and teacher education programs abroad." *Teaching and Teacher Education* 90, 103028. https://doi.org/10.1016/j.tate.2020.103028.

Schleicher, Andreas 2020. *Schooling Disrupted—Schooling Rethought. Presentation from the OECD Forum Virtual Event "Schooling in times of Covid-19."* OECD. https://www.oecd-forum.org/documents/schooling-disrupted-schooling-rethought-presentation-from-the-oecd-forum-virtual-event-schooling-in-times-of-covid-19.

Stephenson, Laura, Robin Dada, and Barbara Harold. 2012. "Challenging the traditional idea of leadership in UAE schools." *On the Horizon* 20, no. 1: 54–63.

Ure, C., Annette Gough, and R. Newton. 2009. *Practicum Partnerships: Exploring Models of Practicum Organisation in Teacher Education for a Standards-Based Profession.* Victoria: Australian Teaching and Learning Council.

Wiseman, Alexander W., and Fawziah Al-Bakr. 2013. "The elusiveness of teacher quality: A comparative analysis of teacher certification and student achievement in Gulf Cooperation Council (GCC) countries." *Prospects* 43, no. 3: 289–309.

Wiseman, Alexander W., Petrina M. Davidson, and Joseph P. Brereton. 2017. "14 Teacher Quality in Gulf Cooperation Council (GCC) Countries." In *International*

Handbook of Teacher Quality and Policy, edited by Motoko Akiba and Gerald Le Tendre, 218–238. Abingdon: Routledge.

Wright, Noeline. 2010. "Twittering in teacher education: Reflecting on practicum experiences." *Open Learning: The Journal of Open, Distance and e-Learning* 25, no. 3: 259–265.

Chapter 7

The Intangibles of Teacher Education in the UAE

Nadera Alborno

INTRODUCTION

This chapter was inspired by a conversation with my research assistant who was collecting interview data for a project about transforming inclusive practices and strategies in online learning environments during the COVID-19 pandemic in 2020. Her pool of participants included three teachers that graduated from the American University in Dubai (AUD) Master of Education (MEd) program, where I teach. In the process of reporting her findings, she remarked, "the graduates of your program seem to have a common language and a common drive." She further explained: "They all used disability-sensitive terms and they spoke about difficulties and barriers, yet they voiced optimism and determination to find solutions.... They all spoke about caring, empathy, connections and relationships." Probing further to understand what distinguished them from other participants, she responded, "it is complicated because it all seems so intangible."

Intrigued by her observations and the reference to something intangible, I decided to research the concept of intangibles in teacher education. What are they? How are they defined? Why do they matter? Results were limited. I came across a plethora of teacher blogs and practitioner essays that mostly described how little attention is given to the intangibles in teacher education and classroom practice, while also arguing for their recognition as fundamental to good teaching (Ankrum 2019; Bates 2020; Gonser 2020). The research literature tended to address teacher dispositions, sometimes as synonymous with the intangibles of education (Harrison et al. 2006; Rinaldo et al. 2009; Talbert-Johnson 2006). In large part, there is no agreement in the literature on how teacher dispositions are defined; however, they are widely discussed as behaviors contingent upon the knowledge

111

and skills acquired in teacher education (Bair 2017; Borko et al. 2007; Diez and Murrell 2010). The Minnesota Educator Dispositions System (MnEDS™) at the University of Minnesota suggests that teacher candidates think about what teachers know and can do in metaphorical terms related to the human body. Thus, one might consider content knowledge as the head and pedagogical skills as the hands. It follows then that dispositions can be considered the heart which pumps blood and gives life to the professional practice of a teacher. Viewed in this way, dispositions are the more intangible aspects of teaching.

This chapter aims to identify and understand the intangible qualities and experiences that matter in teacher education. Given the predominance of literature relating teaching dispositions to the intangible aspects of teaching, I start by unpacking how scholars, teacher education programs, and accrediting agencies address professional teacher dispositions in North America in general and in the United Arab Emirates (UAE) in particular. I include a reference to accrediting agencies because the Ministry of Education and the public tend to value professional programs more when they are accredited by international agencies. The next section focuses on understanding the role of intangibles in teacher education. The final section presents a discussion of how teacher dispositions, especially intangible qualities, can be nurtured in teacher education programs in the UAE.

UNDERSTANDING TEACHER DISPOSITIONS

While most researchers and accrediting bodies agree that content knowledge and pedagogical skills are essential to good teaching, there is a growing consensus among scholars that teacher dispositions matter as well (Da Ros-Voseles and Moss 2007; Carroll 2012; Helm 2006; Murrell et al. 2010; Rike and Sharp 2008). Increasingly, the research tends to conceptualize knowledge, skills, and teacher dispositions as mutually dependent in teacher education; however, they are not deemed as equally important in the literature, by accrediting agencies, or in teacher education programs (Brookhart 2011; CAEP 2019; Guerriero 2013; InTASC 2013; NCATE 2008; Walshaw 2012).

In our prevailing culture of measurement and evaluation, instruments designed to assess what a teacher knows and can do are readily available, even promoted. Such a quantitative focus on knowledge and skills leads to the perception that teaching is a two-dimensional profession—measured and evaluated on only two planes (knowledge and skills). While the role of teacher dispositions may be more difficult to identify and define, it adds an important third dimension to an already complex profession—a depth that can be characterized as intangible.

A review of the literature reveals that there is no clear agreement among scholars regarding the identification and definition of teacher dispositions. For example, Lillian Katz defines "a disposition as a pattern of behavior exhibited frequently . . . in the absence of coercion . . . constituting a habit of mind under some conscious and voluntary control . . . intentional and oriented to broad goals" (Katz 1993, 16). Furthermore, she argues that, unlike attitudes which do not necessarily result in accompanying behaviors, dispositions are deliberate choices. Others concur that teacher dispositions involve "the choice to act or react in characteristic ways in certain situations" (Hollon et al. 2010, 123). On the other hand, Villegas (2007) claims that dispositions are not choices but tendencies to act in a certain manner in given circumstances. Thus, Villegas is suggesting that dispositions are environmentally sensitive.

In ongoing discussions and debates on teacher dispositions, many scholars tend to refer to John Dewey (1922) and his early discussion of dispositions as the underlying motivator and organizer for intelligent behavior. He tended to use words like "disposition" and "habit" interchangeably, leading contemporary scholars to write about dispositions as habits of mind (Katz 1993; Thornton 2006; Nelsen 2015).

In 2000, the concept was introduced in the realm of teacher education by the National Council for Accreditation of Teacher Education (NCATE) as part of the drive for education reform in the twenty-first century. NCATE formally identified professional dispositions in the accreditation standards for teacher education units:

> *Standard 1: Candidate Knowledge, Skills and Disposition.* Candidates preparing to work in schools as teachers or other school professionals know and demonstrate the content knowledge, pedagogical content knowledge and skills, pedagogical and professional knowledge and skills, and professional dispositions necessary to help all students learn. Assessments indicate that candidates meet professional, state, and institutional standards. (NCATE 2008, 12)

Professional dispositions are more clearly conceptualized in the glossary of the framework as follows:

> Professional attitudes, values, and beliefs demonstrated through both verbal and nonverbal behaviors as educators interact with students, families, colleagues, and communities. These positive behaviors support student learning and development. NCATE expects institutions to assess professional dispositions based on observable behaviors in educational settings. The two professional dispositions that NCATE expects institutions to assess are fairness and the belief that all students can learn. Based on their mission and conceptual framework,

professional education units can identify, define, and operationalize additional
professional dispositions. (NCATE 2008, 90)

Two important points can be observed in the above definition: (1) professional dispositions are defined as observable behaviors and therefore measurable; and (2) the definition is flexible allowing teacher preparation programs
to add other dimensions that match their mission and develop means for
cultivating and assessing them. This definition unleashed controversy about
the possibility of ideological bias resulting from the lack of consensus in
defining and operationalizing concepts such as fairness (Borko et al. 2007).
Murrell et al. (2010) further explains that the topic of dispositions is complex and tends to generate political and ideological divide. Later in 2013,
the Council for the Accreditation of Educator Preparation (CAEP), which
replaced NCATE as the official accrediting body, revised the standards for
teacher education programs. In the updated version, professional dispositions
remain in the standards, however, a formal definition has been removed from
the glossary. Without clarity on this concept, teacher education programs are
left to define teacher dispositions according to the vision and mission of their
respective programs.

It is worth mentioning that the CAEP standards are heavily influenced
by the Interstate Teacher Assessment and Support Consortium (InTASC)
standards for teacher licensing and development, which identifies forty-three
distinct dispositions as "critical." This framework describes dispositions as
"habits of professional action and moral commitments that underlie the performances" and "play a key role in how teachers do, in fact, act in practice"
(InTASC 2013, 6). It is interesting to note that the framework articulates
dispositions using language that relates to what a teacher should know and
be able to do. For example, the disposition for standard 7(o) states that "the
teacher values planning," while standard 8(s) states that "the teacher values
flexibility and reciprocity in the teaching." These extracts from the InTASC
framework suggest that values guide behavior. In this matter, Thornton
(2006) observed that educators seldom identify dispositions, instead they
seem to list desirable teacher behaviors "preceded by the word value" (Bair
2017, 225). While the literature reveals a lack of clarity, most scholars agree
that teacher dispositions are an important aspect of professional identity
which can be learned and developed overtime.

Increasingly, scholars continue to explore ways of identifying, developing, and measuring teacher dispositions. For example, in a study about the
challenge of assessing dispositions, Wayda and Lund (2005) developed
a rubric with faculty colleagues who initially identified thirty descriptors. After piloting the rubric with student teachers, they identified five
key areas—all operationalized as values: the teacher candidate (1) values

learning and knowledge; (2) values diversity; (3) values collaboration; (4) values professionalism; and (5) values personal integrity. More recently, Mary Antony Bair (2017) conducted a study at a four-year institution in the Midwestern United States to identify dispositions that matter. She and her team initially recognized twenty-one dispositions which they later reduced to nine dispositions that were valued by all participants: responsive, challenging, reflective, ethical, scholarly, caring, student-centered, fair, and resourceful. In addition, Costa and Kallick (2013) developed a model that named sixteen dispositions referred to as habits of mind interchangeably. Some of these include finding humor, persisting, managing impulsivity, and thinking flexibly. As intended by CAEP, teacher preparation programs are left to identify and define teacher dispositions according to the mission and vision of each program.

Although CAEP is officially a US accreditor, it is not uncommon for teacher preparation programs in the Gulf Cooperation Council (GCC) region to participate in its process of evidence-based accreditation. In addition to international accreditors like CAEP, universities in the countries of the GCC are subject to accrediting processes instituted by local ministries of education. Such entities are also highlighting teacher dispositions as key to teacher effectiveness and school improvement. In fact, Welch, Areepattamannil, and Dickson (2016) conducted a study to develop and validate an instrument designed to assess the professional teaching dispositions based on the professional teaching standards promulgated by the Abu Dhabi Education Council (ADEC) in the UAE Emirate of Abu Dhabi. The study resulted in the Abu Dhabi Professional Teaching Disposition Scale (ADPTDS) which focused on three areas: personality traits, performances of pedagogical values, and behavioral manifestations. In this instance, dispositions were primarily identified as personality traits. In recent years, matters related to school improvement and teacher effectiveness have become a national priority for the UAE (Vision 2021). In 2016, Pearson Education funded a global study of twenty-three countries, including the UAE, to determine the top qualities of effective educators (McKnight et al. 2016). For this purpose, the principal investigator surveyed various stakeholders, consisting of 150 teachers, 150 students, 50 principals, 150 parents, 30 education researchers, and policy makers from the public and private school sectors. The most important quality identified across the full sample of participants was that teachers "need to build trusting, compassionate relationships with their students" (McKnight et al. 2016, 3). Ultimately, the survey results affirmed that the UAE values not only the knowledge and skills that teachers possess but also "dispositions of care and character" (McKnight et al. 2016, 5) that inform good teaching. The surveyed stakeholders emphasized the prominence of teacher dispositions, such as care, patience, compassion, dedication, and relatedness, over

teaching-specific knowledge and skills; thus, suggesting that these dispositions are necessary if children are going to learn and succeed.

In summary, although the literature on identifying and defining teacher dispositions is rightly critiqued for lacking clarity and consensus, it nonetheless
offers guidance for teachers and teacher educators on the framing and cultivation of dispositions as essential qualities of good teaching. Furthermore,
research increasingly confirms that dispositions are teachable. As Cummins
and Asempapa (2013, 110) concluded, "knowledge and understanding related
to professional dispositions can change through the experiences candidates
have during their training."

UNDERSTANDING INTANGIBLE QUALITIES

In a two-year qualitative research project entitled *On Teaching* by Kristina
Rizga, a veteran high school English teacher named Renee Moore posited
that the best teaching practices embody intangible capacities that speak to
the fundamental human needs of all learners—such as empathy, kindness,
and a desire to understand the lives and interests of individual students
(Rizga 2020b). Teacher dispositions are important; they inform what a
teacher knows and does. In other words, teaching requires an orchestration
of all three dimensions: cognition, action, and affect (Richert 2007). Such
dispositions might include appearance, poise, creativity, resourcefulness, as
well as being responsive, reflective, challenging, and scholarly (Bair 2017).
Other dispositions are less tangible, such as inspirational, passionate, caring,
kind, and personal. Intangible qualities go beyond a consideration of how a
teacher behaves to the very heart of who the teacher is. Such a teacher often
provides "something intangible" that influences students, and "sometimes
creates shelter for the soul and a passionate blueprint for living. It is also
the 'something' that may change the lives of students" (Powell-Brown et al.
2014, 67).

In referring to an article by Garrison and Rud (2009) on *Reverence in
Classroom Teaching*, Punya Mishra, a thought leader in education reminds
us that framing teaching as the imparting of knowledge and skills aimed at
goals such as jobs, career, and employability misses something crucial and
fundamental to life and learning—something Garrison and Rud (2009, 2627)
termed as "reverence":

> Although teaching students involves imparting knowledge, it is also a calling
> with other dimensions beyond the cognitive. . . . It is about the formation of
> minds, the molding of destinies, the creation of an enduring desire in students
> not only to know, but also to care for others, appreciate beauty, and much more.

In some sense of the word, teaching is a spiritual, although not necessarily religious, activity.

Although he hesitates to use the word "reverence" in writing about teaching and learning, Mishra acknowledges that educators need to develop a language that more aptly describes the intangible qualities of teaching (Mishra 2011). But first, he suggests, we may want to focus on getting people—educators, teacher educators, accrediting agencies—to acknowledge that "aesthetics and affect" are just as important to good teaching as knowledge and skills (Mishra 2009).

Traditionally, the teacher evaluation process places little to no emphasis on the intangible aspects of teaching and who the teacher is; instead, this process focuses on the observable and measurable behaviors regarding a teacher's content knowledge and pedagogical skills (Rinaldo et al. 2009). Such assessments commonly depend on rubrics and checklists with some narrative. Likewise, teacher preparation programs continue to emphasize knowledge and skills throughout coursework, while paying less attention to the importance of teacher dispositions and their incorporation into the curriculum. Holly Thornton found that memorable and inspirational teachers were those who "exhibited key dispositions that impacted, even determined, how content knowledge and pedagogical skills came to life within the classroom" (2006, 56).

It is true that teacher dispositions, especially those which are intangible qualities, are difficult to measure or even articulate. It is important to keep in mind that researchers in general agree that teacher dispositions matter; however, there is no consensus regarding what they comprise and how to measure them. For this reason, regional communities of research and practice, including teacher education programs, are called upon to articulate teacher dispositions or the personal qualities which best speak to their own culture and context in ways that address local concerns and priorities. Having a shared vision and common language to talk about what matters in our three-dimensional teaching profession benefits everyone. For example, knowing that building "trusting, compassionate relationships" is the most highly regarded personal quality of effective teachers as identified by a variety of stakeholders across the UAE, provides regional teacher education programs with a shared priority (McKnight 2016, 3). Determining how to measure this quality can become a shared endeavor. Keeping in mind no measurement is perfect, especially measurements that try to assess the complexity of individual dispositions and mindsets. Approaching such a task at the program level requires not only organizational support and individual commitment but also a shared understanding that a single rubric or checklist will not suffice. Instead, teacher educators could identify a plurality of measurements to provide evidence for the documentation of teacher dispositions (Duckworth and Seligman 2005; Duckworth and Yeager 2015). As Diez (2006, 69) concurs, "in all good research, triangulation of data sources would be a good idea for having confidence that the data about candidate dispositions is accurate." Furthermore, Mary Diez also supports a program-specific rather than a standardized approach, within "a culture of assessment, using qualitative interpretivist approaches to look at each individual candidate's responses to the challenges of becoming a teacher" (2006, 70).

In summary, let us be mindful of the fact that knowledge and skills are static without the appropriate dispositions to care and communicate well. After all, the quality of influence that the teacher possesses has the power and potential to change a student's life, whereas the measurement of knowledge, skills, and dispositions largely serve as documentation for management and accreditation purposes.

NURTURING THE INTANGIBLES

There is no textbook or curriculum that helps teachers to understand and acquire the intangible qualities of good teaching. Intangibles are not skills, they are not knowledge-based; instead, they are noncognitive capacities (Tough 2012). Nonetheless, they need to be intentionally articulated, operationalized, and nurtured, as well as incorporated in the curriculum. For the education that our children and young people receive depends directly on the quality of the teachers who serve them. Within the context of a carefully crafted supportive environment, teaching dispositions and the intangible qualities of good teaching would likely include an intentional focus on personal relationships, empathy, confidence, and inspiration as essential. How then can they be nurtured and integrated throughout a teacher education program?

First and foremost, teacher educators need an anchoring belief in the positive role that personal relationships play in every aspect of teaching and learning. Understanding the connection between personal relationships and positive outcomes is not necessarily intuitive but it can be learned (Gonser 2020). The process of building caring relationships can be approached in many ways. Modeling is one way to show how to build trusting relationships. For instance, rituals can be established, such as celebrating events in student teachers' lives and having conversations outside the classroom, to create connections that effectively say we care about you and the dreams that you hold (Rizga, 2020a). Teacher educators need not hesitate to share themselves, showing students what it means to be vulnerable and yet strong. Revealing, rather than concealing who we are, has the power to create connectedness and community wherein students—practicing and aspiring teachers—can take risks, find their voices, and lose their fears. In this way, we are demonstrating that lifelong learning is a process of lifelong discovery. To quote Parker Palmer, we teach who we are (Palmer 2017). Emphasizing the importance of relationships, three years ago the School of Education where I teach identified its core value as "Teaching and Learning through Relationships" and intentionally infused it throughout the program. Because of the diversity in our student population, it tends to be a struggle for students to lean in one another lives.

Positive personal relationships are also the foundation upon which the qualities of empathy, confidence, and inspiration can grow. The literature on empathy offers a twofold definition: emotional and cognitive (Batson et al. 1991; Davis 2006; Warren 2018). The emotional aspect of the definition refers to "empathic concern" (the tendency to experience the feelings of others) while the cognitive aspect is characterized as "perspective taking" (the tendency to adopt the psychological view of others) (Warren 2018, 171). Perspective taking is the deliberate action that can lead to empathic concern. In the professional teaching context, the experience and communication of empathy requires knowledge gained from perspective taking, such as who the student is, his/her family, culture, interests, and dreams (Warren 2014).

Examples of perspective-taking activities in a teacher education program might include reflective memos, autobiographical assignments, and structured time for student conversations. Consequently, teacher educators can show teacher candidates the power of empathy by modeling empathic ways of seeing, listening, and responding. It is the teacher who leads individuals to care for the feelings of others in any class, at any level of education. As Carl Rogers (1959) noted, empathy is important in all human relationships.

The qualities of confidence and inspiration are likewise developed within the context of positive relationships and the activity of modeling in the classroom. Great and memorable teachers tend to impart confidence and inspire their students (Rizga 2020a; Powell-Brown et al. 2014; Helm 2007). Confidence comes from an inner sense of accomplishment; it is acquired by surviving risk. When teacher educators create risk-taking learning experiences—written or oral—for the purpose of exploring new ideas and possibilities, teacher candidates have opportunities to find their voice and lose their fears—the fear of failure, the fear of inadequacy, the fear of disappointment. Surviving the risk can generate that inner sense of accomplishment known as confidence. Inspiration is a powerful complement to confidence. According to De Jong and Van der Zee (2009, 12), inspiration represents a kind of motivation that "gives those who are inspired reason to act in a particular way." In effect, an inspiring teacher generates powerful energy; s/he unknowingly ignites a culture of awe, wonder, and curiosity in the classroom. This is confirmed by Powell-Brown et al. (2014, 74) who found that inspirational teachers tend to leave a legacy of impact which ranges from "specific inspirations such as the way to treat other people or regained confidence in oneself, to more broad influences such as career choice."

Any discussion of relationships as dominant among the intangible qualities of good teaching requires a consideration of collegial relationships. Positive and productive relationships among peers are powerful connections. They enable teachers to learn from one another, improve their practice, and access collective wisdom. Teachers need other teachers to succeed (Rizga 2019). They build relationships through the experience of collaboration, participation in peer networks, or in casual meetups as colleagues. Whether in a graduate course, a teacher's classroom, or a local café, finding time to connect with colleagues, share thoughts, and provide mutual support is important not only for a teacher's profession but also for a teacher's well-being (Elmahdi 2017). Attending to relationships in education, be they personal or professional, require ongoing commitment with the understanding that everyone will have different experiences and feelings about the process and the promise of connection (Tannock 2009).

The focus on relationships is also apparent in education reform efforts in the UAE. In 2016, the Education Affair Office (EAO) at the Crown Prince Court in the UAE launched the Qudwa Forum to give teachers a voice in education reform and a place in the heart of the conversation about the future of education in the UAE. In its third edition, the theme for Qudwa 2019 was teaching for global competence. The two-day meetings included a variety of panel discussions, professional workshops, and networking opportunities with educational experts, aiming to promote a culture of collaboration among teachers. Overwhelmingly, teachers acknowledged their need for strong support systems to foster peer learning, collaborative relationships, and continuous development. Following the theme of Qudwa 2019 and using the UAE data from the Teaching and Learning International Survey (TALIS) in 2018 (OECD 2018), the Organization for Economic Co-operation and Development (OECD) was commissioned by EAO to provide practical guidance for improving the quality of teaching and learning. Interestingly, all the lessons concerning teacher professional learning to improve their classroom practices involved nurturing relationships. The lessons focused on implementing systems to (1) provide structured and sustained induction and mentoring for new teachers, (2) encourage peer observation and feedback, (3) facilitate participation in teacher networks for continuous development (OECD 2020).

CONCLUSION

Teaching is complex and the most important elements of the profession seem to remain invisible, sometimes even to the teacher, as the Little Prince profoundly says: "What is essential is invisible to the eye." Content knowledge and pedagogical skill are the essentials of good teaching, but what makes teaching great is often invisible to the eye. This is the work of teaching dispositions which include the intangible qualities of teaching and learning. Teacher education programs will continue to pay attention to theoretical content and focus on structures and routines to develop the necessary skills; however, we cannot forget the all-important third dimension of this noble profession—the dispositions of care and character.

Above all, every teacher education program should be a learning environment rich in caring, supportive, empathetic, and reciprocal relationships between and among individual students as well as faculty. As defined by Nel Noddings (1984, 4–5), reciprocal "caring relations" should define the ethos of the program. In affirming the role that relationships play in the education and practice of teachers, Jane Danielewicz reminds us to keep this in mind:

> In belonging to a caring community, students should receive (and give) attention, and feel known and recognized by others. Being connected to others adds intensity and dimension to the work of learning to teach. (2001, 194)

Most available studies on teaching dispositions and the intangible qualities of teaching and learning were conducted at least a decade ago. This crucial domain of study needs to be given its due and brought to the forefront of education research agendas. Potential pathways for ongoing thinking and research about teacher dispositions need to look beyond the design of measurement tools and pay more attention to articulating, defining, and developing these qualities in local contexts.

In setting out to understand what my research assistant identified as "something intangible" about the teacher education program where I teach, I became immersed in an intellectual journey through volumes of research literature about teacher dispositions and the intangible qualities of teaching and learning. Upon personal reflection, I have come to understand the complexity of teaching more deeply than ever before. Referring to a previously mentioned metaphor, this complexity is not unlike the human body. The head is represented by content knowledge; pedagogical skills are the hands of this endeavor; and the heart is found in the dispositions or intangible qualities of our craft. The interconnectedness of all three aspects is the essence of good teaching. Borrowing from Helm (2006, 118), "Great teachers are the ones with heart . . . big, beautiful, caring hearts."

REFERENCES

Ankrum, Raymond. 2019. "10 intangibles of Good Teaching." https://everybody luvsraymondsedblog.com/2019/02/11/10-intangibles-of-good-teaching/.

Bair, Mary Antony. 2017. "Identifying dispositions that matter: Reaching for consensus using a Delphi Study." *The Teacher Educator* 52, no. 3: 222–234.

Bates, Tony. 2020. "The importance of the 'intangibles' in teaching and learning." *Online Learning and Distance Education Resources.* https://www.tonybates.ca/2020/11/03/the-importance-of-intangibles-in-teaching-and-learning.

Batson, Judy G., Jacqueline K. Slingsby, Kevin L. Harrell, Heli M. Peekna, and R. Matthew Todd. 1991. "Empathic joy and the empathy-altruism hypothesis." *Journal of Personality and Social Psychology* 61, no. 3: 413–426.

Borko, Hilda, Dan Liston, and Jennifer A. Whitcomb. 2007. "Apples and fishes: The debate over dispositions in teacher education." *Journal of Teacher Education* 58, no. 5: 359–364.

Brookhart, Susan M. 2011. "Educational assessment knowledge and skills for teachers." *Educational Measurement: Issues and Practice* 30, no. 1: 3–12.

CAEP (Council for the Accreditation of Educator Preparation). 2019. *2013 CAEP Accreditation Standards.* Washington, DC.

Carroll, David. 2012. "Examining the development of dispositions for ambitious teaching: One teacher candidate's journey." *The New Educator* 8, no. 1: 38–64.

Costa, Arthur L., and Bena Kallick. 2013. *Dispositions: Reframing Teaching and Learning.* Thousand Oaks, CA: Corwin Press.

Cummins, Lauren, and Bridget Asempapa. 2013. "Fostering teacher candidate dispositions in teacher education programs." *Journal of the Scholarship of Teaching and Learning* 13, no. 3: 99–119.

Da Ros-Voseles, Denise, and Linda Moss. 2007. "The role of dispositions in the education of future teachers." *YC Young Children* 62, no. 5: 90–98.

Danielewicz, Jane. 2001. *Teaching Selves: Identity, Pedagogy, and Teacher Education.* New York: State University of New York Press. Suny Press.

Davis M.H. (2006) "Empathy." In *Handbook of the Sociology of Emotions*, 443–466. Boston, MA: Springer.

De Jong, Aad, and Theo Van der Zee. 2009. "Teachers as a source of inspiration in Catholic schools." *Journal of Empirical Theology* 22, no. 1 (2009): 7–29.

Dewey, John. 1922. *Human nature and conduct–An introduction into social psychology.* New York: Henry Holt and Company.

Diez, Mary E. 2006. "Assessing dispositions: Context and questions." *The New Educator* 2, no. 1: 57–72.

Diez, Mary E., and P. C. Murrell. 2010. "Dispositions in teacher education—Starting points for consideration." In *Teaching as a Moral Practice: Defining, Developing, and Assessing Professional Dispositions in Teacher Education.* Edited by Peter C. Murrell Jr., Mary E. Diez, Sharon Feiman-Nemser, and Deborah L. Schussler, 7–26. Cambridge, MA: Harvard University Press.

Duckworth, Angela L., and David Scott Yeager. 2015. "Measurement matters: Assessing personal qualities other than cognitive ability for educational purposes." *Educational Researcher* 44, no. 4: 237–251.

Duckworth, Angela L., and Martin EP Seligman. 2005. "Self-discipline outdoes IQ in predicting academic performance of adolescents." *Psychological Science* 16, no. 12: 939–944.

Elmahdi, Ismail. 2017. "Developing and Nurturing Professional Teaching Dispositions for First Year Students in the Bahrain Teachers College." *International Journal of Pedagogical Innovations* 5, no. 02: 133–141.

Garrison, Jim, and A. G. Rud. 2009. "Reverence in Classroom Teaching." *Teachers College Record* 111, no. 11: 2626–2646.

Gonser, Sara. 2020. "Good teaching is not just about the right practices." *Edutopia*. https://everybodyluvsraymondsedblog.com/2019/02/11/10-intangibles-of-good-teaching/.

Guerriero, Sonia. 2013. "Teachers' pedagogical knowledge and the teaching profession: Background report and project objectives." *OECD Better Policies for Better Lives*, 1–7.

Harrison, Judy, Gary Smithey, Hal McAffee, and Charles Weiner. 2006. "Assessing candidate disposition for admission into teacher education: Can just anyone teach?" *Action in Teacher Education* 27, no. 4: 72–80.

Helm, Carroll M. 2006. "Teacher dispositions as predictors of good teaching." *The Clearing House: A Journal of Educational Strategies, Issues and Ideas* 79, no. 3: 117–118.

Helm, Carroll M. 2007. "Teacher dispositions affecting self-esteem and student performance." *The Clearing House: A Journal of Educational Strategies, Issues and Ideas* 80, no. 3: 109–110.

Hollon, Robert, M. Kolis, S. McIntyre, T. Stephens, and R. Battalio. 2010. "Toward a professional consensus around dispositions: Lessons from practice in teacher education." In *Teaching as a Moral Practice: Defining, Developing, and Assessing Professional Dispositions in Teacher Education,* 117–140. Cambridge, MA: Harvard University Press.

InTASC (Interstate New Teacher Assessment and Support Consortium) 2013. *Model Core Teaching Standards and Learning Progressions for Teachers 1.0: A Resource for Ongoing Teacher Development.* Washington, DC.

Katz, Lilian G. 1993. "Dispositions: Definitions and Implications for Early Childhood Practices. Perspectives from ERIC/EECE: A Monograph Series, No. 4." *ERIC Clearinghouse on Elementary and Early Childhood Education.* https://eric.ed.gov/?id=ED360104.

Rizga, Kristina. 2019. "On Teaching. How to keep teachers from leaving the profession, "*The Atlantic*, September 19, 2019, https://www.theatlantic.com/education/archive/2019/09/teachers-need-other-teachers-succeed/598330/.

Rizga, Kristina. 2020a. "On Teaching. The Craft of Teaching Confidence," *The Atlantic*, September 9, 2020, https://www.theatlantic.com/education/archive/2020/09/teaching-craft-teaching-confidence/616051.

Rizga, Kristina. 2020b. "On Teaching. What is Good Teaching," *The Atlantic*, September 16, 2020, https://www.theatlantic.com/education/archive/2020/09/t eaching-what-good-teaching/616352/.

McKnight, K., J. Yarbro, L. Graybeal, and J. Graybeal. 2016. *United Arab Emirates: What Makes An Effective Teacher?* (Series 4 of 23). London, England: Pearson Education.

Minnesota Educator Dispositions System (MnEDS™). 2021. University of Minnesota. February 1, 2021. https://sites.google.com/a/umn.edu/umn-dispositions-assessme nt-framework/dispositional-strands/what-are-dispositions.

Mishra, Punya. 2009. "A different Language." https://punyamishra.com/2009/02/14/ a-different-language/.

Mishra, Punya. (2011). "The Intangibles of Teaching." https://punyamishra.com/2 011/08/10/the-intangibles-of-teaching/.

Murrell, Peter, Mary Diez, Sharon Feiman-Nemser, and Deborah L. Schussler. 2010. *Teaching as a Moral Practice: Defining, Developing, and Assessing Professional Dispositions in Teacher Education.* Cambridge, MA: Harvard Education Press.

NCATE (National Council for Accreditation of Teacher Education). 2008. *Professional Standards for the Accreditation of Teacher Preparation Institutions.* Washington, DC.

Nelsen, Peter J. 2015. "Intelligent dispositions: Dewey, habits and inquiry in teacher education." *Journal of Teacher Education* 66, no. 1: 86–97.

Noddings, Nel. 1984. *Caring, a feminine approach to ethics and moral education.* Berkeley, CA: University of California Press.

OECD. 2018. *Preparing Our Youth for an Inclusive and Sustainable World.* Paris: OECD Publishing. https://www.oecd.org/pisa/Handbook-PISA-2018-Global-Competence.pdf.

OECD. 2020. *Teaching in the United Arab Emirates: 10 Lessons from TALIS.* Paris: OECD Publishing, https://www.oecd.org/education/talis/Teaching_in_ the_UAE-10_Lessons_from_TALIS.pdf.

Palmer, Parker J. 2017. *The Courage to Teach: Exploring the Inner Landscape of a Teacher's Life.* New Jersey: John Wiley and Sons.

Powell-Brown, Ann Powell-Brown, Dawna Lisa Buchanan Butterfield, and Yuankun Yao. 2014. "Stoking the fire." *Educational Renaissance* 3, no. 1: 65–81.

Richert, A. 2007. "Book review: Deliberating over dispositions." *Journal of Teacher Education*, 58, no. 5: 412–421.

Rike, Cheryl J., and L. Kathryn Sharp. 2008. "Assessing preservice teachers' disposi-tions: A critical dimension of professional preparation." *Childhood Education* 84, no. 3: 150–153.

Rinaldo, Vincent J., Stephen J. Denig, Thomas J. Sheeran, Richard Cramer-Benjamin, Paul J. Vermette, Chandra J. Foote, and Robert Michael Smith. 2009. "Developing the Intangible Qualities of Good Teaching: A Self-Study." *Education* 130, no. 1: 42–52.

Rogers, Carl Ransom. 1959. *A Theory of Therapy, Personality, and Interpersonal Relationships: As Developed in the Client-Centered Framework.* Vol. 3. New York: McGraw-Hill.

The Intangibles of Teacher Education in the UAE 125

Talbert-Johnson, Carolyn. 2006. "Preparing highly qualified teacher candidates for urban schools: The importance of dispositions." *Education and Urban Society* 39, no. 1: 147–160.

Tannock, Michelle T. 2009. "Tangible and intangible elements of collaborative teaching." *Intervention in School and Clinic* 44, no. 3: 173–178.

Thornton, Holly. 2006. "Dispositions in action: Do dispositions make a difference in practice?" *Teacher Education Quarterly* 33, no. 2: 53–68.

Tough, Paul. 2012. *How Children Succeed: Grit, Curiosity, and the Hidden Power of Character.* Boston, MA: Houghton Mifflin Harcourt.

Villegas, Ana María. 2007. "Dispositions in teacher education: A look at social justice." *Journal of Teacher Education* 58, no. 5: 370–380.

Walshaw, Margaret. 2012. "Teacher knowledge as fundamental to effective teaching practice." *Journal of Mathematics Teacher Education* 15, no. 3: 181–185.

Warren, Chezare A. 2014. "Towards a pedagogy for the application of empathy in culturally diverse classrooms." *The Urban Review* 46, no. 3: 395–419.

Warren, Chezare A. 2018. "Empathy, teacher dispositions, and preparation for culturally responsive pedagogy." *Journal of Teacher Education* 69, no. 2: 169–183.

Wayda, Valerie, and Jacalyn Lund. 2005. "Assessing dispositions: An unresolved challenge in teacher education." *Journal of Physical Education, Recreation & Dance* 76, no. 1: 34–41.

Welch, Anita G., Shaljan Areepattamannil, and Martina Dickson. 2016. "The development and validation of the Abu Dhabi professional teaching disposition scale." In *Dispositions in Teacher Education, A Global Perspective*, 183–197. The Netherlands: Sense Publishers.

Part III

WAYS FORWARD IN TEACHER EDUCATION AND DEVELOPMENT

Chapter 8

Reshaping Teacher Education in the Gulf Region

Catherine Hill

INTRODUCTION

Whether we teach in universities or primary schools, we are public scholars by virtue of our profession. As a result, we have a responsibility to contribute to public understanding and relevant debates, as well as to professional practice. As teacher educators in the Gulf region, we need to acknowledge the challenge to embrace this responsibility as urgent. However, we also need to understand that religion, culture, and tradition tend to govern all aspects of society, including education. For example, the countries of the Gulf region and their relevant power structures tend to define the limits of knowledge and truth, creating what the philosopher Michel Foucault calls "regimes of truth" (Lorenzini 2015). As such, efforts to reform or revitalize long-standing programs and practices, such as passive learning and blind obedience, may encounter resistance because some ideas are deemed "beyond question" within regimes of truth (Romanowski and Nasser 2012, 125). Therefore, "going public" with new and transformative concepts of teacher education, such as critical pedagogy, is not without risk. Still, teachers are called to become change agents with the ability to shape the future; as a result, they must first be transformed themselves (Madsen and Cook 2010; Raddawi and Troudi 2018).

The current sociopolitical landscape in the Arab world is deeply fractured by sectarian divisions, conflict, and deep demographic changes because of regional wars and political upheaval. Furthermore, in the Gulf region issues of declining profits from the oil industry, authoritarianism, governance, and accountability have become sensitive and are considered taboo topics that are inappropriate for conversation. Thus, fostering a critical consciousness in this unique context is a challenge that depends upon an educational system that is solid and transformative. Consequently, a teacher education program and pedagogy that holds the promise and the power to affect social change is needed now more than ever before.

This chapter presents the process of building a framework for the reshaping of teacher education in the Gulf region, using the American University in Dubai (AUD), Master of Education program, as a case study. It is based on existing theories and related concepts, specifically, critical consciousness or conscientization (Freire 1970, 1974; Gay 2000; Gay and Kirkland 2003), cultural dialogue (Mullen et al. 2014), and transformative learning (Madsen and Cook 2010; Mezirow 2000), informed by self-reflection (Schon 1983). What follows is a call for radical change in the preparation of teachers, especially in Arab countries where most have been educated in monolithic ways, characterized by rote learning and the passive reception of knowledge (Muasher and Brown 2018; Nasser 2018). Paulo Freire (1996, 53) referred to this type of education as "banking education," wherein the teacher mechanically deposits knowledge into the mind of the learner and anticipates withdrawals during examinations. Such an approach to education is no longer suitable for meeting the challenges of a complex and rapidly changing world. This implies that old ways of thinking and doing, along with underlying assumptions, need to be confronted, examined, unlearned, and transformed into new and informed ways of thinking and acting that are responsive to current realities and the demands of today's world. Freire (1996, 53) called this new way of thinking and learning "liberating education" wherein the teacher and student become colearners sharing information through dialogue and constructing new knowledge together. In this way, even those who might feel bound by traditions can free themselves and develop intellectually (Giroux 2011).

The process of building a framework for transformative learning in teacher education begins with acknowledging that practicing and aspiring teachers must be convinced that they need to change and grow (Apps 1994). To this end, every teacher and/or student teacher needs to engage in a process wherein he/she encounters an event, a person, or a text that triggers self-awareness of inconsistency in thoughts, feelings, and actions leading to a state of discomfort. Through reflective and constructive dialogue, they can be led to confront their assumptions (the good and the bad) and decide what, why, and how their assumptions and perspectives can be revised. In this way, they slowly develop a commitment to new ways of thinking and acting which can be described as critical consciousness. Such a process then leads to the discovery of newfound competencies and deepened understandings. This is the pedagogical framework that gave shape to the master of education (MEd) program established in 2012 at AUD in the United Arab Emirates (UAE). From the onset, the purpose was to build a program that would not only equip students with the knowledge and skills of effective teachers but also inspire them to be and do more. Essentially, we wanted to awaken in them a critical awareness of the power they possess as individuals and as educators to influence lives and social realities. While all MEd students since 2012 were or currently are residents of the UAE, they self-identified as Afghani-French, Algerian, American, Egyptian, Emirati, Indian, Iraqi, Irish, Jordanian, Kenyan, Kuwaiti, Lebanese, Pakistani, Palestinian, Russian, Saudi, Somali-Canadian, Syrian, or Vietnamese-American. Their religious affiliations have included Buddhism, Christianity (Protestant, Catholic, and Maronite), Hinduism, Islam (Sunni and Shia), and Druze. It is hard to imagine a more diverse community of learners. As individuals and as members of a collective, teachers and student teachers alike were encouraged to think for themselves—together.

In summary, this chapter presents a pedagogical framework for reshaping teacher education, informed by research and my experiences in founding and developing the MEd program at AUD. Fundamentally, based on the awakening of critical consciousness, this framework is a reflexive process that begins with the self, extends to the classroom, and moves beyond the school into the wider community. The flow of consciousness from the self to the larger society is a form of engagement and communication with the public, also defined as public scholarship (Graubard 2004). It calls on teachers to be self-aware, knowledgeable of critical issues in the world around them, and responsible agents of change, going beyond the basic competency requirements associated with teacher education in a complex and multicultural world.

What follows is a theoretical explanation of the major concepts that inform critical pedagogy: critical consciousness or conscientization (Freire 1970, 1974), cultural dialogue (Mullen et al. 2014) and transformative learning (Mezirow 2000; Apps 1994), coupled with self-reflection (Schon 1983). Each section also includes practical ideas for application that have proven to be successful for us at AUD. As a teacher educator, I believe that by engaging in cultural dialogue, a teacher and/or student teacher can acquire critical consciousness which can then lead to transformative learning.

CRITICAL CONSCIOUSNESS

Paulo Freire (1974) defined critical consciousness as the ability to intervene in reality for the purpose of changing it. He proposed a developmental cycle of critical consciousness that involved critically analyzing current structures and realities, developing a sense of power or personal agency, and then committing to take some critical action toward positive change (El-Amin et al. 2017).

As such, the concept of critical consciousness or conscientization involves identity reflection, concepts of power, and the social process of questioning one's assumptions (Freire 1974). As a person self-reflects and closely examines his/her realities, perceptions, and contradictions, he/she is given the opportunity to revisit, revise, and replace assumptions and acquire a deeper understanding of self and the world. This understanding then has the power to inform action.

Enacting critical consciousness is a guided process involving multiple insightful moments wherein students come to know themselves by facing their biases, prejudices, attitudes, and beliefs in a particular context of time, culture, and place (McDonough 2009; Sleeter et al. 2004). It requires a willingness to be self-reflective about one's identity, culture, and long-held beliefs. Milner (2003, 196) refers to this reflection process as an act of unlearning that "does not necessarily involve a destination and neither should it follow a linear form."

Honest self-examination is never easy; it requires time for reflection and introspection. Many people tend to lack a healthy self-knowledge because they cannot or will not make time to look inward for various reasons or excuses. As a result, self-awareness can go underdeveloped. "Taking time to reflect—often explicitly—on the events of one's life," said Howard Gardner in a 1997 interview, is the "'*sine qua non*' of effective accomplishment." In other words, unless we intentionally dedicate time for reflection, we risk living superficial lives, limiting personal growth and our ability to accomplish anything as educators and agents of change.

When it comes to growth and human development, self-reflection in teacher education and in life is not an option. It is a fundamental principle and a critical pathway to personal and collective change. The logic is simple. A critical understanding of oneself can lead to a critical understanding of other people and situations, which in turn can lead to critical action for the benefit of others and society. Thus, teachers can become more than mechanically competent; they can become competent in terms of consciousness.

Although not an easy process, getting to know oneself can be learned with guidance, time, and effort. "Until you know yourself," Warren Bennis (2009, 51) wrote, "you cannot succeed in any but the most superficial sense of the word." Therefore, the intentional construction of activities aimed at self-awareness is essential to teacher education, critical consciousness and, ultimately, to social change.

Developing critical consciousness and self-reflection is often challenging for teachers and student teachers in any context. From the author's experience as a teacher educator in the UAE, these challenges often involve a lack of experience in self-reflection and an unwritten and silent acquiescence to an artificial harmony among colleagues. In other words, MEd students tend to hesitate or even resist challenging themselves and each other; thus, missing opportunities that can lead to a deeper understanding. Other obstacles include an overreliance on the statements and viewpoints of scholars as a means of diverting their attention away from the personal work they need to do (Gay and Kirkland 2003; Romanowski and Amatullah 2016). Confronting these challenges or obstacles in a teacher education program requires the teacher educator to provide targeted guidance and intentional modeling (Gay and Kirkland 2003; Nasser 2020).

CULTURAL DIALOGUE

According to Freire (1974), critical consciousness is activated through cultural dialogue wherein one engages in the critical examination of self and context. Cultural dialogue (Mullen et al. 2014) refers to the means we employ to reach critical consciousness, such as difficult conversations, risk taking, close attention, and deep listening. In general, cultural dialogue tends to be deeply personal and often uncomfortable, inviting teachers to reflect on who they are, what they stand for, and what they believe in terms of religion, culture, ethnicity, and disabilities.

In the UAE context, we have learned that teachers can achieve critical consciousness through cultural dialogic assignments and activities. By participating in difficult conversations and engaging in dialogic activities such as an autobiographical essay, teachers and student teachers can acquire a shared vocabulary and an inclusive lens on life. As they are led to appreciate difference and learn to express respect for worldviews different from theirs, they can be pushed to move beyond rhetoric into action. How so? A good place to start is by establishing a safe environment through modeling. At AUD, we begin with frank introductions as teacher educators, willingly presenting ourselves personally and professionally. In this way, we intentionally cultivate an environment characterized by "self-conscious consideration" with the purpose of leading participants to a deepened understanding of themselves and others (Danielewicz 2001, 155–156). Presenting a vision for teacher education along with ground rules for how we communicate and interact in the classroom is also important. How does this work? First, self-revelation helps to set a tone for conversations that are personal and safe. The teacher educators model the discourse so that the students can see and learn how to dignify difference without needing to defend or debate sensitive issues.

Other course activities that promote cultural dialogue include reflective memos, collaborative presentations, and personalized feedback. Reflective memos require MEd students to look inward in discussing the interplay of assigned readings, classroom conversations, and their personal perspectives.

They constitute an inner dialogue which is imperative to the process; however, inner dialogues need to be accompanied by similar dialogues with others which take place during classroom conversations and collaborative activities (Gay and Kirkland 2003).

For collaborative presentations, students need to work in groups of three to five, although they typically prefer working alone or in self-selected pairs. Allowing them to do so may be comfortable but limiting in terms of potential learning and personal growth. Teacher educators need to take care that the practice and experience of collaboration is more than just a catch phrase from the twenty-first-century skills model touted by educators and schools of education worldwide. The challenge of authentic collaboration can be elevated by purposeful planning wherein students learn how to genuinely support one another, build mutual trust, and experience the power of a collective force. The conversations that occur with the self and with others are vital to the entire process. In fact, Mullen et al. (2014) contend that meaningful, critical conversations are essential to fostering professional identity, growth, and development.

Receiving personalized and constructive feedback throughout the process is also crucial to authentic cultural dialogue. This type of feedback includes one-on-one teacher/student conversations based on their progress, the quality of their participation, as well as their emotional and intellectual engagement. Such personalized exchanges can also provide valuable practice in reflection. This also gives the teacher educator a chance to dialogue with each student about what, how, when, and where they might be applying lessons learned.

In a teacher preparation program, each class and activity can become an adventure in developing critical consciousness. Courageous and difficult conversations in the classroom about identity, personal beliefs, and professional practices are important; however, they need to be complemented by deep personal reflection. When dialogic encounters are emotionally honest, they have the potential to help shatter a prevailing culture of silence that exists in the Arab world or in any context where individuals seldom—if ever—talk about religious differences, long-held beliefs and/or biases. Through such dialogic encounters, students can experience self-knowledge as a personal, liberating, and empowering capacity enabling them to become agents of social change in their schools, families, and wider communities.

TRANSFORMATIVE LEARNING

The research literature on transformative learning is rich in content, especially as it relates to adult learning theory. As Madsen and Cook (2010, 128) state, "transformative learning is characterized at the individual level by the development of critical consciousness of personal assumptions . . . at the macro level, transformative learning contributes to broader social progress." Mezirow (1991, 198) suggests that transformative learning is a theory that tries to "describe and analyze how adults make meaning of their experience." More importantly for the purpose of this chapter, Clark (1993, 47) asserts that "transformational learning shapes people; they are different afterward, in ways both they and others can recognize." Thus, the core of transformative learning is change—remarkable and vivid change in the way the individual comes to see himself/herself and others. Transformation then becomes a constant and ongoing process for every lifelong learner who remains critically reflective of his/her assumptions with an openness to making new or revised interpretations of oneself and the world (Mezirow 1990).

While change is the core of transformational learning, Madsen and Cook (2010) remind us that critical reflection is the heart or the driving force. Self-reflection and reflective activities guide the learner to think and behave differently from previously held perceptions. Participating in reflective experiences can help students to understand themselves and others better, while also recognizing wider options in life and other worldviews. As self-awareness increases, the mind opens, and teachers and student teachers personally grow, they are more likely to become active changemakers in their classrooms and the broader society as agents of change.

The research on social change takes us beyond the process of acquiring awareness to "doing" social justice (Iverson 2012; Gay 2002; Gay and Kirkland 2003). While most teacher education programs around the world address the need for self-awareness, cultural responsiveness, and particularly multicultural competencies, there is a growing consensus among researchers that multicultural education today does not go far enough (Gorski 2009; Kumagai and Lypson 2009; Zalaquett et al. 2008). What is needed, they argue, is a more transformative framework, one that empowers teachers as social change agents, inspiring them to work for socially just outcomes. The suggestions proposed in this chapter are designed to meet the need for such a transformative framework.

The teacher education framework under discussion here addresses three essential questions: *what*, *how*, and *why*. The *what* involves the awakening of critical consciousness; the *how* refers to the application of cultural dialogue as a pathway to critical consciousness; and the *why* is embedded in the fact that critical consciousness leads to transformative learning which informs social action. As such, teachers are empowered to bring their own consciousness into the larger society as public scholars. Students who exit teacher education programs with prescribed multicultural competencies, increased knowledge of diversity, and strategies for instruction may be technically able to teach but less transformed as individuals and as teachers who can move social realities forward and actively change lives for the better.

As educators, we are called to be change agents in service to others. In other words, we have a responsibility to acquire a critical consciousness and awaken it in others by carrying our best thinking and research into the world as public scholars. This consciousness inspires people to action, gives them voice and a new way of living, thinking, and learning throughout life. Over the past seven years at AUD, I learned that providing such a transformative experience is possible even among the most diverse group of students, so long as the teacher education program incorporates a critical pedagogy that emphasizes reflection and self-knowledge as the prerequisite for understanding others and how the world works. More than 100 students from different backgrounds and cultures have passed through our teacher education program. A more diverse group is hard to imagine. At present, forty-six students representing thirteen nationalities are enrolled. It is true that most of our teacher education students come from Arab countries and claim a common Arab identity based on language and shared history. It is also true that to some extent, the notion of a common Arab identity acts as a force of unity but unique differences, underlying conflicts, regional personalities, and intersecting loyalties bubble beneath the surface (Barakat 1993). That said, a program and pedagogy that holds the promise of a critical awakening for individuals and offers the power to affect social change is needed here and now more than ever before.

CONCLUSION

This chapter explored a transformative framework for teacher education at AUD in the UAE. All things considered, our journey could be deemed emblematic for other teacher education programs in the GCC region where similar countries are struggling to reform and refine their respective educational systems. Technically, the UAE is a federation of seven hereditary monarchies or Emirates—not unlike other GCC countries. Rulers govern, security is tight, cultural traditions run deep, families are strong, services are plentiful, and religion influences relationships and social behaviors. Within such a structured society, people are less inclined to explore alternate realities or different ways of living and learning. Expressions of free and independent thinking do exist but within a dominant culture of silence and acceptance. The kind of education posited here is urgently needed. Awakening critical consciousness empowers teachers to overcome the silence and achieve socially just outcomes to benefit all, not just the privileged few.

REFERENCES

Apps, J. W. 1994. *Leadership for the Emerging Age. Transforming Practice in Adult and Continuing Education.* San Francisco, CA: Jossey-Bass Publishers.

Barakat, Halim. 1993. *The Arab World: Society, Culture, and State.* California: University of California Press.

Bennis, Warren G. 2009. *On Becoming a Leader.* New York: Basic Books.

Cammack, Perry, and Marwan Muasher. 2016. *Arab Voices on the Challenges of the New Middle East.* Washington, DC: Carnegie Endowment for International Peace.

Cammack, Perry, Michele Dunne, Amr Hamzwy, Marc Lynch, Marwan Muasher, Yezid Sayigh, and Maha Yahya. 2017. *Arab Fractures: Citizens, States, and Social Contracts.* Washington, DC: Carnegie Endowment for International Peace.

Clark, M. Carolyn. 1993. "Transformational learning." *New Directions for Adult and Continuing Education*, no. 57: 47–56.

Danielewicz, J. 2001. *Teaching Selves: Identity, Pedagogy and Teacher Education.* Albany, NY: State University of New York Press.

El-Amin, Aaliyah, Scott Seider, Daren Graves, Jalene Tamerat, Shelby Clark, Madora Soutter, Jamie Johannsen, and Saira Malhotra. 2017. "Critical consciousness: A key to student achievement." *Phi Delta Kappan* 98, no. 5: 18–23.

Freire, Paulo. 1970. *Pedagogy of the Oppressed.* New York: The Seabury Press.

Freire, Paulo. 1974. *Education for Critical Consciousness.* London: Sheed and Ward Ltd.

Freire, Paulo. 1996. *Pedagogy of the Oppressed (Revised).* New York: Continuum.

Gardner, Howard. 1997. "Multiple intelligences as a partner in school improvement." *Educational Leadership* 55, no. 1: 20–21.

Gay, G. 2000. *Culturally Responsive Teaching: Theory, Research and Practice.* New York: Teachers College Press.

Gay, G. 2002. "Preparing for culturally responsive teaching." *Journal of Teacher Education* 53, no. 2, March/April: 106–116.

Gay, Geneva, and Kipchoge Kirkland. 2003 "Developing cultural critical consciousness and self-reflection in preservice teacher education." *Theory into Practice* 42, no. 3: 181–187.

Giroux, Henry A. 2011. *On Critical Pedagogy.* UK: Bloomsbury Publishing.

Gorski, Paul C. 2009. "What we're teaching teachers: An analysis of multicultural teacher education coursework syllabi." *Teaching and Teacher Education* 25, no. 2: 309–318.

Graubard, Stephen Richards. 2004. *Public Scholarship: A New Perspective for the 21st Century.* New York: Carnegie Corporation of New York.

Iverson, Susan VanDeventer 2012. "Multicultural competence for doing social justice: Expanding our awareness, knowledge, and skills." *Journal of Critical Thought and Praxis* 1, no. 1: 62–87.

Kumagai, Arno K., and Monica L. Lypson. 2009. "Beyond cultural competence: Critical consciousness, social justice, and multicultural education." *Academic Medicine* 84, no. 6: 782–787.

Lorenzini, Daniele. 2015. "What is a 'Regime of Truth'?" *Le foucaldien* 1, no. 1. 10.16995/lefou.2.

Madsen, Susan R., and Bradley J. Cook. 2010. "Transformative learning: UAE, women, and higher education." *Journal of Global Responsibility* 1, no. 1:127–148.

McDonough, Kathy. 2009. "Pathways to critical consciousness: A first-year teacher's engagement with issues of race and equity." *Journal of Teacher Education* 60, no. 5: 528–537.

Mezirow, Jack. 1990. "How critical reflection triggers transformative learning." *Fostering Critical Reflection in Adulthood* 1, no. 20: 1–6.

Mezirow, Jack. 1991. *Transformative Dimensions of Adult Learning.* San Francisco, CA: Jossey-Bass Publishers.

Mezirow, Jack. 2000. *Learning as Transformation: Critical Perspectives on a Theory in Progress. The Jossey-Bass Higher and Adult Education Series.* San Francisco, CA: Jossey-Bass Publishers.

Milner, H. Richard. 2003. "Teacher reflection and race in cultural contexts: History, meanings, and methods in teaching." *Theory into Practice* 42, no. 3: 173–180.

Muasher, Marwan and Nathan J. Brown. 2018. "Engaging society to reform Arab Education: From schooling to learning." Carnegie Endowment for International Peace. https://carnegieendowment.org/2018/10/11/engaging-society-to-reform-arab-education-from-schooling-to-learning-pub-77454.

Mullen, Carol A., J. Kenneth Young, and Sandra Harris. 2014. "Cultural dialogue as social justice advocacy within and beyond university classrooms." In *International Handbook of Educational Leadership and Social (in) Justice*, Vol. 29, 1145–1168. Dordrecht: Springer.

Nasser, Ilham. 2018. "The State of Education in the Arab World." The Arab Center, Washington DC, http://arabcenterdc.org/policy_analyses/the-state-of-education-in-the-arab-world/.

Nasser, Ilham. 2020. "Mapping the terrain of education 2018–2019: A summary report." *Journal of Education in Muslim Societies* 1, no. 2: 3–21.

Raddawi, Rana, and Salah Troudi. 2018. "Critical pedagogy in EFL teacher education in the United Arab Emirates: Possibilities and challenges." *TESOL International Journal* 13, no. 1: 79–99.

Romanowski, Michael H., and Ramzi Nasser. 2012. "Critical thinking and Qatar's education for a new era: Negotiating possibilities." *The International Journal of Critical Pedagogy* 4, no. 1: 118–134.

Romanowski, Michael H., and Tasneem Amatullah. 2016. "Applying concepts of critical pedagogy to Qatar's educational reform." *Critical Questions in Education* 7, no. 2: 77–95.

Schon, D. A. 1983. *The Reflective Practitioner: How Professionals Think in Action.* New York: Basic Books.

Sleeter, Christine, Myriam N. Torres, and Peggy Laughlin. 2004. "Scaffolding conscientization through inquiry in teacher education." *Teacher Education Quarterly* 31, no. 1: 81–96.

Zalaquett, Carlos P., Pamela F. Foley, Kenyon Tillotson, Julie A. Dinsmore, and David Hof. 2008. "Multicultural and social justice training for counselor education programs and colleges of education: Rewards and challenges." *Journal of Counseling and Development* 86, no. 3: 323–329.

Chapter 9

Critical Consciousness in TVET Teacher Professional Development

A Framework for Sociopolitical Agency in the Arabian Gulf

Samah Abdulhafid Gamar

INTRODUCTION

This chapter forwards a critical pedagogical approach to teacher professional development in the Arab states, with a particular focus on the development of *conscientization* (Freire 2000), or critical consciousness, in educators working in the technical and vocational education and training (TVET) sector in the Arabian Gulf. Rooted theoretically in positivism and human capital economics, vocational education has historically focused on practical skills development and competence attainment through technocratic, neoliberalist approaches that rely on observable, verifiable means to meet labor market needs—rather than the preparation of students for general citizenship (Kincheloe 1999; Giroux 2005; Sukhan 2012). Over the past century, TVET has assumed a purpose separate and apart from the individual's intellectual inquiry and critical abilities (MacIntyre 1964); instead, it has chiefly been concerned with narrowly defined job training in the interest of national economic advantage and social efficiency (Daniels 2018; Nash 1972). Technical and vocational education has adopted a largely "uncritical response to industry demand for skilled labour [that focuses] on fueling productivity, efficiency, and economic growth through skills training" (Bedi and Germein 2016, 125), which principally ignores social aspects (Anderson 2009; Arenas and Londono 2013) and the promotion of critical agency.

This study problematizes the TVET sector's preoccupation with instrumental and functional skills development for the labor market, to the exclusion of constructivism and critical inquiry for active citizenship. It argues for the integration of critical pedagogies in technical and vocational education in general terms, and more explicitly advocates for professional development that advances critical consciousness that works to equip vocational teachers to bare systemic social incongruences and inequities within the world of work. When TVET teachers engage in dialogical practices and participate in reflexive explorations of hegemonies through critical self-narratives, or autoethnographies, this study argues, they can facilitate a more humanistic, transformative, and emancipatory education for vocational learners.

In the context of the Gulf Cooperation Council (GCC), a region undergoing rapid socioeconomic transformation, this incorporation offers an alternative theoretical construct and mode of practice that can prepare learners to navigate complex power struggles, tensions, and inequities in work settings, as it equips them with applied and technical occupational skills.

The study begins with a brief overview of the foundations of TVET, globally and in the Arab region, along with the aims and structures that have been used to distinguish it—rightly or falsely—from general higher education. Having situated technical and vocational education within this context, it dons a critical pedagogical lens to examine contemporary social justice issues that challenge TVET's capacity to empower vocational students. Shining a light directly on issues relevant to GCC countries, it contends that vocational teachers ought to play a role in nurturing critically reflective learners who are cognizant of structures and forces within the workplace that can disempower, dispossess, and marginalize. Finally, it argues that the practice of conscientization in teacher professional development can serve as a mechanism for preparing vocational educators to model forms of agency in and outside of workplace environments in the GCC.

DEFINING TECHNICAL AND VOCATIONAL EDUCATION AND TRAINING

The term "TVET," or Technical and Vocational Education and Training, was formalized at the World Congress on TVET in 1999 in Seoul, Republic of Korea, making it the most common of a diverse set of terms used for applied, career-oriented education. Various other terms have been used to describe elements of the field comprising TVET, including apprenticeship training, vocational education, technical education, technical-vocational education (TVE), occupational education (OE), vocational education and training (VET), professional and vocational education (PVE), career and technical education (CTE), workforce education (WE), and workplace education (WE). These terms are commonly and interchangeably used in various geographic regions around the world. Although TVET carries a diverse set of names across nations, it is generally understood as education and training that provides practical, hands-on competency development relevant to occupational environments. The World Congress formally refers to it as any education, training, or learning activity that manifests in the attainment of knowledge, understanding, and skills for the primary purpose of employment or self-employment. The United Nations Educational, Scientific and Cultural Organization (UNESCO) provides a comprehensive definition referring to TVET as "aspects of the educational process involving, in addition to general education, the study of technologies and related sciences, and the acquisition of practical skills, attitudes, understanding and knowledge relating to occupants in various sectors of economic and social life" (UNESCO and ILO 2002).

Definitions for TVET intersect around a characterization involving learning and skills development for the preparation of participants for the world of work (Maclean and Wilson 2009).

Defining characterizations of technical and vocational education often draw from legislature which establish and govern policies related to the aims and mechanisms of the vocational education sector. According to the Carl D. Perkins Career and Technical Education Act from the US Department of Education, the primary purpose of technical and vocational education is to equip individuals with the academic and occupational skills required for the labor market (Perkins Collaborative Resource Network 2018). The legislature, which was originally established in 1963 as the Vocational Education Act, states that its purpose lies in enabling the United States to be more competitive in the global economy through occupational and academic training programs intended to prepare participants for employment.

After establishing TVET's essential role to the economy, the Australian government defines vocational education as training which prepares individuals for employment through the acquisition of qualifications and specific skills required for the workplace (Australian Skills Quality Authority 2018). Germany, which has one of the world's most established vocational systems, refers to VET as one which provides systematic competency development to engage individuals in skilled occupations for "a changing working world"; one which also qualifies them with essential occupational experience (Vocational Training Act, Federal Ministry of Education and Research 2005). Within the United Kingdom, "vocational qualification," rather than TVET, is used to refer to general or technical skills acquired for a specific job or workplace component. Although vocational education in the UK originally emerged from independent bodies, such as City and Guilds, today, it is fully legislated under the Technical and Further Education Act of 2017.

With one of the most advanced TVET systems in Asia, Singapore's Institute of Technical Education Act of 1992 was established with the function of establishing provision for technical and further education for those whose aim is to be employed in commerce or industry. It defines its mandate as presiding over training and development in technical skills (Singapore Statutes Online 2018).

Within the Middle East and North Africa (MENA) region, Egypt—which has the largest population and is most significantly impacted economically by the TVET sector—strives to have TVET "pave the way to successful careers for young people" and "guarantee a skilled work force for the economy" (UNEVOC). Clear in its definition of TVET is the preparation of members of society for production to fuel the economy. Tunisia, also an Arab nation with a rapidly growing demographic of young people, defines TVET as skill-based professional training geared to meet the needs of the economy. Government legislature and reforms in the education sector define it as a mechanism to "equip the economic enterprise with the tools to improve its productivity and competitiveness" (AUP Report 2017).

In the Arabian Gulf region, the United Arab Emirates' (UAE) National Qualifications Authority (NQA) via its Vocational Education and Training Awards Council (VETAC) defines TVET as knowledge and skills for economic and social development via the preparation of individuals for careers, with a priority for those skills related to new and emerging technologies (National Qualifications Authority 2019). In Qatar, though no formal TVET legislation has yet been passed, strategy committees under the Ministry of Education and Higher Education are in the midst of formulating a definition aligned to UNESCO, which would work within a new Education and Training Sector Strategy and a Qatar Qualifications Framework (Gamar 2017).

Worldwide, nations have converged on a common understanding of technical and vocational education, this being a focus on (a) occupational skills, and (b) primarily for employment and economic development. Though UNESCO ties TVET to the acquisition of skills for social life, in addition to economic life—a clear mandate tying technical and vocational education to sociocultural, political, and civic life is presently absent from both mainstream literature and government legislature.

These definitions of the TVET sector contrast significantly with descriptions of traditional academic education. In fact, since the nineteenth century, a binary system emerged such that vocational education predominantly focused on psychomotor skills, often limited to repetitive tasks that require little independent thinking, while "academic" education nurtured cognitive and affective skills that culminated into "knowledge" (Sharp 1996). This dichotomy can be witnessed until today, and quite overtly, within the GCC. The UAE's Technical and Vocational Education's official website states that the sector aims to "produce" ten Emiratis for every university graduate to achieve a sustainable economy, recruiting Emiratis "who aspire to succeed but experience challenges with academic studies" (UAE Government Portal, "Technical and Vocational Education"). Such a statement imparts that TVET is for a demographic of learners *other than* those who are capable of "academic" learning requiring higher order cognitive and abstract thinking.

Relegated to the margins of the education sector, defined not by what they can do but what they are perceived as being incapable of, vocational learners are often swept into a technocratic, rigidly structured, singularly focused system that does not celebrate or acknowledge their capacity to critically think and reflect as contributing citizens of a complex national society. This system is dominated by discourse that treats its participants as variables within an economic system—not as empowered members of a social community who are required within and outside of their professional environments to strive for the public good.

I will return to this dominant narrative, inspecting its underlying ideology, and challenging it through a critical pedagogical lens that promotes critical awareness—but first, it is important to briefly explain where vocational education lies in the sector's evolutionary continuum within the GCC.

TECHNICAL AND VOCATIONAL EDUCATION IN THE GCC: SAMPLE COUNTRY FRAMEWORKS

In the Middle East, technical and vocational education came into existence only in the late twentieth century when many MENA nations gained independence. After the discovery of oil and gas reserves in the 1970s, countries in the GCC initiated large-scale accelerated social and economic transformation efforts. The extensive investment in ambitious national strategies in the six GCC countries is recognized as a significant catalyst in the region's reform of its education systems—a shift often referred to as an educational renaissance (Al-Mujaini 2018). Nations which heavily depended on semi-skilled and skilled migrants and expatriate workers to achieve their massive reform efforts erected vocational education systems to build internal capacity to fuel their rapidly developing economies (Al-Ali 1993; Bahgat 1999; Bilboe 2011; Al-Mujaini 2018). These GCC TVET systems were largely modeled upon British, European, Australian, and North American frameworks, along with their structural and curricular deference to industry and instrumental skills development for economic efficiency.

Across the GCC, similar approaches and skills frameworks were adopted to entrench vocational education in support of economic development. Within these structures, emphasis on skills development to meet industry needs and labor shortages can be seen. Education reforms in Saudi Arabia, for instance, established key regulatory bodies for TVET such as the Saudi Skills

Standards (SSS) and the Technical and Vocational Training Corporation (TVTC) under the Ministry of Education. Whereas the SSS was tasked with developing fit-for-purpose qualifications aligned to the National Occupation Skills Standards (NOSS) along with executing external assessments and accreditation, the mandate for building an advanced system for job skills training programs by engaging international training providers fell to the Colleges of Excellence (CoE) project. Looking closely at the SSS, we see that descriptors and indicators focus on the same limited manual competencies that are common across global TVET systems. Along with disabling the vocational learner from participating meaningfully and critically in professional environments and in all facets of public life, this articulation of TVET in terms of restrictive instrumental job skills works to further stigmatize vocational educational pathways as a "subordinate discipline" in Gulf societies (Kennedy 2011, 172). With this vocational education focus solely on industrialization to meet national economic goals, the transformative potential of TVET in addressing larger societal issues that are tightly interwoven within occupational settings is neglected.

Vocational education in Kuwait is similarly structured under the governance of the Ministry of Education's Public Authority for Applied Education and Training (PAAET) which develops skills aligned to the needs of the national labor force ("TVET Country Profile: Kuwait" 2018). PAAET defines its authority and objectives as providing technical and professional skills development for middle levels of employment in order for Kuwait to become competitive and assume a role in economic and social progress ("About PAAET," n.d.). With the development of skilled and semi-skilled labor being the highest priority for the country (Al-Ali 2014), much of the attention of vocational and technical institutions in Kuwait has been dedicated to responding to the operational requirements of industry (Al Badir 2013) in order to build national workforce capacities and reduce heavy reliance on expatriate labor. Within this framework, quality education from ministerial and labor market perspectives is defined as having a philosophy, strategies, and planning structures "thoroughly assimilated by management, instructors, staff, students, and industry" with success or failure being defined by "industries' perception of the quality of graduates" (Al-Ali 2014). Absent from vocational skills and quality assurance frameworks are references to the development of individuals who have the knowledge, skills, and values to be active, socially cognizant, and critically reflective members of a community. As ministerial documentation details practical and technical skills required by employers across sectors and establishes metrices to gauge the success of their adoption exclusively through employer lenses, it remains silent on competencies required to nurture responsible, socially aware citizens who will resist forces that silence, marginalize, or disempower, as they make positive contributions in their workplaces and society at large.

Like most of the GCC's TVET systems, Qatar's vocational education falls under the Ministry of Education and Higher Education's authority, with the nation in the midst of establishing a formal and integrated vocational structure linked to its recently released Qatar Qualifications Framework. The Qatar National Vision 2030, National Development Strategy (NDS), and Education and Training Sector Strategy 2018–2022 (ETSS) all emphasize the importance of skilled workers for a diverse, knowledge-based economy (Oxford Business Group). Since 2002, the country's national technical college has offered up to thirty vocational and technical qualifications in the fields of industrial trades, engineering technology, IT, business and health sciences. A recent study of its curricula (Gamar, n.d.) indicates standards and outcomes primarily within the psychomotor domain in strict alignment to technical skills required by industry. Cognitive skills such as critical analysis and evaluation, as well as affective competencies arising from values, beliefs, and interests are not reflected in the pedagogical model.

Under the purview of the Ministry of Manpower, Oman's Occupational Standards and Testing Centre (OSTC) has worked to establish standards of performance in the vocational education sector in collaboration with the German Agency for Technical Collaboration (GTZ). The standards, which define "what an individual needs to do, know and understand in order to carry out a particular job role or function" (Oman Occupational Standards Center) focus exclusively on what it deems as skills necessary for increased productivity and improved quality for employers. According to detailed National Occupational Standards (NOCs) for trades and technical fields such as welding, facilities maintenance, manufacturing engineering, instrumentation, and health, safety, and environment (HSE), the skills standards are defined in partnership with the public and private sectors and represent "statements of effective performance . . . against clear and agreed-upon objectives," which employers can use to assess workers (National Occupational Standards: Sultanate of Oman Ministry of Manpower). Standards defined with exclusive focus on employer and labor market needs, rather than holistically with the student-citizen in mind calls to question the human capital economic ideology underpinning vocational education, especially with respect to its appropriateness in Arabian Gulf societies (Shaw 2000).

Across the GCC, the emphasis on vocational education serving national economic interests is unmistaken. Though each of the six member countries is undergoing social transformation, the education sector—especially the vocational education sector—has not been leveraged in ways that create transformative social movement. This potential is within means through critical pedagogical approaches, as will be presented in the ensuing sections, following a presentation of the implications of human capital economic theory in formative, rapidly evolving nations that make up the GCC.

IMPLICATIONS OF HUMAN CAPITAL
THEORY IN GCC TVET SYSTEMS

As forwarded in the beginning of this chapter, this exploration problematizes the technical and vocational education sector's preoccupation with instrumental skills development for the labor market—one that pursues national economic prosperity to the exclusion of cultivating critical, reflective citizens who strive, in their various job capacities, for a more socially just world starting with their immediate work environments (Kincheloe 1990). The dominant conceptualization of TVET, globally and within the GCC, imparts that it is a form of training for the mere pursuance of an occupation required for national prosperity. This stance was advocated by Snedden at the turn of the previous century—one in which workers are encased within an inflexible system of labor while having minimal to no understanding of the meaning and impact of their work (Snedden 1977; House 1921) and which renders them ill-prepared to diagnose and respond to work-based hegemonic structures (Giroux 2005).

The existing prevalent conceptualization of TVET has historically and habitually confined it to the mechanical and technocratic (Kincheloe 1999, 384; Orr 1994)—drawing heavily from Prosser and Snedden's market-driven social efficiency model (1977). By virtue of the GCC's borrowing of TVET frameworks from nations which, in the wake of two world wars, had an imperative to rebuild industries, initiate and support new markets, meet national economic needs and compete globally, all while integrating influxes of immigrants, GCC TVET systems have mirrored—seemingly without question—the underpinning human capital theoretical construct of twentieth-century vocational education. However, this has not passed without some criticism.

The dominant human capital ideology, which strives to establish education for economic growth and global supremacy by supplying workers for businesses (Spring 2011), imparts a conceptualization of vocational education as "irreducibly and without unnecessary mystification . . . the pursuit of an occupation" (Two communications 1977, 34)—one that is determined by and for national economic advantage. Kincheloe (Kincheloe 2008, 55) argues that the conservative, neoliberal, capitalist agenda driving current vocational education has created a knowledge imperialism and an epistemological absolutism where the empire promotes a positivist, formal, intractable, decontextualized, universalistic, reductionistic, one-dimensional intellectual climate "devoted to free market economics, globalized economic imperialism, [and] geo-political expansionism."

As GCC countries compete to establish knowledge-based economies by fueling rapidly expanding industries and ambitious national development projects, they have depended heavily on a TVET sector shaped by human capital ideology. As these young states with newly acquired wealth shape their national identities and vie for prosperity, and as they utilize education systems as an essential component of massive growth and modernization plans, they can offer mechanisms to nurture citizens who can think and act critically in and outside of work environments. As Kincheloe argues (1999, 384), we cannot expect "workers to be passive in civics but active in the pursuit of corporate values." Simply put, vocational learners' value systems cannot be activated when it serves corporate or market interests, yet deactivated or repressed where it involves such matters as ethical stewardship and advocacy for equity in the workplace.

Several regional considerations provide compelling reasons for rethinking vocational education formulated solely upon human capital economic theory that places instrumental skills development and labor market alignment above all other educational aspirations. These contextual factors encompass structures that make oppressive social relations and systemic inequity more prevalent and members of society more vulnerable to marginalization and oppression. Significant wage disparity, working conditions that make expatriate and foreign workers vulnerable to exploitation and abuse, cultural and socioeconomic stratification, barriers to equitable access to health and human services, informal and formal segregation of community groups are but a few examples of challenges across the Arabian Gulf states that prompt for alternative vocational models that support practical occupational competencies that simultaneously incorporate cognitive and affective skills that nurture the development of a responsible, critically aware member of society.

Shaw (2000), Al-Harthi (2011), and Belwal (2017) highlight the problem of a selective, labor-focused, human capital theory-based education system in the GCC noting that a high proportion of contracted migrant workers, accelerated national capacity-building schemes within a complex sociopolitical, cultural, and demographic context make it inappropriate for the region. Such a framework and curricula predominantly focus on skills development that is disconnected from the sociocultural and political contexts in which workers live and act as it places its ultimate objective the alignment of individuals' skills with labor market requirements that have been standardized and packaged in curricula for uniform and consistent application. Across the GCC this has oft reflected in narrowly defined student learning outcome statements reverently aligned to qualifications frameworks and occupational standards in heavily prescribed curricula that focus on demonstratable motor actions

(Gamar, n.d.). In so doing, vocational curricula discount the rich social contexts students come from and hinder their participation in the formation of
democratic social systems in and outside of the workplace (Giroux 2005).

CRITICAL PEDAGOGY AND
VOCATIONAL EDUCATION

A counter visage of vocational education is a progressive democratic conceptualization forwarded by John Dewey (1916). In the Deweyan philosophy of
vocational education, learners are prompted to not only develop psychomotor skills relevant to occupational scopes of practice but also encouraged to
gain cognitive and affective skills that develop their higher order and critical thinking skills along with their capacities to perceive, respond to, value,
and act in accordance with those values (Krathwohl, Bloom, Masia 1973).
Dewey's conceptualization led to new forms of critical vocational pedagogies that fused his early advocacy for critical agency in career-oriented
education with the teachings of Paolo Freire (1990). Among other scholars,
critical pedagogues like Kincheloe (1995, 1999) and Lakes (1997, 2005)
challenged the functional model of TVET, arguing for social reconstructivist
approaches that integrated "liberatory dialogue, active citizenship, reflective thinking, relevant learning experiences, and participatory, democratic
decision-making" (Adams and Adams 2011, 93).

A critical vocational pedagogy challenges the dominant narrative of
technical and vocational education as an unintellectual endeavor that func-
tions strictly for the whims of the marketplace. Aldossari's (2020) study
highlights that the perception of TVET as offering dead-end credentials, ill-
preparedness for white-collar jobs, suited for those from low social-economic
demographic groups, and involves manual labor that requires low intellectual
ability, dominates public perception in the Gulf. This has led to deep stigma-
tization of TVET and a further perpetuation of its aims as an instrumental
tool for economic advancement, rather than for collective social prosperity
through liberatory approaches.

Critical vocational pedagogues conceptualize TVET institutions, and all
educational institutions, as serving an incredibly important social and moral
role within society. Technological and career-oriented colleges and centers
nurture citizens—and those citizens have voices that can speak up against
hegemony in the forms of workplace gender bias, low or inequitable wage
distribution, physically or emotionally unsafe work conditions, infractions
on employee dignity and basic rights, deterrence of self-direction, self-
expression, or career progression, and lack of opportunities for intellectual

stimulation and growth. On this, Giroux states, "the official discourse of schooling depoliticizes the notion of culture and dismisses resistance" (2001, 66)—though clearly, workplace environments necessitate acts of social agency and resistance against inequity.

Educators within the TVET sector have the capacity to counter this dominant and abusive narrative, to adopt a more holistic, humanistic view of TVET education for the worker as a whole—not for what that worker will produce in capital gains. Giroux (2011) resounds this reasoning that education is not just an economic agency for preparing participants to contribute to the development of their economies, but also a political tool that can be wielded. In advocating for critical vocational pedagogy, we treat TVET institutions and their programs as contexts for cultural politics (McLaren 2007). We urge for this in the GCC, understanding that the region is undergoing rapid social, political, and economic transformation and where heavy investment in education has been and continues to be a significant propellant in that change.

Contextual factors specific to the GCC implore us to advocate for critical approaches to vocational education. The special case of being rentier states, where a limited few are involved in the generation of wealth from natural (oil-based) sources and where the remainder of society is involved in its distribution or utilization (Beblawi 1987, 385; Lanthaler 2021) is one such key contextual factor that shapes the entire Gulf economic system. The heavy reliance on unskilled migrant workers who are tied to the kafala or sponsorship system, the huge divide between management and workers, the national capacity-building schemes that inherently distinguish between nationals and nonnationals, and the predominance of prescriptive job roles that are often determined by nationality as opposed to education or abilities—all account for the need to specially integrate critical vocational pedagogies in the TVET sector, in opposition to the dominant human capital approach.

TEACHING FOR CRITICAL CONSCIOUSNESS AND AGENCY

Freire (2015) repels the notion of learners as "educands"—passive objects at the receiving end of information that is deposited into them like money into a bank, later to be withdrawn with utmost precision during assessment exercises. He argues that educators must recognize that students are intellectuals with their individual right to think and value, and so, an educator's role involves empowering learners to understand that they signify the act of meaning-making. Students render meaning to a particular matter when they analyze it using their own individual lens, and so must be prompted to examine cultural processes through their own set of experiences and realities (Giroux 2005). Freire states:

> [A] theoretical understanding of the practice of political education, which, if is to be progressive, must . . . take careful account of the reading of the world being made popular by groups and expressed in their syntax, their semantics, their dreams and desires. (2015, 12)

And so, another mechanism for transformative education is the practice of reading the world, listening carefully and considering the multidimensionality of phenomena.

The aim of engaging vocational learners in a process of intellectual and critical inquiry that equips them with the tools to become more aware of their socio-politico-economic contexts—and respond to various forms of struggle in those spheres—requires deliberate critical pedagogical methods to be used by teachers. As this chapter has thus far posited, highly regimented vocational curricula that focuses entirely on motor skills in reverential fidelity to occupational standards leaves little to no room for activating students' cultural awareness and their understanding of their place in a grand social and economic structure. However, vocational educators can contest these restrictive mechanisms in the classroom and employ ways of engaging learners in connecting meaningfully, critically, with various structures in the workplace.

Conscientization, or critical consciousness, as forwarded by Paulo Freire (1974), is an exercise of metacognition for the purpose of baring factors which restrict liberation and sustain inequity (Jemal 2017). Freire advocates for educators who are critically conscious of ideology and use powerful lenses to question hegemonic constructs, but he advises that educators do this with the virtue of humility for one's own biases and subjectivities. Giroux (2001) asserts that learners can be made to be conscious of the selections of knowledge for which they are exposed, and to take command and reject to be objects of control. Conscientization, then, calls on educators and the learners they teach, to practice a heightened form of awareness of social mechanisms that work to prop dominant frameworks.

Critical awareness can be enacted by educators through many different approaches—one of which is through the exercise of critical autoethnographies. In engaging in critical autoethnographic acts, I contend that vocational educators will be more prepared to model to vocational learners how they themselves can become more critically conscious workers and citizens.

CRITICAL AUTOETHNOGRAPHY AS A
FORM OF CONSCIENTIZATION

Autoethnography emerged from the qualitative research tradition and endeavors to describe and interpret personal experience for the aim of understanding cultural practice (Ellis 2004). Auto denotes the independent or self in the methodology, ethno relates to culture, and graphy signifies the study or analysis of such. The study of the self within a cultural context and/or for cultural realization is, by definition, the purpose and also the process of ethnography (Ellis and Bochner 2010). It is what is enacted and what manifests. Richard Pinner (2018, 95) calls it, quite simply, "evidence-based reflection," while Ellis and Bochner (2000, 733) define the methodology as "an autobiographical genre of writing and research that displays multiple layers of consciousness, connecting the personal to the cultural" (as cited in Humphreys 2005, 841). Deborah Reed-Danahay (2017, 145) describes autoethnography as examining the dichotomies of individual against his/her culture, personal insight against objective observation, and closeness versus proximity. She also posits that autoethnography "reflects a view of ethnography as both a reflexive and a collaborative enterprise, in which the life experiences of the anthropologist and their relationships with others 'in the field' should be interrogated and explored."

Autoethnographic exercises, then, can be understood to be a self-reflexive methodology concerned with connecting the self to social structure through personal narrative (Anderson 2006). Autoethnography stands in stark opposition to the positivist paradigm and challenges the epistemological and ontological claims made by the positivist era (Kuhn 1996). In postmodernism, consideration of subjectivity in research was made. Rather than hide behind the guise of pure objectivity, which is untenable and arguably self-delusional, autoethnography embraces value-centered, socially conscious, and politically cognizant research (Bochner 1994, 21–41) through ethnographic, autobiographical accounts. As Wall (2016, 1) advances, autoethnography supports "non-traditional ways of knowing" that rejects positivist skepticism of diverse ways of attaining knowledge.

Autoethnography has not always held this label, but has been referred to using different terminologies, most closely as the methodological approach of reflexive sociology termed by Pierre Bourdieu (1997). Reflexivity, here, is the act of something turning back upon itself (Turner 1974), resulting in an exposition of itself (Bourdieu 1992). Reflexive sociology requires of the researcher efforts in creativity and sociological imagination (Adams 2008) where he/she steps out of their immediate social reality to examine how they think, feel, and what they believe about a phenomenon in order to understand the experiences of others. Reed-Danahay (2017, 145) elucidated that autoethnography is "both a reflexive and a collaborative enterprise, in which life experiences of the anthropologist and their relationships with others 'in the field' should be interrogated and explored." Hence, the researcher-practitioner's interactions within their context as related to a particular phenomenon, and its examination, is central to autoethnography.

Gouldner (1989) purported that the ultimate charge of autoethnography is to deepen the professional scope of the researcher/teacher with new sympathies and understandings so as to advance his/her consciousness to a higher level. The product of any autoethnographic study, Garfinkel (1967) states, is a deeper consciousness of the sociological work at hand, through the transformation of the self and his or her praxis. In this way, an educator employs autoethnography to establish a heightened consciousness of the self and its situatedness in a particular social reality to realize a new way of seeing and practicing.

Autoethnography involves narrative storytelling, which relates the researcher's personal reflections and experiences to an examination (Foster et al. 2006). It requires writing about oneself as a research-practitioner (McIlveen 2008), placing him/her within a social context (Reed-Danahay 1997, 2017). The approach compels the researcher to be critical about personal lived experiences while addressing a selected phenomenon. The human-environment interaction that is central to qualitative research is, more specifically in autoethnography, an interface between the researcher-educator himself/herself and their physical and cultural context (Ellis, Adams, and Bochner 2011).

Critical autoethnography builds on the traits of analytical autoethnography, contesting social and cultural contexts in order to seek change (Reed-Danahay 2017). It assumes a stance of "cultural critique" (Marcus and Fischer 1986). Adams (2017, 79) highlights the key characteristics of this type of autoethnography, positing that it makes "vital and often unforeseen connections between personal experiences and cultural experiences; identify manifestations of power and privilege in everyday practices . . . [and] discern social injustices and inequities" with a commitment to challenge social inequity, endorse confrontation and opposition of injustice and advance solutions for these. In other words, critical ethnography is a narrative-driven form of qualitative inquiry whose purpose is to change the phenomenon being observed. This is a form of agency.

One of the commitments of critical ethnography that Adams, Jones, and Ellis (2015, 229) mention is that "critical autoethnography involves both a material and ethical praxis." According to Jones (2015, 229), "doing critical autoethnography engages us in processes of becoming and because of this, shows us ways of embodying change." Knowing, doing, and transforming all three defining features of this form of autoethnography.

Autoethnographic practice in teacher professional development can be a powerful tool to building critical self-awareness in vocational educators, immersing them in processes that require them to oscillate between personal narrative and reflective examination. As Ellis (2007, 14) states, "Doing auto-ethnography involves a back-and-forth movement between experiencing and examining a vulnerable self and observing and revealing the broader context of that experience." Personal stories and introspection are relayed in the first person with frequent interjections of analysis.

Writing conventions are minimal for autoethnography, where the researcher-practitioner's voice is more important than academic and schol-arly construction (McIlveen 2008). To tell the story, the research-practitioner can use archival data and self-observation presented through memoirs, photographs, diaries, and other methods (Delany 2004). Guidelines for auto-ethnographic practice include writing that is comprehensive, transformative, and expository—informing the readers of experiences they, the readers, have not encountered, through epiphanies, or stories of deep insight that have impacted the writer/teacher's life (Bochner and Ellis 1992). As McIlveen stated, autoethnography "has the potential to act as a stimulus for profound understanding of a single case and, moreover, act as a stimulus to open new intellectual vistas for the reader through a uniquely personal meaning and empathy" (2008, 5).

Most individuals have encountered dominance and repression in some form or another, and within those experiences lie rich sources upon which to build critical consciousness. As forwarded by Ali-Khan and Siry (2011), edu-cators must engage in dialogical practice, learning through dialogue (Freire and Macedo 1996), and this exercise must be inclusive of TVET teachers and administrators who participate in self-dialogue as a starting point for criti-cally analyzing the place for democratic education. Ultimately, this exercise of reading the self enables one to commit to transformative education and the practice of reading the world (Freire 2015).

CONCLUSION

The GCC's vocational education systems have largely adopted and propagated a human capital economics ideology for skills development that directly mirror technical labor market skill requirements to the exclusion of nurturing voca-tional learners as citizens within rapidly transforming societies replete with complex socio-politico-economic factors. National technical and vocational frameworks in Gulf countries perpetuate the narrative of vocational education that serves industry needs with industrial, manual labor. Despite the incred-ible opportunity for vocational systems in the GCC to play a role in orienting students to the complex sociopolitical terrain that is the workplace—as a microcosm of the larger society—and rather than strive to prepare learners for navigating challenges that relate to power and privilege through critical reflection, the sector's focus has and remains to be on socially decontextualized demonstrations of mechanical skills that assume sterile, apolitical conditions.

This chapter has argued that the mobilization of learners toward critical consciousness as a form of reclaiming agency ought to be a priority in vocational education systems, and teacher professional development frameworks in GCC countries. In the integration of critical autoethnographic practices in teacher professional development a more holistic, humanistic TVET pedagogy can be forwarded in the vocational classroom to prompt students to understand where they are in the sociocultural and economic landscape and what role they can play in resisting hegemonies. As Giroux states, "a theory of critical literacy necessitates a more profound understanding of how the wider conditions of the state and society produce, negotiate, transform, and bear down on the conditions of teaching so as to either enable or disable teachers from acting in a critical and transformative way" (2005, 159). Educators working within the TVET sector must find ways to engage in their own exercise of reflexivity, seeking to excavate through personal histories from which to draw critical lessons.

This chapter aims to provide a foundation for further scholarly efforts in holistic and humanistic TVET pedagogies where practical skills development and the studies of technologies and applied sciences are inclusive of critical pedagogies where consciousness is awakened and channeled toward social action. Rather than the prevalent technocratic human capital ideology, this study hopes to instigate dialogue on the need for the promotion of citizenry and social good, just as economic gain is vested in, through technical and vocational education.

Ultimately, this study argues for critical progressive democratic educational praxis where teachers adopt critical reflection as an exercise of metacognition for the purpose of baring factors which restrict liberation and sustain inequity in occupationally focused education. This chapter's aim lies in illuminating ways for increased integration of critical pedagogical, and social justice-oriented practices in vocational education.

REFERENCES

"2017–18 Annual Report." 2018. *Australian Skills Quality Authority.* https://www
.asqa.gov.au/resources/publications/2017-18-annual-report.
"About the Public Authority for Applied Education and Training." n.d. http://paaetwp
.paaet.edu.kw/scf/paaet/.

Adams, Tony E. 2017. "Critical Autoethnography, Education, and a Call for Forgiveness." *International Journal of Multicultural Education* 19 (1): 79. https://doi.org/10.18251/ijme.v19i1.1387.

Adams, Tony E., Stacy Holman Jones, and Carolyn Ellis. 2015. *Autoethnography: Understanding Qualitative Research*. Oxford, England: Oxford University Press.

Al Badir, Anfal Fouad. 2013. "Investigating the Skills-Gap in the Kuwaiti Labour Market: Perspectives from Policy Makers, Employers, Graduates, and Higher Educational Institutions." PhD Thesis, University of Manchester.

Al-Ali, Salah. 2014. "Are Lecturers Transferring the Necessary Skills Needed for the Workplace? The College of Technological Studies, Kuwait—A Case Study." *Journal of International Education and Leadership* 4 (2): 1–10.

Al-Ali, Salahaldeen. 1993. "Technical and Vocational Education in Kuwait." *The Vocational Aspect of Education* 45 (1): 15–23.

Al-Mujaini, Amal Obaid. 2018. *An Overview of the TVET System in the Sultanate of Oman: An Investigation on Modules of Work-Based Learning (WBL) Programmes Implementation for Youth in Oman*. Beirut: UNESCO Regional Bureau for Education in the Arab States.

Ali-Khan, Carolyne, and Christina Ann Siry. 2011. "Writing We: Collaborative Text in Educational Research." *Critical Pedagogy in the Twenty-First Century: A New Generation of Scholars*. Edited by Curry Malott and Bradley J. Porfilio. Charlotte, NC: Information Age.

Anderson, Damon. 2009. "Productivism and Ecologism: Changing Discourses in TVET." *Work, Learning and Sustainable Development: Opportunities and Challenges*. Edited by John Fien, Rupert Maclean, and Man-Gon Park. Vol. 8. Dordrecht, Netherlands: Springer.

Anderson, Leon. 2006. "Analytic Autoethnography." *Journal of Contemporary Ethnography* 35 (4): 373–95. https://doi.org/10.1177/0891241605280449.

Arenas, A., and F. Londono. 2013. "Connecting Vocational and Technical Education with Sustainability." *International Handbook of Research on Environmental Education*. Edited by Robert Murrell Stevenson, Michael Brody, Arjen E. J. Wals, and Justin Dillon. New York: Routledge.

Bahgat, Gawdat. 1999. "Education in the Gulf Monarchies: Retrospect and Prospect." *International Review of Education* 45 (2): 127–36. https://doi.org/10.1023/a:1003610723356.

Bedi, Gitanjali, and Susan Germein. 2016. "Simply Good Teaching: Supporting Transformation and Change through Education for Sustainability." *Australian Journal of Environmental Education* 32 (1): 124–33. https://doi.org/https://doi.org/10.1017/aee.2015.52.

Belwal, Rakesh, Pushpendra Priyadarshi, and Mariam Humaid Al Fazari. 2017. "Graduate Attributes and Employability Skills." *International Journal of Educational Management* 31 (6): 814–27. https://doi.org/10.1108/ijem-05-2016-0122.

Bilboe, Wendy. 2011. "Vocational Education and Training in Kuwait: Vocational Education versus Values and Viewpoints." *International Journal of Training Research* 9 (3): 256–60. https://doi.org/10.5172/ijtr.9.3.256.

Bochner, Arthur P. 1994. "Perspectives on Inquiry II: Theories and Stories." *Handbook of Interpersonal Communication.* Edited by Mark L. Knapp and Gerald R. Miller. 2nd ed. Thousand Oaks, CA: Sage.

Bourdieu, Pierre. 2003. "Participant Objectivation." *Journal of the Royal Anthropological Institute* 9 (2): 281–94. https://doi.org/10.1111/1467-9655.00150.

Daniels, Leslie. 2018. "An Exploration of How Discourses of Efficiency and Social Justice Shaped the Technical and Vocational Education and Training (TVET) Sector with Special Reference to TVET Colleges." PhD Thesis, Stellenbosch University.

Delany, Samuel R. 2004. *The Motion of Light in Water.* Minneapolis, MN: University Of Minnesota Press.

Ellis, Carolyn. 2004. *The Ethnographic I: A Methodological Novel about Autoethnography.* Walnut Creek, CA: AltaMira Press.

Ellis, Carolyn. 2007. "Telling Secrets, Revealing Lives: Relational Ethics in Research with Intimate Others." *Qualitative Inquiry* 13 (1): 3–29. https://doi.org/10.1177/1077800406294947.

Ellis, Carolyn, Tony E. Adams, and Arthur P. Bochner. 2011. "Autoethnography: An Overview." *Forum: Qualitative Social Research* 12 (1). https://doi.org/10.17169/fqs-12.1.1589.

Ellis, Carolyn, and Arthur P. Bochner. 2000. "Autoethnography, Personal Narrative, Reflexivity: Researcher as Subject." *Handbook of Qualitative Research.* Edited by Norman K. Denzin and Yvonna S. Lincoln. 2nd ed. Thousand Oaks, CA: Sage. Quoted in Michael Humphreys. 2005. "Getting Personal: Reflexivity and Autoethnographic Vignettes." *Qualitative Inquiry* 11 (6): 840–60. https://doi.org/10.1177/1077800404269425.

Freire, Paulo. 2000. *Pedagogy of the Oppressed.* 50th anniversary ed., New York, NY: Bloomsbury.

Freire, Paulo. 2015. *Pedagogy of Hope: Reliving Pedagogy of the Oppressed.* New York, NY: Bloomsbury.

Freire, Paulo, and Donaldo Macedo. 1996. "A Dialogue: Culture, Language, and Race." *Breaking Free: The Transformative Power of Critical Pedagogy.* Edited by Pepi Leistyna, Arlie Woodrum, and Stephen A. Sherblom. Cambridge, MA: Harvard Educational Review.

Gamar, Samah Abdulhafid. 2017. "Vertical Permeability between Vocational and Higher Education: A Case Study of a Qatar Technical Institute's Role in Facilitating Transition to Higher Education for Trades Students." *International Journal of Training Research* 15 (3): 204–13. https://doi.org/10.1080/14480220.2017.1374665.

Garfinkel, Harold. 1967. *Studies in Ethnomethodology.* Englewood Cliffs, NJ: Prentice Hall.

Giroux, Henry A. 2001. *Theory and Resistance in Education: Towards a Pedagogy for the Opposition.* Westport, CT: Bergin & Garvey.

Jemal, Alexis. 2017. "Critical Consciousness: A Critique and Critical Analysis of the Literature." *The Urban Review* 49 (4): 602–26. https://doi.org/10.1007/s11256-017-0411-3.

Kincheloe, Joe L. 1999. *How Do We Tell the Workers? The Socioeconomic Foundations of Work and Vocational Education.* Boulder, CO: Westview Press.

Kincheloe, Joe L. 2008. *Knowledge and Critical Pedagogy: An Introduction.* New York, NY: Springer.

Kuhn, Thomas S. 1996. *The Structure of Scientific Revolutions.* 3rd ed. Chicago, IL: University of Chicago Press.

Langthaler, Margarita. 2021. *Vocational Education for Industrialisation. The Case of Oman in a Regional Perspective.*

MacIntyre, A. C. 1964. "Against Utilitarianism." *Aims in Education: The Philosophic Approach.* Edited by T. H. B. Hollins. Manchester: Manchester University Press.

Maclean, Rupert, and David Wilson, eds. 2009. *International Handbook of Education for the Changing World of Work: Bridging Academic and Vocational Learning.* Dordrecht, The Netherlands: Springer.

Marcus, George E., and Michael M. J. Fischer. 1986. *Anthropology as Cultural Critique: An Experimental Moment in the Human Science.* Chicago, IL: University Of Chicago Press.

McIlveen, Peter. 2008. "Autoethnography as a Method for Reflexive Research and Practice in Vocational Psychology." *Australian Journal of Career Development* 17 (2): 13–20. https://doi.org/10.1177/103841620801700204.

McLaren, Peter. 2007. *Life in Schools: An Introduction to Critical Pedagogy in the Foundations of Education.* Toronto, Canada: Irwin.

Ministry of Education. 1979. "Kuwait: Department of Technical and Vocational Education, Technical and Vocational Education in Kuwait, Public Relations Unit."

Orr, David W. 1994. *Earth in Mind: On Education, Environment, and the Human Prospect.* New York, NY: Island Press.

Reed-Danahay, Deborah, ed. 1997. *Auto/Ethnography: Rewriting the Self and the Social.* Oxford, England: Berg.

Reed-Danahay, Deborah. 2017. "Bourdieu and Critical Autoethnography: Implications for Research, Writing, and Teaching." *International Journal of Multicultural Education* 19 (1): 144–54. https://doi.org/10.18251/ijme.v19i1.1368.

Shaw, Ken E. 2000. "Human Capital Formation in the Gulf and MENA Region." *Mediterranean Journal of Educational Studies* 6 (1): 91–106.

Spring, Joel H. 2011. *The Politics of American Education.* New York, NY: Routledge.

"Technical and Vocational Education (TVET)—the Official Portal of the UAE Government." 2021. U.AE. January 11, 2021. https://u.ae/en/information-and-services/education/technical-and-vocational-education.

"TVET Country Profile: Kuwait." 2018. UNESCO-UNEVOC. https://unevoc.unesco.org/wtdb/worldtvetdatabase_kwt_en.pdf.

United Nations Educational, Scientific and Cultural Organization, and International Labour Organization. 2002. *Technical and Vocational Education and Training for the Twenty-First Century: UNESCO and ILO Recommendations.* Paris, France: UNESCO.

Wall, Sarah Wall. 2016. "Toward a Moderate Autoethnography." *International Journal of Qualitative Methods* 15 (1): 1–9. https://doi.org/10.1177/1609406916674966.

Chapter 10

Removing Cultural Barriers and Advancing an Asset-Based Pedagogy in Higher Education

Fatima Hasan Bailey, Jenny Eppard,
and Herveen Singh

INTRODUCTION

With the onset of national agendas and educational reform, many tertiary institutions in the United Arab Emirates (UAE) have objectives and outcomes, which include providing students with the analytical skills they need for career readiness, leadership, and decision-making (UAE 2010). As the UAE is advancing toward raising the country's national priorities, which includes education, to an internationally recognized benchmark, changes in teaching and learning are imminent. To support student learning, this involves university faculty enabling and empowering students to become active lifelong learners, and productive citizens who are capable of contributing to their society and communities. University faculty in the UAE are expected to steer Emirati students away from rote memory as the primary tool of learning and encourage them to become critical thinkers and innovators (Chapman et al. 2014).

Historically, the educational model in the UAE was rooted in educational practices with an emphasis on rote, passive, and hierarchical learning with a focus on religion and community-level oral storytelling (Freimuth 2014; Russell 2004). While there are remnants of this type of traditional learning still in place, the UAE is transitioning to a focus on entrepreneurship and innovation, which requires active learning and critical thinking (Saji & Nair 2018). Local and international standardization may improve service and teaching quality at institutions, however, localized cultural nuances need to be respected and protected (Li 2016). Kirk and Napler (2009) stated that nations that try to reform education face the following challenges: "expansion versus quality, regional versus local needs, resolving questions of equity and equality, inequity and inequality, and developing an indigenous system" (543–544). This idea of meeting local needs while developing a localized educational system is significant in the context of education in an increasingly diverse environment such as the UAE.

Over the years, Gulf Cooperation Council (GCC) countries such as the UAE have experienced a rapid growth in their higher education sector, this led to the recruitment of expatriate faculty (Chapman, et al. 2014). Western-trained (expatriate) university faculty who embark on teaching in higher educational institutions in GCC countries, the UAE in particular, need to be explicitly and sufficiently prepared for unique teaching experiences with their Emirati students (Austin, et al. 2014). Expatriate university faculty should be aware, cognizant, and capable so as to facilitate the best type of learning experience appropriate for the GCC region. Carefully developed and sustained strategies and structures that promote positive student learning experiences are key. Many in the field of higher education contend that this can be achieved through the implementation of an asset-based pedagogy, such as a culturally relevant pedagogy (CRP).

This chapter notes the educational changes that are taking place in higher education in the UAE and the expectation for initiatives to be implemented at the tertiary level. Thus, the question for faculty teaching in the UAE is how to best respond to the changes? This chapter seeks to explore and answer the following inquiries: how can faculty innovate and move beyond CRP toward a teaching and learning approach that seeks to perpetuate and foster Emirati cultural norms and values as integral parts of students' learning experience; and is there an outcome-oriented approach, faculty can take toward teaching and learning in higher education settings where the culture of most students do not mirror the faculty. This will be accomplished by outlining underlying assumptions and viewpoints of faculty and students regarding teaching and learning. This chapter addresses various factors and significant influences, which impact teaching and learning experiences, as it presents an overview of the literature. This chapter will be informed through data collected from an empirical study conducted within the context of this research. The chapter will highlight emergent themes for critical analysis. Thereafter, the chapter will conclude with key recommendations that may inform future policies and/or initiatives. Ultimately, this chapter attempts to bridge the gap on this subject within the existing literature and provide new knowledge that has implication for a "sustainable change" in higher education.

CULTURALLY RELEVANT PEDAGOGY IN THE UAE

In comparison to other cultural groups, Middle Eastern Arab students, particularly those of Emirati descent, face challenges in their learning as a result of cultural, racial, and religious misunderstanding (Mahrous & Ahmed, 2010). It is essential for faculty to have cross-cultural interaction by first being well aware of their students' backgrounds and reflecting on experiences that can help improve their learning outcomes. Faculty teaching in the UAE needs to be more culturally aware and informed of the Emirati culture, in order to create a more engaging and thriving learning environment. Culturally informed faculty who incorporate culturally sensitive teaching practices, also known as culturally relevant pedagogy, seek to incorporate educational practices that respond to all students from diverse cultural backgrounds (Ladson-Billings, 2014). The effective implementation of CRP minimizes the cultural discontinuity for students from different linguistic and cultural backgrounds (from faculty teaching their courses). Through the implementation of CRP, faculty become more responsive, passionate, and engaged in teaching practices that support their students' needs and identities and that promote meaningful and powerful learning experiences (Ladson-Billings, 2014).

There are numerous studies that have addressed the importance of advancing educational practices and policies that mirror students' diverse cultures, as well as the need to focus on how students from the Middle Eastern culture respond (Austin, et al. 2014; Freimuth, 2014; Blaik-Hourani, Diallo, & Said, 2011). The use and advancement of asset-based pedagogical approaches is a nuance worthy to examine and explore. Our chapter focuses on studies which explore how such approaches such as CRP, for example, are about being responsive to the cultural ways, language, and literacies that Emirati students bring into their classrooms, and how these places and spaces for learning may perpetuate, foster, deepen, and/or extend student's learning and yield favorable outcomes.

The current literature and research that explores expatriate faculty supporting the teaching and learning of Emirati students in this way is emerging (Austin et al. 2014). In order to fully explore this, we will first turn our attention to expatriate faculty teaching experiences, highlighting their roles, responsibilities, and practices in higher education classrooms.

TEACHING AND LEARNING IN THE UAE

The UAE is committed to developing an innovative education system wherein its graduates think critically, are workforce-ready, and thrive within globally competitive markets (Saji & Nair, 2018). The national focus on innovation has prompted the UAE to reexamine its education systems and fortify its commitments to developing an informed citizenry capable of championing the UAE's national agenda for generations to come. Historically, the education system in the UAE was based on a banking model approach that emphasized rote learning, religion, and oral storytelling (Freimuth, 2014; Russell, 2004). In 2017, the Ministry of Education announced the following objectives in its "Strategic Plan":

1. Ensure inclusive quality education including preschool education.
2. Achieve excellent leadership and educational efficiency.
3. Ensure quality, efficiency, and good governance of educational and institutional performance, including the delivery of teaching.
4. Ensure safe, conducive, and challenging learning environments.
5. Attract and prepare students to enroll in higher education internally and externally, in light of labor market needs.
6. Strengthen the capacity for scientific research and innovation in accordance with the quality, efficiency, and transparency standards.
7. Provision of quality, efficient, and transparent administrative services, in accordance with the quality, efficiency, and transparency standards.
8. Establish a culture of innovation in an institutional working environment.

The above Ministry of Education Strategic Objectives signals the UAE's commitment to instituting a quality assured educational system committed to equipping graduates with the knowledge, skills, and capabilities required to propel the UAE national agenda. While quality assurance and standardization may improve some elements related to educational services and teaching, it should not be at the cost of foregoing cultural assets or heritage. Li (2016) cautions that while standardization may improve service and teaching quality at institutions, localized cultural nuances must be respected and protected (Li 2016). Respecting and safeguarding cultural nuances within educational systems and especially during educational reform can be a daunting task. Critical questions arise such as, what are cultural nuances? How do teachers and administrators protect these cultural nuances? And, how are cultural nuances accounted for in curriculum, teaching, and leadership? If culture is to have a central role in education, critical questions like these must play a vital role in informing educational reform agendas. Kirk and Napler (2009) adequately noted that nations that try to reform education often encounter the following challenges: "expansion versus quality, regional versus local needs, resolving questions of equity and equality, inequity and inequality, and developing an indigenous system" (543–544, as noted in Singh et al. 2021). Within the UAE context developing an educational system that accounts for the Indigenous population is of paramount importance. Emiratis (the Indigenous people) represent approximately 10 percent of the population, with the remaining 90 percent being expats.

LANGUAGE AND COMMUNICATION CHALLENGES

In efforts to expedite the UAE's global position as a world leader, the government has imported foreign skilled labor in many social sectors. Given the transient nature of the workforce in the UAE, the English language was readily adopted as the language of choice to communicate across ethnic and linguistic differences. The quick adoption of English as the Lingua Franca within the UAE has impacted the use of Arabic across the country. Sarah Hopkyns (2014) recognizes the impact of the power of English as a double-edged sword, "Although the global power of English brings with it great opportunities, progress, increased knowledge and a sense of excitement, there are also notable concerns about the negative effects such a powerful language has on local languages and cultures" (Hopkyns 2014, 1). The ultimate cost of this double-edged sword is the loss of the Arabic language.

The loss of the Arabic language is of critical importance as culture and language are closely intertwined. Proponents of culturally responsive pedagogy recognize that language informs and explicates culture and vice versa. In her definition of cultural identity, Sperrazza states that it is "a continuously fluid concept that depends on the individual's linguistic connection to a particular language or languages, which also includes personal experiences involved in those languages" (Sperrazza 2012, 298). Within the federal universities, the UAE has established English as the official language of instruction. In this way, students are in a constantly fluid state between English spoken within the classroom and Arabic within their private circles of family and friends. Expat educators committed to CRP would be wise to recognize the English language's dominance and its impact on student identity. In recognizing the global power of English and its potential to subordinate the Arabic language (and thus culture), expat faculty could reflect on *how* their approaches to teaching and learning, including curriculum and assessments, are constructed to provide students with opportunities to reflect on their cultural identities within the space of fluidity.

Making curriculum adjustments to allow students to reflect on the fluidity of their identities require faculty to allow space for students to articulate their thoughts, reflections, and possible internal conflicts that may arise. As educators, we must eagerly anticipate student responses and be poised to engage with them critically and support students as they "negotiate conflict in order for cultural injustice to be transformed into pedagogical instances of individual agency as students understand their own identities by questioning the role of English in a postcolonial context" (Sperrazza, 2012, 299). Examining the global dominance of English (in relation to Arabic and its impact on identity) allows students to see how power is operationalized and explore ways to leverage it. This is not simply a novel exercise. As students begin to understand their relationship to English, they are then positioned to examine how the UAE is situated as a competitive global leader while committed to maintaining its heritage, language, and religion.

CULTURAL CLASHES

Most UAE educators are expatriates with varying degrees of cultural knowledge, experience, and competence. This should be considered when pushing for educational reform. Raven (2011) identified a potential clash of cultures between the collectivist ways of being in Emirati culture versus expat educators who may approach education from an individualistic paradigm. This potential clash of cultures, coupled with the UAE's historical approach to teaching and learning from a banking model with an emphasis on rote learning, has implications for students' preferences for learning and educators' pedagogical teaching methods. Emerging from the literature, table 10.1 identifies possible differences in student and teacher perspectives, conceptualizations, and teaching and learning expectations.

Table 10.1 Higher Educational Approaches for Teaching and Learning in the UAE

Teaching Approaches and Student Learning Patterns	How Does This Translate in the Classroom?	Sources
There are several teaching approaches and preferred patterns of learning which are visible: 1. Rote learning 2. Passive learning 3. High-stakes testing 4. Collaborative activities 5. Oral activities 6. Scaffolding 7. Hierarchical	In the classroom, students often prefer: 1. Slideshows summaries over text-based information 2. Paired and teamwork activities 3. Giving presentations over writing 4. Constant scaffolding 5. Teacher as the center and source for information	Rapanta (2014) Russell (2004) Halawah (2011) Freimuth (2014) Sonleitner & Khelifa (2005) Engin & McKeown (2012)
Teachers' Possible Conceptualization of an Idealized Learning Environment 1. Focus on reading 2. Active learning	Expect students to: (1) read academic texts; (2) participate in interactive classrooms	Freimuth (2014) Zajda & Rust (2016)

Source: Table created by authors using collected data.

This table reveals that there are a range of faculty and students' conceptions with regards to teaching and learning. While there are marked differences between teaching approaches, methods and conceptualizations in higher education, with regards to the UAE, the table highlights that rote teaching and learning along with banking model is still preferred over other methods such as developing funds of knowledge. Additionally, university students' learning preferences and expectations still tend to focus more on passive learning. The question therein is: are faculty coming into UAE tertiary institutions aware of this? If so, how does this inform their pedagogical approaches and methods? And if not, what are the implications for how faculty set up expectations and experiences for "successful" teaching and learning?

GLOBALIZATION

Globalization has expedited the dominance of the English language worldwide. Globalization of the English language is further fortified by recruiting Western-trained educators in federal institutions responsible for educating Emiratis to be workforce-ready. However, there has been a concern with the transference of Western educational theories and practices (Garson, 2005; Hallbach, 2002; Saudelli, 2012), as well as the likelihood of "embedded western values into foreign countries" (as noted in Saudelli 2012, 104). In this way, expat educators run the risk of "exporting methodologies" (Hallbach, 2002, as quoted in Saudelli 2012, 104) to foreign countries without examining the implications for the host country they have been recruited to teach in. This "exporting methodologies" approach is complex and warrants caution as it lends itself to cultural clashes rooted in differing beliefs and value systems.

TEACHING METHODOLOGIES AND PEDAGOGIES

The exporting of methodologies manifests in several ways. In examining Emirati student encounters with Western teachers, Diallo (2014) identifies four ways exported methods may trigger student resistance. First, Diallo identifies course textbooks as biased: "Textbooks are not innocent or neutral but are fundamentally ideological in the sense that they are produced by particular vested linguistic, socio-political and cultural agendas" (Diallo 2014, 9). Second, Diallo identifies student reactions to course texts and resources as sites of resistance to Western indoctrination; student responses included striking out or shading out women dressed in an unexpected way and articulating the female characters clothing as *haraam*, or prohibited (Diallo 2014). Third, Western culture including lifestyle, politically sensitive issues, and gender issues were identified as possible sites for tension and resistance within the classroom (Diallo 2014). Specifically, when discussing sensitive topics, the gender of the faculty member matters. Diallo references faculty experiences in which female students engaged with sensitive issues with a female educator (e.g., a book review on Chekhov's *The Lady with the Dog*), however, would not do the same with a male educator (discussing *Metamorphosis* to an all-female class) (Diallo 2014). Lastly, Diallo (2014) identifies engaging in discussions related to politics can be challenging, especially if it contradicts the established political and spiritual views of the country. While discussions like these may be viewed as a routine exercise related to fortifying critical thinking and debating skills in Western universities, it may be problematic and result in the faculty member's termination (Diallo 2014).

A UNIVERSITY CASE STUDY IN THE
UNITED ARAB EMIRATES

This chapter further explores these aspects and elements through a real-life situation via a case study. Ten faculty members who had been in the Emirates for under two years and ten students who had been at this particular university for under one year agreed to participate on a voluntary basis in a mixed methods study. Student volunteers were recruited when visiting student advising courses. The researchers did not know any of the student participants before the study. Instructors were recruited by word-of-mouth and through email due to time constraints and logistical issues sampling could be categorized as convenience sampling. All the faculty and two of the researchers gained their degrees in the United States or the United Kingdom. Subjects taught by the faculty interviewed for the study included education, life skills, art history, computer science, and media. Tables 10.2 and 10.3 provide more in-depth information about the participants. Student participants were all UAE nationals aged 18 and older who had been educated at government, private, and international schools. Arabic was the first language of all students interviewed. Their level of English was within the range of the university's average of between IELTS 5 and 5.5, which indicates that the student needs extra language support in an academic environment (Setting IELTS entry scores, n.d.).

Table 10.2 describes the types of training that faculty members had with pedagogy before their appointment at the university. Some of the faculty members were education scholars, while other faculty members had content expertise without formal training in pedagogical approaches to teaching and learning, and others had departmental (internal) professional development training to include but were not scholars of pedagogy.

Table 10.2 Backgrounds of Teacher Participants

Faculty Participants	
Experience with Teaching and Learning	*Description of experience*
1. Trained and experienced educators	1. Obtained a degree in education, which included preservice practicum/ field experiences in K–12 classrooms
2. Possess some teaching and learning experience	2. Received a certificate in teaching and learning, involved with educational centers and/or K–12 in some capacity
3. Possess content knowledge; pure content specialists	3. No previous training in teaching and learning

Source: Table created by authors using collected data.

Table 10.3 Backgrounds of Student Participants

Student Participants	
Previous Experience with Western-Trained Faculty Members	*Description of Experience*
1. Lots of interaction with expatriate teachers who were trained in countries with an individualistic culture	1. Attended a British or American private school in the UAE and/or attended an international university previously
2. Some interaction with expatriate teachers who were trained in countries with an individualistic culture	2. Attended a British or American school at some point but finished schooling at an Arabic-centered school
3. Limited interaction with expatriate teachers who were trained in countries with an individualistic culture	3. Attended a government school

Source: Data based on author survey.

Table 10.2 is significant for various reasons. Regarding faculty participants, table 10.2 demonstrates that not all faculty members were well trained or experienced; faculty had a range of training and experience in education. This could not influence how well the faculty members adapted to the teaching environment or current context. Regarding student participants, table 10.3 demonstrates the depth of experience students had with Western educational systems. Some had exclusively attended Western private schools in the UAE, some had been to both Western private schools and government schools, and others had only attended government schools during their K–12 years. Lastly, this table shows that students had different exposure to educational contexts. Some were used to learning within a Western context with Western teachers, while others had little to no contact to educational environments that differed from the UAE government schools.

ANALYSIS

Upon analysis, an asset-based pedagogy, particularly CRP, was the lens which helped determine the themes and codes present. The qualitative data from the interviews was analyzed using inductive content analysis which is the process of analyzing data by creating open codes which are combined with other codes when appropriate. These codes translate into themes and categories. To analyze this data, the researchers independently and collectively identified categories and subthemes that emerged from the interview questions. The researchers analyzed the data separately and together to ensure reliability (Creswell 2014).

FINDINGS

A number of themes emerged from the content analysis. Faculty members reported the following issues when working with students: culturally divergent views toward teaching and learning practices, misunderstanding the learning needs of the students, and not fully understanding students' motivations for learning. In addition, the findings further showed that: (1) collaborative learning and relationship building is integral to teaching and learning in this environment; (2) a pathway from traditional (banking), namely rote learning, models of teaching and learning to integrated models is needed; (3) differentiated learning should be central when teaching classes; (4) students need to feel empowered so that mistakes are seen as learning experiences rather than consequential errors.

One faculty member stated the following about cultural differences between teachers and students by emphasizing how different the local (Emirati) students are from other students they had taught in a different context:

> Like [in] Asian cultures teachers are revered. You do not challenge what the teacher says so the classroom culture is not a place for open discussion or debate. . . . These are the most respectful students that I have ever taught.

Open debate with teachers is not acceptable and perhaps causes students to feel a level of discomfort when asked to discuss their opinions. Not only did this faculty member discuss the cultural differences between students and faculty members, they also highlighted the cultural differences within Emirati culture due to generational differences. They further explained:

> They are also primarily first-generation college students so they haven't had experience with the norms because they haven't had parents or grandparents

with the experience so it is not a lived experience. The challenge with that is that while education might be respected by families, the specific norms of what is expected is not clear or understood.

The assumption is that while students understand the shift in demand from the previous generation, their families may not. For example, there is a balancing act between being a successful, career-oriented woman while continuing to play an integral role in family life. So, while individual faculty members may not have the power to focus on student-life balance, the university as a whole may want to consider instructional and curricular changes that holistically embeds aspects of this (Ojo, Falola and Mordi 2014).

Other students seemed to understand the lived experiences of their peers. They would often intervene and support students when they felt like there was a need. One faculty member explained:

> It's a very communal society and they take that into account. A whole group of girls will come into your office to plead the case for one of the other students even in situations of academic integrity. The family unit and society come first. There are levels of importance and higher education is not always at the top. It's important but not at the same level of importance as other things.

This quote demonstrates that the faculty member viewed student deference to teachers as both positive and negative. She appreciated the amount of respect given to faculty members but found students' reluctance to engage in classroom interaction as a barrier to learning. This aligns with a study conducted by Sonleitner and Khelifa (2005) who found that students often work better collaboratively and will visit faculty member's offices in groups. Perhaps collaborative learning as part of Emirati culture could be viewed as an asset rather than a shortcoming (Castagno & Brayboy, 2008).

While some students and faculty agreed that learning was demonstrated through application, some students focused solely on the grade. One student reflected that learning was "when I want to share it. Tell it to someone who does not know it" and that making mistakes was necessary in the learning process. "You have to make mistakes to learn. I prefer to make a mistake at the start. It's better." This shows that students are perhaps in greater alignment with faculty members as to what an ideal teaching and learning environment should look like, which includes safety when making mistakes. However, students' focus on achieving an "A" grade still serves as a barrier to engaging with the subject matter as faculty members had to readdress the purpose of learning and emphasize the importance of the application of learning. For example, one student stated that "an A is a good grade . . . a B is a bad grade." This focus on high grades was also highlighted in a study conducted by Freimuth (2014). A shift from extrinsic motivation to intrinsic motivation takes time to change and the spectrum is not easily defined. However, faculty members who are enthusiastic about their subject and can scaffold materials so that students can follow demonstrate the benefits of intrinsic motivation (Halawah, 2011).

Another issue that faculty members highlighted was the need to focus on intrinsic motivation from the beginning. One faculty member stated:

> I get students to open up at the start about their goals and aspirations. Not the short-term but the longer-term too. Students seem to think there is one major employer [the government]. They (the one major employer) would employ only Nationals . . . I try to tell them regardless of that you still need to know why you are doing something. Not just to graduate. I try to hit the intrinsic motivation aspects of being a professional for yourself.

Like with the focus on getting "A" grades as opposed to being able to apply knowledge, some students attended university with the aim of solely getting the degree to get a job. However, they need to understand that being effective and productive at a job means understanding how to apply the knowledge they have learned.

FACULTY PARTICIPANT RECOMMENDATIONS

Based on the data collected in this study, four suggestions and potential treatments can be made using data collected during the interviews:

(1) Collaborative Learning and Relationship Building Are Integral to Teaching and Learning

One faculty member highlighted the following as successful teaching and learning strategies in his class:

> Teaching strategies include project-based learning, group theory, group work, collaboration and student-centered topics. Letting students explore their own interests is effective in innovation coming up with an innovation in UAE society that they can develop.

Collaborative learning as an effective teaching and learning strategy in the UAE was backed by Halawah (2011) who stated that Emirati students work better in an educational environment when they are in groups than they do individually.

(2) Differentiated Learning Should Be Central When Teaching Classes

One faculty member discussed how differentiation was needed in classes due to language understanding and personality traits:

> Here if I give too many concepts they can't get this. Learning in a language other than their own. It's harder for them. I really want to assess but I tell them it will help them. Second, when I break them into groups, I try to engage with the less extraverted students so I can get the less verbal students to present their ideas.

Stafin (2008) also recommended more differentiation of instruction for a successful classroom in the UAE.

(3) Utilizing Funds of Knowledge While Moving Away from Banking Models Is Imperative

One faculty member stated that students relied on memorization as a primary learning strategy. A focus on rote learning in Emirati learning environments was also highlighted in a paper written by Ashencaen Crabtree (2010). For example, one faculty member emphasized this point when she said: "Actively engaged—does not happen here. They read the day before, memorize, spew back and then forget." However, she further explained that this may change: "it will change. Anytime I have a complaint, I just look at how far the country has come." She went on to provide an example of an innovative activity that she had used successfully with the students: "I made them do a 2 minute silent movie but it has to tell a story silently. A couple were screamingly funny."

Some students also want a more interactive and diverse learning experience. One student stated the following: "They (teachers at K12 schools) liked to give us activities, I learned more from activities than from things written on board." However, she continued to describe how the faculty members at the university compare with her K12 teachers: "More presentation and explaining . . . there is a PowerPoint—the teacher explains—I review the PowerPoint. It works for me but for some of my friends it doesn't. It would be better if there were more activities." This shows that at least some students have transitioned to a preference for active learning.

Even though faculty members and students recognized that active learning was preferential to rote learning, there were still some faculty members who claimed that the students needed a certain amount of rote learning. However, this could also be due to language issues where students relied on a certain amount of memorization to support their understanding of concepts in a second language.

(4) Students Need to Feel Empowered So That Mistakes Are Seen as Learning Experiences Rather Than Consequential Errors

This was evident through the data collected. Specifically, faculty reported that students were reluctant to answer questions and engage in activities for fear of making mistakes and being ostracized. One faculty member highlighted the need to model using mistakes as a reflective teaching tool:

> Mistakes—as learning opportunities. This has travelled with me since preschool. My expectation is that students will make mistakes because if they know this info already why am I even here. Sometimes consistent mistakes have to do with how I am teaching it so I use it as an opportunity to reflect on my own teaching.

The students' responses were mixed. Some saw mistakes as learning opportunities but also as a source of embarrassment. One student stated the following: "I do not want to participate after I've made a mistake. It's my fault. I feel people laugh at me." It is interesting to note that both students had limited exposure to Western-educated teachers.

DISCUSSION

Western teaching pedagogical practices often reflect the norms of monolingual, Euro-centric/white, middle-class education, which excludes students who come from diverse cultural and linguistic backgrounds (Diallo, 2012). Students who are excluded from these norms are often viewed through a deficit lens, which means that faculty may quickly and arbitrarily attribute poor academic performance to diverse student ethnic and/or cultural groups (Alnawar 2015; Ashencan 2010). Viewing students through such a lens creates a disservice and disruption to the teaching and learning process. One way to address this is through cultural adjustments of expat faculty. These types of adjustments are especially necessary when teaching in a different cultural context. Asset-based pedagogical approaches come into play as a necessary adjustment.

Western teaching pedagogical practices will sometimes situate cultural diversity and culture in odd ways. Hopkyns (2014) argues that culture is fluid. Culture is not static, rather it is dynamic and ever-changing. Faculty that embrace this notion can start to change their lens, views, and open up to having powerful teaching experiences to stimulate significant interactions with Emirati students. A mechanism that prompts faculty to question how educators can meaningfully utilize the culture of their students as a resource for classroom learning is needed. Advancing asset-based pedagogical approaches and practices, while addressing factors that inhibit, impede, or impact Emirati students' learning experience is one way to address this concern.

ADVANCING ASSET-BASED PEDAGOGICAL APPROACHES AND PRACTICES THROUGH CROSS-CULTURAL ADJUSTMENTS

Although educational practices and philosophies in the UAE are attempting to catch up with the latest reforms, cultural considerations must be taken into account at the same time. For example, independent learning rather than collectivist approaches could be divergent from the normal cultural practice. In the UAE, traditional Bedouin values, for instance, may conflict with educational pressures toward promoting learner autonomy and openness (Raven 2011). Furthermore, Raven (2011) argued that collectivist practices of local Emirati culture could conflict with the independent learning preferred by other expatriate cultures. Faculty need to recognize this along with the ways in which cultural aspects of a given group (i.e., collectivism) impact teaching and learning within the classroom (Engin & McKeown 2011). Iyer (2015) argues that in Western cultures, "students are encouraged to make mistakes and are seduced into errors which they reflect upon" (247) and that originality is highly praised, whereas in collectivist cultures learners are encouraged to conform to rules and regulations that are highly regulated.

Faculty should consider the cultural and linguistic challenges Emirati students face to communicate in their classes. Faculty should reflect on what they can do to address some of those challenges. Cultural misunderstandings happen, therefore, cross-cultural adjustments of faculty are critical (Austin et al. 2014). Familiarizing oneself with cultural values of students and how those might or might not be aligned with a faculty member's expectations is another way to remove cultural barriers. Faculty can make a conscious effort to develop intercultural agility as they learn about communication barriers from the students' point of view and discover ways to create a more welcoming line of communication (Sonleitner and Khalifa 2005).

ADVANCING ASSET-BASED PEDAGOGICAL APPROACHES AND PRACTICES THROUGH PEDAGOGICAL ADAPTATIONS

Another important faculty adjustment is pedagogical adaptation as it involves exploring teacher-student dimensions while teaching. Faculty that learn how to balance traditional teaching orthodoxies with more progressive ones are making progress. The best pedagogical adaptation is the implementation of a CRP. It enables and challenges faculty to rethink about what they do and why. CRP affords faculty with the opportunity to embrace and consider perspective differences of both their students and themselves. Additionally, it promotes progressive ideologies which include social competence, academic success, and critical consciousness (Ladson-Billings 1995). Teachers who embrace CRP develop and promote cultural competence, flexibility, and adaptability (Castagno & Brayboy 2008). Meeting halfway, reaching and teaching students through culturally rich and relevant ways bridge critical connections and relationships between faculty and students. CRP stems as a result of a qualitative shift in learning that is of interest and relevance to students, in addition to the multiple learning styles of students.

Faculty who adhere to traditional pedagogical paradigms and norms, which promote teacher-centered approaches must challenge their beliefs about teaching practices. Western-trained teachers can best support and accommodate their students if they adapt their positionality, choice of teaching material, textbooks, and culturally relevant pedagogical practices, to accommodate the cultural space (epistemologies, cultural and religious values) of their Emirati students (Austin et al. 2014; Blaik-Hourani, Diallo, & Said 2011).

CONCLUSION AND RECOMMENDATIONS: ONWARD AND UPWARD

We conclude this chapter with key recommendations for teaching by example through removing cultural barriers via a series of approaches and strategies. It is important to note that both faculty and students play integral roles in removing cultural barriers. Open communication and mutual collaboration to understand the context for learning is critical toward mitigating cultural clashes. Reevaluating and adjusting (unrealistic) expectations so as to be more appropriate and in line with the cultural context is an important process for expatriate faculty to undergo. Faculty should reflect on how they can help students feel more at ease communicating and expressing their learning experiences with them. Faculty should consider adopting a more student-centered communication-style approach.

It is incumbent upon both the expat university and the expat educator to understand the context in which they operate. Universities seeking to recruit Western-trained faculty must do their due diligence in understanding the teaching and learning implications of faculty formally trained in secular democracies. During the onboarding process of new faculty, universities must be obligated to orient new faculty to the culture of the university along with clearly defining teaching and learning expectations. Conversely, faculty must seek out understanding concerning the sociopolitical and cultural contexts in which they have been hired to teach in. Prior to joining an institution, faculty would be wise to actively seek out an understanding of the boundaries within which they are expected to teach and cautiously take into account the educational needs of their Emirati students.

Faculty should develop intercultural ability and agility in order to move across cultures in a way that is not just tolerant of conflicting perspectives, but that is accepting, considerate, and deeply respectful of students' lived experiences. Embracing the cultural richness and cultural diversity afforded in the classroom is one way to bring faculty and students together. Western-trained faculty should consider inviting Emirati students to a discussion on what they deem are pertinent ways to "teach and reach them" in addition to successful cross-cultural teaching strategies to use in higher educational settings.

Along with developing intercultural ability is the need for faculty to implement asset-based pedagogical approaches as learning has to be sustainable. To motivate students, learning should be renewed and imbued with a sense of empowerment. Beyond just CRP, culturally sustaining and revitalizing practices (CSRP) may ultimately allow, invite, and encourage best practices that in turn enable students' learning to flourish. It is plausible that such approaches may provide students with opportunities to not only use their cultural practices from home in school, but to maintain them. This in turn will motivate and engage students in learning. Additionally, it may be a mechanism that connects faculty and students in powerful ways as it bridges existing divides and disconnects. Implementing CSRP in a way which not only makes learning relevant, but also revitalizes and sustains Emirati culture in higher education classrooms is a promising practice. If faculty go beyond implementing a CRP to include sustaining and revitalizing instructional strategies and practices, a rich and robust culturally sustaining and responsive pedagogy can emerge.

REFERENCES

Alnawar, Hassan J. 2015. "Raising Teachers' Cultural Knowledge of Middle Eastern Students in the Classroom." Capstone Projects and Master's Theses. 504. https://digitalcommons.csumb.edu/caps_thes/504.

Alsharari, N. M. 2018. "Internationalization of the higher education system: An interpretive analysis." *International Journal of Educational Management* 32, no. 3: 359–381. https://doi.org/10.1108/IJEM-04-2017-0082,

Ashencaen Crabtree, Sara. 2010. "Engaging students from the United Arab Emirates in culturally responsive education." *Innovations in Education and Teaching International* 47, no. 1: 85–94.

Austin, A. E., Chapman, D. W., Farah, S. et al. 2014. "Expatriate academic staff in the United Arab Emirates: the nature of their work experiences in higher education institutions." *High Education Policy* 68: 541–557. https://doi.org/10.1007/s10734 -014-9727-z.

Blaik-Hourani, R., Diallo, I., & Said, A. 2011. "Teaching in the Arabian Gulf: arguments for the deconstruction of the current educational model." In Christina Gitsaki (Ed.), *Teaching and Learning in the Arab World* (335–355). Lausanne Switzerland: Peter Lang Publishing Co.

Chapman, D., Austin, A., Farah, S., Wilson, E., & Ridge, N. 2014. "Academic staff in the UAE: Unsettled journey." *Higher Education Policy* 27: 131–151.

Creswell, John W. 2014. *A Concise Introduction to Mixed Methods Research.* Thousand Oaks, California: SAGE Publications.

Diallo, I. 2014. "Emirati students encounter Western teachers: tensions and identity resistance." *Learning and Teaching in Higher Education: Gulf Perspectives* 11, no. 2: 9.

Engin, Marion, and McKeown, Kara. 2016. "Motivation of Emirati Males and Females to Study at Higher Education in the United Arab Emirates." *Journal of Further and Higher Education* 41, no. 5: 678–691. doi:10.1080/0309877x.2016.1159293.

Freimuth, H. 2020. "Who are our students? A closer look at the educational and socio-cultural influences that have shaped Emirati students." *The KUPP Journal* (3): 37–48. Retrieved December 1, from http://www.kustar.ac.ae/source/academics /prepprogram/kupp-journal-issue3-june2014.pdf 2014.

Garson, Bonnie. 2005. "Teaching abroad: A cross-cultural journey." *Journal of Education for Business* 80, no. 6: 322–326.

Halawah, I. 2011. "Factors influencing college students' motivation to learn from students perspectives." *Education*, 132, no. 2: 379.

Halbach, Ana. 2002. "Exporting methodologies: The reflective approach in teacher training." *Language Culture and Curriculum* 15, no. 3: 243–250.

Hopkyns, Sarah. 2014. "The effect of global English on culture and identity in the UAE: A double-edged sword." *Learning and Teaching in Higher Education: Gulf Perspectives* 11, no. 2: 1.

Hopkyns, Sarah. 2017. "A conflict of desires: global English and its effects on cultural identity in the United Arab Emirates" (Doctoral dissertation, University of Leicester).

James, A. & Shammas, N. 2018. "Teacher care and motivation: a new narrative for teachers in the Arab Gulf." *Pedagogy, Culture & Society* 26, no. 4: 491–510. DOI :10.1080/14681366.2017.1422275.

Ladson-Billings, Gloria. 2014. "Culturally Relevant Pedagogy 2.0: a.k.a. the Remix." *Harvard Educational Review* 84, no. 1: 74–84.

Li, J. 2016. "Chinese University 3.0 in a global age: History, modernity and future." In P. C. I. Chou & J. Spangler (Eds.), *Chinese Education Models in a Global Age: Transforming Practice into Theory* (pp. 15–35). Singapore: Springer.

Ojo, Ibiyinka Stella, Hezekiah Olubusayo Falola, and Chima Mordi. 2014. "Work life balance policies and practices: A case study of Nigerian female university students." *European Journal of Business and Management* 6, no. 12: 3–14.

Paris, D. & Alim, H. 2014. "What are we seeking to sustain through culturally sustaining pedagogy?" A loving critique forward. *Harvard Educational Review* 84, no. 1: 85–100.

Rapanta, C. 2014. "'Insha' Allah I'll do my homework': adapting to Arab undergraduates at an English-speaking University in Dubai." *Learning and Teaching in Higher Education: Gulf Perspectives* 11, no. 2: 8.

Raven, J. 2011. "Emiratizing the education sector in the UAE: Contextualization and challenges." Education, Business and Society: Contemporary Middle Eastern Issues.

Russell, A. 2004. "Zayed University students' teaching and learning beliefs and preferences: An analysis based on the surface versus deep learning approach." Learning and Teaching in Higher Education: Gulf Perspectives, 1. Accessed December 30, 2020 http://www.zu.ac.ae/lthe/vol1/lthe01_01.html.

Saji, B. S., & Nair, A. R. 2018. "Effectiveness of innovation and entrepreneurship education in UAE higher education." *Academy of Strategic Management Journal*, 17, no. 4: 1–12.

Saudelli, Mary Gene. 2012. "Unveiling Third Space: A Case Study of International Educators in Dubai, United Arab Emirates." *Canadian Journal of Education* 35, no. 3: 101–116.

Setting IELTS entry scores. (n.d.). Accessed February 18, 2021, from https://www.ielts.org/for-organisations/setting-ielts-entry-scores.

Solloway, A. 2016. "English-medium instruction in higher education in the United Arab Emirates: The perspectives of students" (Doctoral dissertation). Retrieved from Open Research Exeter.

Sonleitner, N., & Khalifa, Mohammad. 2005. "Western-educated faculty challenges in a Gulf classroom." *Learning and Teaching in Higher Education: Gulf Perspectives* 2, no. 1, 1–21.

Sperrazza, Lelania. 2012. "A clash of cultural identities in the UAE." *International Journal of Arts & Sciences* 5, no. 7, 297.

Stafin, S. 2008. "Arab tertiary student perspectives of effective teachers." *Learning and Teaching in Higher Education: Gulf Perspectives* 5, no. 2. http://www.zu.ac.ae/lthe/lthe05_02_saafin.htm.

Standards: for Institutional Licensure and Program Accreditation. 2019. Accessed February 1, 2021 https://www.caa.ae/caParisa/images/Standards2019.pdf.

UAE National Agenda. 2021. "*Education Vision 2021.*" Abu Dhabi: UAE. 2010. Accessed January 5, 2021. https://www.vision2021.ae/en/national-agenda-2021.

Website, MOE. 2021. "Ministry of Education Strategic Plan 2017–2021." Ministry of Education. Accessed March 14, 2021. https://www.moe.gov.ae/En/AboutThe Ministry/Pages/MinistryStrategy.aspx.

Zajda, J. & Rust, V. 2016. "Current research trends in globalization and neo-liberalism in higher education." In J. Zajda & V. Rust (Eds.), *Globalisation and Higher Education Reforms* (pp. 1–19). Switzerland: Springer.

Chapter 11

Stimulating High Intellectual Challenge through Culturally Responsive Pedagogy

United Arab Emirates Educator Perspectives

Nadeem A. Memon, Deborah Price,
Deborah Green, and Dylan Chown

INTRODUCTION—COHESIVE SOCIETY
AND PRESERVED IDENTITY

Preserving local culture and heritage is a national priority in the United Arab Emirates (UAE). For the past seven years, "Cohesive Society and Preserved Identity" has been one of the six national priorities of the UAE National Agenda 2021 (UAE Vision 2021). Within national policy, the majority expatriate and diminishing local Emirati populations in the country have remained a central consideration. Fostering a "cohesive society" is intended to create an "inclusive environment" where expatriates feel welcome in sharing diverse beliefs, cultures, and religious practices. Social cohesion, however, is coupled within a social fabric that exemplifies the UAE's national identity, culture, heritage, and traditions. The two-pronged commitment of social cohesion and preserved national identity remain, and likely will continue to define the UAE's social context.

In the private education sector, this commitment is equally reflected in performance standards and curriculum. For example, in the Dubai School Inspections Bureau (DSIB) protocol, one of the six overall indicators in school performance is "Students' personal and social development" that includes a measure of "Understanding of Islamic values and awareness of Emirati and world cultures" (DSIB Inspection Reports 2019). Schools are measured on their ability to display an appreciation of the UAE and its

179

traditions, demonstrate a solid understanding of Islamic values, and nurture pride of students' individual and world cultures. Sample enactments of this commitment by schools rated "Outstanding" by the DSIB include educational initiatives that promote Islamic values of tolerance and kindness (e.g., outreach programs to help the needy in Ramadan); national celebrations including National Day, Flag Day, and Commemoration Day; and school displays, student projects, and assemblies that reflect pride in world cultures (DSIB Inspection Reports 2019). With respect to curriculum, private schools are expected to integrate UAE Social Studies curriculum expectations in a cross-curricular manner within the school's existing social studies program. Outstanding schools exemplify this through high levels of critical thinking with respect to issues of the environment and economic development in the UAE. Similar sentiments can be found in performance standards and curriculum approaches by the Abu Dhabi Department of Education and Knowledge (ADEK) that oversee private school inspections in the province, and the Ministry of Education (MoE) that supports public schools across the country.

Despite the commitment toward social cohesion and national identity described through DSIB protocol, both public and private schools in the UAE are challenged by an increasingly pervasive educational context of accountability and performativity. The very National Agenda 2021 that prioritized preserving identity also lists a "First Rate Education System" as a national priority—of which seven of twelve key performance indicators, relate to student performance on international assessments related to math, science, and reading. The Organization for Economic Co-operation and Development's (OECD) Programme for International Student Assessment (PISA) and International Association for the Evaluation of Educational Achievement (IEA) Trends in International Mathematics and Science Study (TIMSS) international assessments also feature as a core focus on DSIB school inspection reports, with a dedicated section related to what is referred to as the "National Agenda Parameter." Significant pressure on schools, educators, and particularly students, is a reality in the UAE whereby school inspection reports are publicly available, school ranking is commonplace, school choice is market-driven, and educational quality is primarily measured by student performance. A narrow focus on measuring subjects deemed "core" (e.g., math, science, and language) places significant implications on pedagogical and curriculum innovation, educator efficacy, and student well-being, at the expense of educational priorities such as cultural understanding that we would argue are inextricably linked. It is not uncommon, for example, to see statements such as the following in the inspection reports of schools ranked "Outstanding": "Program results are impressive across all subjects. Students are less successful in Islamic Education and Arabic than in other subjects" (DSIB Inspection Key Findings 2018–2019). Notably, the 2016 analysis of UAE school inspections reports found that not one private school in the UAE that was already ranked "Outstanding" had achieved a subject ranking of "Outstanding" in Islamic Education or Arabic (ADUKG Road to Outstanding). In the same vein, in 2018, less than 50 percent of ninth-grade students attained high skills in Arabic language on the national MoE test in both public and private sectors (UAE Vision 2021). School inspection reports and national test results consistently illustrate how schools that perform academically and meet accountability standards are able to circumvent commitments to UAE culture and heritage with mediocre attempts of preserving national identity and fostering social cohesion. In the Australian context, similar pressures where schools must "ascribe to the narrow vision of education promoted by performative demands" has led to a "degrading of curriculum and pedagogy" and the sidelining of the "social, creative, aesthetic, cultural, moral and spiritual aspects of students' development" (Keddie 2017, 383).

This chapter thereby centers the perspective of educators in the UAE in relation to employing culturally responsive pedagogy (CRP) as essential within their educational philosophy and practice. For the UAE education context, we employ CRP to provide an important theoretical shift in the way the two-pronged national priorities of fostering social cohesion while acknowledging the relevance of local culture and heritage are achieved. We posit that CRP's commitment to learner lifeworlds, that is, "the subjective nature of everyday life" including their embodied, spatial, relational, and past, present, and future experiences (Connelly 2015, 119), provides the necessary language to acknowledge the complex identities of both expatriates and local Emiratis and the intersecting narratives in a globalized world. We rely on the conceptual frame of CRP with the hope that it may offer the necessary theoretical shift from conventional intercultural efforts that are commonly enacted in schools as celebratory cultural awareness initiatives to authentic pedagogies advocating social cohesion and preserving identities. CRP extends conceptions of intercultural understanding by proposing the task is not just about "learning from diversity" or "building cultural understanding," rather that the cultural and religious ways students know the world are learning assets educators need to draw upon.

As chief investigators of a Department of Foreign Affairs and Trade (DFAT), Council of Australia-Arab Relations (CAAR) grant in 2020, we conducted "educator roundtables" at two universities providing teacher education programs (one public and one private), and four private schools in the UAE. The empirical data in this chapter is composed of the voices of 350 educators exploring "Cultural Preparedness to Teach in the Middle East." This study is an extension of the collaborative work the coauthors contribute to CRP at the University of South Australia, including membership with the Centre for Research in Educational and Social Inclusion (CRESI) in

Adelaide, Australia. Collectively, the coauthors contribute to the Education Futures Unit initiative, committed to embedding CRP across preservice and in-service teacher education and research programs. Additionally, one of the coauthors (Memon) previously worked in the UAE as an education consultant with a focus on professional development for educators on CRP, most notably as a coauthor of ADEK's "My Identity" curriculum (EdArabia 2015) for all private schools in Abu Dhabi. Together, the experience of the local context and collective expertise in CRP facilitated critical discussions during the educator roundtables of this study.

This chapter will begin with a conceptual description of CRP to establish the lens through which the coauthors have approached and analyzed the data. The methodology will then follow describing how, where, and when "educators roundtables" took place. The findings organize educator perspectives around key themes that include a particular emphasis on existing practices, contextual challenges, and essential aspirations that were expressed about the potential of CRP in the UAE. The chapter concludes with an analysis of educator voice in relation to a robust conception of CRP and how responsive pedagogy can be embedded pedagogically to stimulate high intellectual challenge within high-stakes educational contexts, while prioritizing the preservation of national identity and further fostering and achieving sustained social cohesion.

CONCEPTUALIZING CULTURALLY RESPONSIVE PEDAGOGY

This study is located at the confluence of several intersecting areas of research within the larger field of education, and more specifically, teacher education and preparation. The geneses of our theoretical underpinning are within the literature archive of critical pedagogy, purposefully drilling down into additional conceptual frames of "New Pedagogy Studies" (Green 2003) and "Culturally Responsive Pedagogy" (Hattam & Zipin 2009; Morrison, Rigney, Hattam, & Diplock 2019). We argue that together these can assist in situating our analysis of educator perspectives on pedagogical practice across private and public schooling in the UAE in ways that stimulate high intellectual challenge within a high-stakes educational context, while not losing sight of national identity and sustained social cohesion priorities. They offer a lens not only responsive to the national policy commitment around appreciation of local culture and heritage in schools in the UAE, but to critical engagement with orientations and practice deliberations around intercultural understanding.

Important to this study, New Pedagogy Studies seek to advance and invigorate debates inside of critical pedagogy (Hattam & Zipin 2009) and stimulate "new movements in pedagogical thinking" to link classroom practice with both educative and ethical purposes (Hattam & Zipin 2009, 298). Our situatedness within New Pedagogy Studies (Green 2003) is further motivated by the shift from related themes associated with curriculum as the site for struggle around justice, to that of pedagogy (Hattam & Zipin 2009). This reflects the important lens that we applied to this study, by leading with and mobilizing a more expansive view of pedagogy to center educational practice (Hattam & Zipin 2009).

CRP as our principle conceptual frame is an extension of critical and new pedagogies. CRP reflects and enables a further theoretical shift to lift our analysis beyond the reifying of culture in cultural awareness approaches, and for avoiding foreclosed assumptions for a curriculum-centric insertion of additional intercultural content, to allow deeper considerations on pedagogical opportunities that draw on diverse, rich and complex cultural traditions. We understand CRP to be authentic pedagogies capable of recognizing and respecting local knowledges and local lifeworlds of learners. CRP is inclusive of the cultural and religious ways learners know the world, and as learning assets for the diverse largely expatriate educator population. This was viewed as a necessary lens for our inquiry on educator perspectives on employing CRP within the UAE.

CONCEPTUALIZATION OF CULTURALLY RESPONSIVE PEDAGOGY

We rely on a nuanced conceptual description of CRP to establish the lens through which the coauthors have approached and analyzed the data. We contend that

> CRPs respond to students' identities by respecting, valuing and drawing on these attributes and rich histories and lived experiences, provide a powerful foundation for not only deeper learning in educational settings, but also relevant connections with lifeworlds beyond the classroom for life-long learning. (Price & Green 2019 in Price, Green, Memon, & Chown 2020, 42)

We understand CRP as "those pedagogies that actively value, and mobilize as resources, the cultural repertoires and intelligences that students bring to the learning relationship" (Morrison et al. 2019, v). This is neatly encompassed in what Morrison et al. (2019) outline as the principles of CRP, as involving "high expectations; quality relationships; diversity as an asset; connected to students' life-worlds; and socio-political consciousness" (20–22). We add to this, a respect for the religious identities and ways of knowing of learners, what Memon and Chown (forthcoming) argue expands CRP to include being "religiously responsive."

The conceptualization of CRP in this study also entails a significant and explicit orientation of cultural humility (Tervalon & Murray-Garcia 1998) over cultural competence. This is purposeful in avoiding a detached notion of mastery over skills and information about cultures (Tervalon & Murray-Garcia 1998). This conceptual orientation, we argue, allows for critical reflexivity and critical reflection, necessary if intercultural understanding is to be a "truth seeking encounter, a 'process of mutual transformation' which goes beyond trying to understand the 'other' but reaches out to a new level of mutual self-understanding" (Hanezell-Thomas 2018, 12). Cultural humility over cultural competence in this study is premised on our concern that essentialized or decontextualized "knowing" about culture or religion may impede rather than assist in "getting to know" learners' unique lifeworlds, or in identifying learner strengths and that of local communities. For our educators, whose perspectives we sought, this does not inquire into their "knowing" of culture or religion, rather from an orientation of humility (Carey 2015; Freire 1998; Nolan 2016; Reid 2017), it allows exploration of educator perspectives on forms of relationality they employ in "getting to know" their learners and their lifeworlds. With reference to teaching in diverse environments, Reid (2017) argues that educators who lack humility to look and learn, before they teach, can only reproduce what they already know, limiting the learning of learners. We are convinced with Reid (2017), who argues, "humility is necessary if educators are to find out how to learn from and with their learners" (211). Aligned with research on CRP (Esteban-Guitart & Moll 2014; Morrison et al. 2019), we approach this study foregrounded with the belief that local contexts count, that orientations of humility facilitate asset-based views and relationships that enable asset-based pedagogies, and encourage critical reflection, and that engagement with lifeworlds and high intellectual challenge are complementary.

EDUCATOR ROUNDTABLES IN THE UAE: METHODOLOGY

The coauthors facilitated "educator roundtables" at four schools and two universities in Dubai between January 20 and 24, 2020, to share conceptions of CRP and gain understandings of the Gulf context in being responsive in culturally diverse classrooms. "Educator roundtables" supported our aspirations to learn from educator voices and foster dialogue between the diverse lived and professional experiences of the educators we met.

Our methodological approach of "educator roundtables": (a) acknowledged the unique contexts and experiences of particular school sites; and (b) facilitated

discussions across the varied professional experiences of the participating educators (Ladwig & White 1996). The approach also reinforced for participants
that a participatory culture is necessary for school reform (Cushman 1995) and
with the intent that collegial critical reflective discussions will foster owner-
ship and commitment toward change (Ladwig & White 1996). Roundtables
were held for approximately two hours and were co-facilitated by the coauthors through a combination of whole group and small group discussions.
Roundtables began with a whole group discussion on "who are our learners?"
to unpack the lived experiences, home cultures, and expressions of identity of
the students in our classrooms. Small group roundtables were then facilitated
by each of the four coauthors with the following conceptual frames:

a. What Does Being Culturally Responsive Mean? (Deborah Price)
b. It's about Pedagogy Not More Curriculum (Deborah Green)
c. Drawing on Learning Assets (Dylan Chown)
d. Complexity within Diversity (Nadeem Memon)

Small group roundtables returned for a "Consolidating of Big Ideas" whole
group discussion and concluding by discussion on "Implications for Practice."
Schools and universities were identified through the first coauthor's existing
professional relationships with educators and academics in the region. All
of the participating schools in both contexts were from the private sector
whereas universities included both public and private sector institutions and
particularly Schools of Education. The number of participating educators in
each group varied anywhere between 25 and 100. A total of 220 participants
were involved in the educator roundtables.

Data from the roundtables were captured through written brainstorming
on large chart paper in whole groups discussions and on individual sticky
notes for individual reflection. Participant names were kept anonymous
throughout the written reflective exercises. All reflective brainstorming was
collected and transcribed to form the data corpus of this study. Transcriptions
were then analyzed and thematically organized using key concepts related to
CRP, such as learning assets, learner diversity, deficit thinking, performativity, and so on. Analysis of the data acknowledged that educational practice
occurs in particular classrooms that are located in particular communities and
sociopolitical contexts. Our analysis of the data intended to make visible the
dispositions and knowledges that inform educational decision-making and
practices of the educators we met (Edwards-Groves & Grootenboer 2015).
The chapter now turns toward educator perspectives from the roundtables.
Educator voices are italicized and often captured through short phrases as
opposed to long quotations in order to draw on collective responses shared
during group brainstorming.

EDUCATOR PERSPECTIVES:
UNDERSTANDINGS, OPPORTUNITIES,
AND CHALLENGES

Engaging in conversations with those entrusted with education in the UAE, including teacher educators, preservice and in-service teachers, professional staff, school leaders, and researchers, uncovered an overwhelming aspiration toward CRP that embraces deeper relationships, connectedness, and sense of belonging within diverse educational communities. Prioritizing CRP in educational philosophy and practice was advocated as affording inspiration of high intellectual challenge within all students, thereby enhancing academic achievement, social cohesion, and preservation of national identity, a recognized national priority. Emerging from these dialogic interactions were three key priorities in aiming to apply CRP as an educator within the UAE:

1) a strong desire to deeply examine the notion of CRP within local contexts in aiming to come to shared understandings, responsibility, and commitment to inform future educational practice
2) aspirations to focus on the opportunities that CRP affords and the enabling factors that translate CRP's theory into educational practice as a way of increasing high intellectual challenge, educational engagement, and connectedness
3) importance of identifying challenges to enacting CRP, with shared commitment and problem-solving to create new possibilities and recommendations for future policy and practice

In applying CRP to our conversations with educators, we began by sharing our local histories, contexts, and lived experiences, before inviting educators to share their histories and experiences as well as those of their learners. In modeling CRP, we began to learn from one another, acknowledge the richness of diversity within each community, and build initial trusting and collegial relationships (Price et al. 2020). This enabled critical dialogue across the three themes and five subthemes that will now be explored in detail with implications for applying CRP in educational practice.

Theme 1: Understandings of CRP That Inform Shared
Responsibility and Commitment

As learner contexts become ever-increasingly diverse in culture, linguistic, gender, religion, and ability, educators need to move away from being trapped into adopting mono-cultural approaches to acknowledging that particular forms of teaching advantage learners and others forms disadvantage some learners (Morrison et al. 2019). Conversations with UAE educators revealed that for some, CRP was "not new" rather was seen as "quality education" and "best practice." They explained that with increasing internationalism, "people are relocating more than ever in the history of humanity. Diversity is the new culture." Recognizing diversity within diversity is important and while it is impossible for an educator to know everything about every culture, it is crucial that a learner's lifeworld, for which culture is an important part, is embedded in their learning. The common challenge raised by participants was in how to fully achieve this goal particularly within contemporary UAE visions that advocate a knowledge economy arguably underpinned by an educational climate prioritizing performativity, standardized testing, and accountability. Central to this was to work toward a deep shared understanding of CRP as there were a range of definitions presented.

CRP is often defined in literature as a "socially mediated process" that is "related to students' cultural experiences" (Irvine 2010, 58); that is, learning is holistic, anti-deficit, and socially and culturally mediated (Rizvi & Lingard 2009; Wink & Putney 2002). Embracing this, many educators in the UAE highlighted the importance of relationships and listening to individuals and "valuing the child," while "try[ing] to know more from the child" as being key in defining CRP. Being aware of cultural values and beliefs was central in participant dialogue along with valuing, acknowledging, and not judging differences and creating an environment of acceptance. The words "appreciate," "respect," and "accept" were common themes expressed by participants.

By engaging in rich dialogue in defining CRP, educators began shifting from initial references of surface-level cultural awareness and multicultural educational approaches of "accepting different cultures" or teaching about "clothes, food and society" or "making one day for all different cultures." They also began critiquing their own language with potential negative tones of having to "deal with diversity" to learning from other cultures. Through the roundtable discussions, we felt a critical consciousness began to emerge where participants began acknowledging how CRP required more than "learning from diversity" but rather requires an "ethically responsible pedagogy" that is beyond tokenistic cultural days and toward drawing on who and what shapes learners lived experiences authentically. In the words of some participants, CRP involves "recognizing the teachable moments as they occur" and promoting truth-seeking encounters to foster mutual self-understanding that includes "cultural enrichment through openness that is two way rather than cultural responsiveness." This requires critical consciousness, cultural humility, and self-reflection of one's own history, lifeworld experiences, cultural values and beliefs, and positionality, as well as—in the words of our participants—"listening, learning from them [learners] without holding judgement," "putting ourselves in other's shoes" and learning about the "many layers within the same culture" that are foundational to codesigning teaching and learning experiences.

In fostering shared understandings of CRP, educators were asked to formulate what they believed to be the underpinning principles of CRP. Their responses are outlined as follows with participant collective perspectives captured in italics:

- Promote continual responsiveness to local histories and lifeworld experiences as "culture is living, changing, developing" and to reflect "lifelong learning" of educators and learners.
- Apply cultural humility in understanding and "prioritizing connecting lifeworlds and funds of knowledge" to facilitate the "cultural asset-based" perceptions of learners and approaches to teaching and learning.
- Foster "authentic" "relationships," "connectedness" and mutual self-understandings.
- "Value perspectives, lenses, awareness of cultural constructs in meaning," and "various ways of viewing the world, living, being."
- Advocate "high expectation for depth . . . culture, respect, relationships and reconciliation."
- Promote "safe," "critically reflective," and "dialogical" encounters and interactions that embrace "languages" are "student-centered" and empower "voices."
- Promote "integrity" where "teachers believe" in embedding CRP and "live what we are teaching."
- Necessitate equality through advancing equity: "to be equal to one another" and "teaching without making hierarchy . . . ignoring cultures" to "create a world where we live together peacefully" which requires mobilizing resources to address inequities.

The passion for being able to apply these principles in practice was critically debated, particularly raising the local and global contextual sociopolitical influences that both enable and challenge the translation of CRP's theory into everyday educational practice and with a central tenet of how to sustain local knowledges, cultures, and histories that are foundational to the local contexts.

Theme 2: Enabling Factors Translating CRP Theory into Educational Practice

What was noticeable in engaging in critical dialogue with educators in the UAE was the proposition that embedding CRP's principles and application to educational policy and practice was core to advance high intellectual challenge and academic achievement. By drawing on the diverse, rich, and complex cultural traditions, local knowledges, and local lifeworlds of learners, learners see themselves and their local histories and lived experiences in their education and learning experiences. The following are factors UAE educators felt enabled them to do CRP.

Enabler 1: Embracing Diversity and Culture as Assets. Gay (2010, 26) defines CRP as teaching "to and through [students'] personal and cultural strengths, their intellectual capabilities, and their prior accomplishments"; something that was echoed in the practices of the educators that we spoke with, who viewed culture as an asset and an entry point for learning. Valuing all learner's cultural heritage and seeing this as an asset enables all learners to be visible in the curriculum thus differing from cultural competence which is "a set of congruent behaviors, attitudes and policies that come together in a system or agency or among professionals that enable effective interactions in a cross-cultural framework" (Cross et al. 1989, iv).

Across the UAE the passion to embrace CRP and the local culture was noticeable, with many educators highlighting the need to "appreciate other cultures, norms and traditions." Yet, there was a sense for some that the "teacher needs to be the holder of all knowledge" suggesting there is a need to "learn more" and "read about my student's culture and also know different words." Considerable debate on how this challenges educators who already experience accountability with high expectations on high-stakes testing results within their diverse classrooms. The affordances of CRP were thereby central in collegial problem-solving conversations in supporting educators to increase their efficacy to integrate pedagogies that support their learning and knowledge of all learner's backgrounds, histories, culture, that is, the "virtual backpacks" (Thompson 2002) they bring to their educational settings. Participating educators expressed that when they have the flexibility to be facilitators of dialogue as opposed to being pressured to teach to the test, they are able to increasingly stimulate intellectual challenge. Many emphasized wanting to draw on the "voice and agency of students" in "negotiation in learning and assessment," "promoting openness, curiosity," and "engag[ing] them [learners] in research and finding solutions." CRP's commitment to flipping the discourse from culture as a barrier to viewing lifeworld experiences as assets resonated with UAE educators we felt. There was a concerted recognition that CRP could deepen learning through solving real-world problems that matter to learners. As one participant claimed, "diversity is an asset . . . embrace it."

Enabler 2: Applying Affective Pedagogies: "Care and Know the Students." It is well documented that educators are drawn to the relational profession due to a deep care for building strong connections and commitment to positively making a difference in young people's lives, both academically and their well-being. We note the role CRP plays in supporting learner well-being understanding that:

Wellbeing is diverse and fluid respecting individual, family and community beliefs, values, experiences, culture, opportunities and contexts across time and change. It encompasses intertwined individual, collective and environmental elements which continually interact across the lifespan. Wellbeing is something we all aim for, underpinned by positive notions, yet is unique to each of us and provides us with a sense of who we are which needs to be respected. Our role . . . is to provide the opportunity, access, choices, resources and capacities for individuals and communities to aspire to their unique sense of wellbeing, whilst contributing to a sense of community wellbeing. (Price & McCullum 2016, 5–6)

It was suggested by participants that CRP has the potential to positively influence learner well-being through prioritizing and embedding their cultural and religious identities within their education across curriculum, pedagogy, and assessment.

Specifically, CRP supports learner well-being through applying "ethics of care," whereby the dignity and integrity of learners is honored (Starratt 2014) through open and trusting relationships (Harris et al. 2019). Many of our participants reflected similar sentiments regarding the enabling factors for CRP. The affective dimension of participants' professions offered them an opportunity to be "compassionate," to show "empathy by understanding and sharing knowledge in a respectful manner considering cultural differences" and "allowing others to tell narratives in a safe way." Participants continued by emphasizing that a commitment to an affective pedagogical practice not only involves listening to learners and learning more about individuals but also developing empathy for differences in beliefs, values, and worldviews. Participants particularly felt that a national commitment in the UAE of a "family-focused society" reflects the ethics of care and affective pedagogies they aspire for.

Enabler 3: Drawing from Learner Lifeworlds. Among the themes of discussion during our educator roundtables was the fostering of a strong sense of belonging as being critical for academic success and well-being (Baumeister & Leary 1999). Employing teaching practices that value the learner and their lifeworlds is, therefore, critical to success. Literature highlights the need to ensure all learners are successful and educators need to employ pedagogical approaches that ensure that their cultural and behavioral norms are reflected in their pedagogy and curriculum (Gay 2002). It is commonly cited that learners engage when their lifeworlds are the focus of planning and their funds of knowledge are drawn upon, for some, religion is a part of their "virtual schoolbag" (Thompson 2002). We felt that the idea of drawing on learner lifeworlds resonated for the educators we met. Many spoke about co-construction and codesign of learning that they already do and could appreciate how the ideas of lifeworlds are embedded in such dialogical processes.

For example, during discussions some participants responded with the following: "Every learner has their own lifeworlds . . . experiences of culture . . . big part for us," that is, "through lived experiences of students, merged and layered experiences" and "when you know the learner worlds . . . more connections" in learning and relationships are opened. Participants began to collectively appreciate that learner cultures and by virtue lifeworlds require dialogue and facilitated opportunities for meaning-making. Matthews (2019) identifies, "all knowledge is heavily grounded in a cultural worldview. We simply need to recognize this and see it as an opportunity for students to move freely within their worldview . . . to engage with ideas and concepts" (146). This shifts a "rigid, objective discipline focus . . . to a creative process in which students can engage in . . . thinking and express their ideas through their own language and creativity" (Matthews 2019, 146).

Theme 3: Challenges to CRP in the UAE

Challenge 1: Dangers of Essentializing Culture. The diversity across and within educational contexts posed challenges for some educators, including the "diversity within culture" and changing "cultural dynamics," influenced by "generational change." While preserving local culture and heritage was understood to be a national priority, issues of generational change were posed. For example, one participant shared "that our culture does not accept new things for example, before many years it was not accepted that women work for many families." In the words of another educator, "to introduce a new trend to the society with a specific culture they have followed for years like the education of a woman, they were angry with me . . . didn't have a positive response." Additionally, concerns were also raised of sensitivities of essentializing Emirati culture as one or similarly other expatriate cultures being assumed to be one and the same. Deeply underpinning discussions were questions in relation to how to approach "culturally sensitive" topics with learners, educators, and local communities, given diversity of individual worldviews, beliefs, values, and norms.

In advancing the potential affordance of CRP to address these concerns, the Ethics of Justice approach, advocates for "the rights of individual staff and students and also the fair distribution of resources" and challenges educators to meet the needs of all students, while also promoting "ethics of critique, ask[ing] educators to adopt a critical stance that questions which groups or individuals are privileged or disadvantaged by current systems" (Harris et al. 2019, 251). Applying a whole school inquiry approach to addressing these issues collectively was suggested by some participants and to "start to see real life and purpose in curriculum" through a culturally diverse lens. Other suggestions that participants brainstormed to respond to this challenge of essentializing cultures included applying CRP across the curriculum, using an ethical critique to question biases, and critically approaching mandated curriculum for what worldviews are informing particular perspectives. Matthews (2019) reinforces the ideas collectively raised by UAE educators in a similar vein: "All knowledge is heavily grounded in a worldview. We simply need to recognize this and see it as an opportunity for students to move freely within their worldview to engage with [discipline] thinking" (146).

Challenge 2: Constrained by Performativity Demands. While prioritizing commitment to learner achievement, educators consistently described feeling constrained by high-performativity expectations within school contexts. This was compounded by efforts at accommodating both the diversity of learner populations and the preserving of the local population's history and culture. In applying ethical critique, educators questioned, "How do we define success?" "How do we push back against the qualitative/scientific model that doesn't recognize let alone value diversity?" as reflected with the challenges of standardized assessments, high-stakes testing, and prescriptive syllabus. Being solution focused, some educators recognized that "changing the way that students learn and teachers teach" is needed. That is, by providing open-ended and inquiry-based learning rather than traditional teacher-directed models, would over time, "gradually . . . provide higher grades." We felt there was a shared sentiment among participants that lifeworld pedagogies of CRP can stimulate high intellectual challenge and stronger professional commitment. As described by some participants, CRP facilitates a "strength-based curriculum approach" that is centered on "relationships," "expectations," and learner "lifeworlds." Participants expressed that seeing diversity as an asset will help educators in the UAE to recognize the need to be upfront and be intentional in planning from beginning.

CONCLUSION

This chapter began by acknowledging UAE's commitment toward fostering social cohesion and intercultural understanding with an ongoing recognition for local culture and heritage. Both private and public schools along with teacher education programs in the UAE play a critical role in working toward this national commitment. Using a theoretical lens of CRP, we sought to explore what enables or constrains educators from enacting pedagogy that is culturally responsive in the UAE. Through a series of educator roundtables, we discovered an overwhelming aspiration among educators in the UAE toward embracing the diverse lifeworlds of their learners. The foundational thinking of CRP was not new for the educators we met. There was an appetite for embracing learner cultural assets, enacting reflexivity, and promoting well-being. However, educators felt constrained by an educational context of performativity and accountability. Educators expressed that the potential of high intellectual challenge through a responsive pedagogy is hindered by pressures to perform. Through engaging with educators, we left with a sense of optimism that CRP may positively contribute toward drawing on the diverse lived experiences of expatriate educators and learners while at the same time serving as a lens through which the complexities within Emirati national heritage can be understood. Each of our roundtables reflected this two-pronged priority in the UAE. CRP allowed for the intersections between the common binaries of public/private schools, Emirati/expatriate experience, and local/global cultures to manifest. CRP is commonly used to address minoritized learners in Western contexts; however, in this chapter, the discussions with educators in the UAE illustrate the potential of CRP to be used as a pedagogical framework to preserve the cultural heritage of the ruling minority, while fostering social cohesion among a diversifying expatriate majority.

REFERENCES

Carey, M. 2015. "The limits of cultural competence: An Indigenous Studies perspective." *Higher Education Research & Development*, 34(5), 828–840.

Connelly, L. M. 2015. "Life-Worlds in Phenomenology." *Medsurg Nursing,* 24(2), 119–120.

Cross, T. L., Bazron, B. J., Dennis, K. W., & Isaacs, M. R. 1989. *Towards a culturally competent system of care: A monograph on effective services for minority children who are severely emotionally disturbed.* Washington, DC: Georgetown University Child Development Center.

Dubai Schools Inspection Bureau (DSIB) Inspection Reports (Searchable by year) https://www.khda.gov.ae/en/DSIB/Reports.

Dubai Schools Inspection Bureau (DSIB) Inspection Key Findings 2018–2019 https://www.khda.gov.ae/Areas/Administration/Content/FileUploads/Publication/Documents/English/20190526094359_InspectionKeyFindings2018-2019_En.pdf.

Dubai Schools Inspection Bureau (DSIB) Inspection Reports https://www.khda.gov.ae/DISB/AttachmentDownload.aspx?DOC_ID=UmMaH%2bnXeS8%3d.

Ed Arabia October 2015 https://www.edarabia.com/111664/emirati-culture-to-be-part-of-adec-curriculum/.

Esteban-Guitart, M. S., & Moll, L. C. 2014. "Funds of Identity: A new concept based on the Funds of Knowledge approach." *Culture & Psychology*, 20(1), 31–48.

Freire, P. 1998. "Fourth letter: On the indispensable qualities of progressive teachers for their better performance." In P. Freire (Ed.), *Teachers as cultural workers: Letters to those who dare teach* (pp. 71–98). Abingdon, UK: Routledge.

Gay, G. 2010. *Culturally responsive teaching: Theory, research, and practice.* New York, NY: Teachers College Press.

Gay, G. 2002. "Preparing for culturally responsive teaching." *Journal of Teacher Education,* 53(2), 106–116.

Green, B. 2003. "An unfinished project? Garth Boomer and the pedagogical imagination." *Opinion: Journal of the South Australian English Teachers' Association,* 47(2), 1324.

Harris, J., Ainscow, M., Carrington, S., & Kimber, M. 2019. "Developing inclusive school cultures through ethical practices" (Chapter 10). In L. Graham (Ed.), *Inclusive Education for the 21st Century: Theory, Policy and Practice.* Routledge, London and New York.

Hattam, R., & Zipin, L. 2009. "Towards pedagogical justice Discourse Studies in the Cultural Politics of Education: 'Symposium 1: Global/National Pressures On Schooling Systems. The Andrew Bell Lecture Series' and 'Symposium 2: Re-Designing Pedagogy,'" 30(3), 297–301.

Henzell-Thomas, J. 2018. *The Power of Education,* International Institute of Islamic Thought. ISBN: 1565645685, 9781565645684.

Irvine, J.J. 2010. "Culturally relevant pedagogy." *Education Digest,* 75(8), 57–61.

Keddie, A. 2017. "School autonomy reform and public education in Australia: implications for social justice." *The Australian Education Researcher,* 44, 373–390.

Matthews, C. 2019. "Maths as storytelling: Maths is beautiful" (Chapter 7). In K. Price & J. Rogers (Eds.), *Aboriginal and Torres Strait Islander Education: An Introduction for the Teaching Profession.* Cambridge: Cambridge University Press.

Memon, N., & Obaidat, M. 2017. "Road to Outstanding: A Qualitative Analysis of School Inspection Reports," Abu Dhabi University Knowledge Group, United Arab Emirates.

Morrison, A., Rigney, L.-I., Hattam, R., & Diplock, A. 2019. "Toward an Australian culturally responsive pedagogy: A narrative review of the literature." Retrieved from Australia: https://apo.org.au/sites/default/files/resource-files/2019/08/apo-nid 262951-1392016.pdf.

Nolan, E. A. 2016. "A critical analysis of multiculturalism, cultural competence, and cultural humility: An examination of potential training opportunities for pre-service teachers." (Doctor of Education thesis), George Fox University, Newberg, OR.

Price, D. & McCallum, F. 2016. "Wellbeing in education" (Chapter 1). In F. McCallum & D. Price (Eds.), *Nurturing Wellbeing Development in Education: From Little Things Big Things Grow.* London & New York: Routledge. ISBN: 978-1-138-79382-8.

Price, D., & Green, D. 2019. "Inclusive approaches to social and citizenship education." *The Social Educator,* 37(2), 29–39. ISSN: 1328-3480.

Price, D, Green, D, Memon, N & Chown, D. 2020. "Richness of complexity within diversity: educational engagement and achievement of diverse learners through culturally responsive pedagogies." *The Social Educator,* 38(1), 42–53.

Reid, J.-A. 2017. "Conclusion: Learning the humility of teaching 'others'—preparing teachers for culturally complex classrooms." In C. Reid & J. Major (Eds.), *Global teaching: Southern perspectives on teachers working with diversity* (pp. 209–229). New York, NY: Palgrave Macmillan.

Rizvi, F., & Lingard, B. 2009. *Globalizing Education Policy*. Florence, UK: Routledge.

Starratt, R. J. 2014. "The purpose of education" (Chapter 4). In C. M. Branson & S. J. Gross (Eds.), *Handbook of Ethical Educational Leadership*. New York: Routledge.

Tervalon, M., & Murray-Garcia, J. 1998. "Cultural humility versus cultural competence: A critical distinction in defining physician training outcomes in multicultural education." *Journal of Health Care for the Poor and Underserved,* 9(2), 117–125.

Thomson, P. 2002. *Schooling the rustbelt kids. Making a difference in changing times*. Crows Nest, NSW: Allen & Unwin.

UAE Vision 2021 https://www.vision2021.ae/en/national-agenda-2021.

UAE Vision 2021 https://www.vision2021.ae/en/national-agenda-2021/list/card/percentage-of-students-with-high-skills-in-arabic-according-to-national-tests.

Wink, J., & Putney, L. 2002. *A Vision of Vygotsky*. Boston: Allyn & Bacon.

Index

Note: *Italic* page number refer to figures and tables.

197

differentiated learning, 171
digital devices, 98
diglossic (language), 40, 41
distributed leadership, 100
diversity, 8, 9, 11, 14
Dubai, 111
"Dubai Disability Strategy 2020," 77
Dubai School Inspections Bureau
    (DSIB) protocol, 179–80

educands, 149
Education Affair Office (EAO), 120
educational discourse: complexities and
    challenges in, xiv–xvi; trends in,
    xii–xiv
educational policy, 57
educational practice, translating CRP
    theory into, 188–91
educational reform, 57, 58
educational system: implications of, xiii;
    in Oman, 57–58; of UAE, 76
Education and Training Sector Strategy
    2018–2022 (ETSS), 142, 145
education systems: challenges for, 93–
    96; before pandemic, 94–96; Western
    norms and expectations for, 95
educator, 193; within TVET sector,
    149; in UAE, 181; understandings,
    opportunities, and challenges,
    186–92
educator roundtables, in UAE, 184–85
Efthymiou, Efthymia, 81
Egypt, 28, 142
Elhoweris, Hala, 81
Ellis, Carolyn, 151–53
Ellis, Viv, 102
Emam, M. M., 60, 71
Emirati culture, 164, 168, 173;
    collaborative learning of, 169
Emiratis, 142–43, 160, 161, 181
Emirati schools, unqualified/low-
    qualified teachers in, 95
Emirbayer, M., 61
emotional and behavioral difficulties,
    59

"empathic concern," 119
empathy, literature on, 119
empirical research, 58, 61, 62, 72
English language, xv, 23, 41, 163–64;
    assessment in, 40
essentialize(ing), 184, 191–92
essential workers, 101
ethics, 24
"ethics of care," 190
Ethics of Justice approach, 191
ethnography, 3, 7, 18, 151–53
etiquette(s), 4
evaluation, 112, 117
Everington, Judith, 25
evidence-based accreditation, 115
evidence-based reflection, 151
exemplary knowledge, 28
expatriate, xiv, xv
"exporting methodologies," 165
extremist(ism), 14
extrinsic motivation, 170

face-to-face classrooms, 98
faculty: cultural and linguistic
    challenges Emirati students, 173;
    intercultural ability and agility
    development, 175; promote teacher-
    centered approaches, 174
faculty teaching, 161
"family-focused society," 190
Faour, Muhammad, 44
feedback, 134
female, 60, 63
First Rate Education System, 180
focus group, 82, 83
formal education system, 39
Foucault, Michel, 129
free association narrative method, 28
Freimuth, H., 170
Freire, Paulo, 130, 131, 133,
    148–50
Fullan, Michael, 101

Gaad, Eman, 76, 79, 81
Gallagher, Kay, 94, 101, 103

qualitative interviews, 28
quantitative, 61, 65, 72
Qudwa Forum, 120
Question-Response-Evaluation format, 47, 48
Quran/Quran memorization, 4, 21; reflection on teaching, 31–32; teachings of, 31

Raven, J., 164, 173
Reading Panel, 51
recitation, 42, 47, 51
recruitment, teacher, 101–2, 104
Reed-Danahay, Deborah, 151
reflective dialogue, 130
reflective memos, 133–34
Reflective Model, 105
reflexive sociology, 151
reflexivity, 151; autonomous, 26, 31; defined as, 26; element of, 27
reform, educational, 57, 58
Reid, J.-A., 184
religiosity, 12
remote teaching, 101
research methodology, 27–28
responsive pedagogy, in new teaching setting, 30–31
reverence, 116–17
Reverence in Classroom Teaching (Garrison and Rud), 116–17
Reyes, Luis, V., 81
Riis, Ole, 30
Rizga, Kristina: *On Teaching,* 116
Rogers, Carl, 119
Romanowski, Michael H., 95
Rosehart, Paula, 103, 104
rote learning, 162, 164, 168, 171
Rud, A. G.: *Reverence in Classroom Teaching,* 116–17
Ruppar, A., 61, 62
Ryan, Mary, 27

Sadhra, Sarine, 103, 104
El-Saharty, Sameh, 94, 96, 106
Sahin, Abdullah, 24

Salamanca Statement and Framework for Action on Special Needs Education (1994), 58
salary cuts, in private sector, 101–2
Salman bin Hamad Al Khalifa (Prince), 97
Saudi Arabia: education reforms in, 143–44; school system in, 96
Saudi Skills Standards (SSS), 143–44
school leadership, 99–101
schools: development in educational systems, 57; educational reform in, 57
school support, mediation effect of, 68, *70*
SEL. *See* social emotional learning (SEL)
self-assessment, 32
self-awareness, 130, 132, 135
self-narratives, 140
self-reflection, 130, 131, 135; critical consciousness and, 132–33; in teacher education, 132
semi-structured interviews, 28, 84
SEN. *See* special educational needs (SEN)
SEND. *See* special educational needs and disabilities (SEND)
sensory impairments, 59, 86–87
servant leadership, 100
Services for Educational Development, Research and Awareness for Inclusion (SEDRA), 78
Shaw, Ken E., 147
Sheikh Zayed Bin Sultan Al Nahyan, 76
Shiite Muslims, 13
short-term goals, 100–101
short vowels, 41
Sikes, Pat, 25
Singapore's Institute of Technical Education Act (992), 141–42
single item measures, 63
Siry, Christina Ann, 153
skill-based professional training, 142

About the Editors and Contributors

ABOUT THE EDITORS

Naved Bakali completed his PhD in Educational Studies from McGill University, Canada. He is an assistant professor of anti-racism education at the University of Windsor. Prior to this, he served as an assistant professor of education at the American University in Dubai. He also serves as a nonresident research fellow with trends research and advisory and he's a senior research fellow with Yaqeen Institute for Islamic Research, as well as a research affiliate with the Canadian Network for Research on Terrorism, Security and Society. He has been the recipient of major national and departmental grants and awards in recognition of his work. Naved has published extensively in the field of multicultural and diversity education, equity education, and Muslim youth identity in the post-9/11 context. He is the author of *Islamophobia: Understanding Anti-Muslim Racism Through the Lived Experiences of Muslim Youth* (Brill Sense 2016) and the coeditor of *Coloniality, Race, and Securitisation: The Rise of Global Islamophobia in the War on Terror* (Manchester University Press, forthcoming).

Nadeem A. Memon is a senior research fellow in the Centre for Islamic Thought and Education (CITE) in Education Futures at the University of South Australia (UniSA). He is currently the program director for an online accredited graduate program in Islamic pedagogy offered through UniSA. His research focuses on teacher education with particular emphasis on Islamic pedagogy, comparative faith-based schooling, philosophy of religious education, and culturally relevant and responsive teaching. He is the author of *A History* *of Islamic Schooling in North America* (Routledge 2019) and the coeditor of two books: *Philosophies of Islamic Education: Historical Perspectives and Emerging Discourses* (Routledge 2016) and *Discipline, Devotion, and Dissent: Jewish, Catholic, and Islamic Schooling in Canada* (Wilfrid Laurier University Press 2013). Prior to joining CITE/UniSA, Nadeem spearheaded the design and implementation of an online teacher certificate program, the Islamic Teacher Education Program (ITEP), in collaboration with the University of Toronto.

ABOUT THE CONTRIBUTORS

Nadera Alborno is an associate professor of education at the American University in Dubai. Her current research interest includes culturally competent teacher education with a focus on the development of inclusive education in the UAE. She is also active in the empowerment of people with disabilities through education and employment from a human agency perspective. In addition, Dr. Alborno works with local communities to spread awareness regarding the rights of people with disabilities and advises organizations regarding inclusive policies and practices. As an active member of the American Education Research Association (AERA) and a contributor to British journals, she has published articles, book chapters, and case studies addressing the challenges in the UAE and GCC context.

Ali Hussain Al-Bulushi is the director of Community Service and Continuing Education Center at Sultan Qaboos University, where he also serves as an associate professor.

Mariam Alhashmi is an assistant professor in the College of Education at Zayed University. Her academic interests include the philosophy of Islamic education and its implications for curriculum development and teacher growth. Mariam completed her PhD at the British University in Dubai specializing in educational management and leadership with a focus on the philosophy of Islamic education. She started her career in the field of education as a teacher, then as an assistant head of a kindergarten school. Then she worked as a head of the national curriculum for a group of schools focusing on the teaching and learning of the Arabic, Islamic studies, and UAE social studies curricula. Prior to joining Zayed University, she worked as the director of Curriculum and Instruction at Emirates National Schools, responsible for overseeing all areas related to teaching and learning of twenty schools across the United Arab Emirates.

Fatima Hasan Bailey is a researcher, teacher educator, and full-time faculty member at Zayed University. She provides professional mentorship and coaching for in-service practitioners in the Al Jalila Foundation, Ta'Alouf Program for Career-Based Teacher Development. She provides clinical supervision for preservice teachers completing their teacher preparation program. Dr. Bailey previously held positions as a director, school development manager, principal, and vice principal in P–12 schools in the United States and the UAE. Dr. Bailey has an active research agenda. She has written several book chapters and articles in line with her research interests. She disseminates her research and presents at local, regional, and international conferences. Dr. Bailey was recently featured as a faculty scholar at Zayed University. She is an awardee of the distinguished California Legislature: "Teachers of Excellence Award." She is a recipient of the prestigious Gordon Allport Prize for Outstanding Papers on Intergroup Relations, Society for the Psychological Study of Social Issues.

Lucy Bailey is an associate professor and head of Education Studies at the Bahrain Teachers College (BTC) in the University of Bahrain. She is part of the BTC's Leadership Centre and served on the national working group on the collaboration of applied learning. She chairs the cycle 1 DAC which is currently revising the teacher education curriculum of cycle 1 teachers for government schools. She was previously an associate professor at the University of Nottingham Malaysia, where she was program coordinator for the MA Education. She has written extensively about the internationalization of education, including studies of various aspects of international schooling, the internationalization of higher education, and the schooling of students who are refugees or asylum seekers.

Dylan Chown is a lecturer in the Centre for Islamic Thought and Education (CITE) in Education Futures at the University of South Australia (UniSA). His research focuses on teacher education and school renewal, with emphasis on Islamic pedagogy and culturally and religiously responsive pedagogy, as well as educational inclusion. Dylan is also an active member of UniSA's Centre for Research in Educational and Social Inclusion (CRESI) and Pedagogies for Justice Research group. Dylan coordinates courses in an online accredited graduate program in Islamic pedagogy offered through UniSA. Prior to joining UniSA, Dylan was a member of an International network of educators on the Islamic Teacher Education Program (ITEP), a project of Razi Ed (Canada/UAE). Dylan's PhD research focuses on the exploration of Islamic pedagogy in practice, based on a case study of an Australian K–12 Islamic school. He was a coeditor of the book *Islamic Schooling in the West: Pathways to Renewal* (Palgrave MacMillan).

Maria Efstratopoulou is an associate professor of Special Education at the United Arab Emirates University (UAEU). Before joining UAEU, she was a senior lecturer at BG University in the UK in Special Education and Inclusion. Her research interests are in motor behavior and assessment for children with emotional, behavioral, and developmental disorders, and she has clinical and educational experience working with children with autism, ADHD, CD, DCD, and mental health problems. She is an active researcher with international cooperations for more than fifteen years in the field of special education, psychomotor therapy, and child psychology. She is the author of four books in special education and has published many research articles in peer-reviewed journals. She is a core member of the EFP (European Framework in Psychomotor) in Research and she acts as an editorial board member and senior reviewer for several peer-reviewed journals in the field of education.

Mahmoud Mohamed Emam is a professor and Head of the Department of Psychology at Sultan Qaboos University, College of Education. He holds a PhD from the University of Manchester and a master's from the University of London, UK. He obtained two Fulbright scholarships at the University of Kansas and University of Florida in the United States. He obtained a number of grants from His Majesty's Research Trust in Oman and other internal grants from Sultan Qaboos University, and the Centre for Specialized Studies in Egypt. He previously served as the head of the Assessment Unit at the College of Education and was a member of the Accreditation Steering Committee whose efforts led to the accreditation of the teacher education program at Sultan Qaboos University by CAEP. He has a number of published articles in peer-reviewed international and regional journals.

Jenny Eppard has a PhD in Instructional Technology from the University of Virginia in the United States and a master's degree in International Education from George Washington University. She is an experienced English as a Second Language teacher with a professional background in teaching a variety of ESL students in terms of age, proficiency, and background. She has headed several research projects on using the iPad with students in the English foundations program at Zayed University. Currently, her research topics include reading on the iPad, flipped learning, XMOOCs in the UAE, online collaborative tools to support content reading, vocabulary-centered apps, student e-portfolios, interactive documentaries, and online informal learning.

Mohammed Adly Gamal graduated in 2001 with a BA in Arabic language and Islamic studies from Dar al-Ulum, Cairo University. Since then, he has been teaching Islamic studies and Arabic language in international schools across the GCC nations, and currently, he works as a teacher at Qatar

Foundation. Additionally, he is an early-career researcher with interests in the sociology of religious education, international schooling, and the educational policies of identity formation. He holds a master's degree from the University of Keele, UK, in International Education. Mr. Mohammed Adly Gamal is a member of BERA (British Educational Research Association) and CSSE (Canadian Society for the Study of Education).

Samah Abdulhafid Gamar is an educator and critical pedagogue who has worked in the higher education and government sectors in Canada and Qatar for twenty years. She holds graduate degrees from the United States and Canada and currently serves as the director of Teaching, Learning and Assessment at the Doha Institute for Graduate Studies. She has previously served as the vice president—Academic at College of the North Atlantic—Qatar. Her academic research is driven by a commitment to education reform in the Arab region that works toward liberation and empowerment through transformative education policy and practice. Her work has advocated for the integration of conscientization, or critical self-awareness, as a form of sociopolitical agency across higher education, but in particular, the technical, vocational education and training (TVET) sector.

Deborah Green is a program director: Bachelor of Primary Education (Honors) and a senior lecturer: Humanities and Social Science Education at the University of South Australia. Her research projects address persistent bullying, cyberbullying, turning points, resilience, inclusive education, culturally responsive pedagogies, and disability studies. She is an active member of the Centre for Research in Educational and Social Inclusion (CRESI) group, Executive Committee member of Social and Citizenship Education Association of Australia Inc., and executive secretary of HaSS SA.

Ahmed Hassan Hemdan is an associate professor at the Department of Special Education, College of Education, United Arabic Emirates University. He received his PhD from the University of Arizona in Special Education/Gifted. He is currently the editor-in-chief of the *International Journal for Research in Education* (IJRE), UAEU. His research interests include assessment and education of gifted and talented students, developing and adapting assessments to the Arabic culture for students with special needs, designing and adapting enrichment programs for gifted and talented students, and the educational psychology of preschool children. He is currently a member of several professional associations such as the World Council for Gifted and Talented Children (WCGTC, UAE Delegate), the American Psychological Association (APA), the European Council for High Ability (ECHA), and the Arabic Council for the Gifted and Talented (ACGT). He has led several national research grants in the fields of special and early childhood education. He has won several national and regional awards for his scholarly achievements.

Catherine Hill is a dean and an associate professor of the American University in Dubai, School of Education. She began her career as a high school teacher of history and Spanish. In higher education, she has taught courses in education, sociology, and public administration, and held a number of academic appointments, including director of Graduate Programs in Educational Leadership and associate dean in the College of Arts and Sciences at Villanova University. Most recently, she worked two years as a principal writer and special assistant to the CEO and superintendent of the School District of Philadelphia. She has conducted research, written widely, and given talks on issues concerning children of conflict, multicultural learning environments, and the purpose and philosophy of higher education. Her academic pursuits and personal interests have led her to spend considerable time in South America, Lebanon, India, Europe, the United Kingdom, and Dubai.

Jessica Tsimprea Maluch is an assistant professor of education at the American University in Dubai, where she works closely with preservice and in-service teachers to support their professional growth. She received her doctorate from Humboldt University in Berlin, Germany, MEd from Harvard Graduate School of Education, and BA from Wellesley College. For the last twenty years, she has worked in a variety of roles in the education sector in the United States, the Middle East, and Europe. She has taught in the English (ESL) and language arts classroom at the middle school, secondary, and postsecondary levels, been an educational adviser and program developer, and worked as an educational researcher and trainer. Her research and publications focus on issues of multilingualism, language development, and assessment.

Ashraf Moustafa is instructor of Special Education at the United Arab Emirates University. He holds a PhD and a master's degree in special education, a subspecialty in sensory disabilities, has field experience in the field of special education for more than twenty years, during which he worked in Abu Dhabi Education Council schools before joining the UAE University. He has clinical and educational experience working with children with sensory impairment, LD, autism, and ADHD. His research interests are in sensory impairment and assessment for children with sensory impairment, developmental disorders, and learning difficulties. He is the author of three books in special education about assistive technology for students with visual impairment and adjustment behavior of the blind. He was awarded the Sheikh

Khalifa Education Award in 2015, as the best specialist for people with disabilities in the Arab world. He also won the Sharjah Award for Educational Excellence in the year 2020, as the best applied educational researcher for students with learning difficulties.

Deborah Price is a research degree coordinator and senior lecturer: Inclusive Education and Wellbeing at the University of South Australia (UniSA) Education Futures. She is an executive member and portfolio lead: Partnerships for the UniSA Centre for Research in Educational and Social Inclusion (CRESI) and member of the Pedagogies for Justice Research Group. Her educational research focuses on inclusive education; disability; educator and learner wellbeing; social justice; culturally and religiously responsive pedagogy; curriculum; initial teacher education; bullying and cyberbullying; youth studies and voice; capabilities and strengths-based approaches; codesign, inquiry, and participatory action-based research. Currently, she is the president of the Australian Curriculum Studies Association (ACSA); further details can be found at https://people.unisa.edu.au/Debbie.Price.

Herveen Singh is the head of Quality Assurance and Accreditation at Zayed University in the United Arab Emirates. She is also an assistant professor with the College of Education at Zayed University. Her areas of research interests are in quality assurance and accreditation; decolonial studies in educational leadership; faculty development; equity in hiring, retention, and promotion; organizational change management; and stakeholder engagement in educational leadership and schooling in diverse contexts. Herveen has led curriculum development teams and developed programs at the bachelors, masters, and doctoral levels in education, policy, and business areas. Herveen has conducted quantitative and qualitative studies with Canadian school boards and organizations at local, provincial, and federal levels. Specifically, she has led teams in designing curriculum, programming, and assessment for federally funded research projects involving over 2,000 students from across the province of Ontario in Canada. She has also conducted district-wide research for the second largest school board in Canada, involving over 1,500 government employees.

Hanada Taha Thomure is the endowed professor of Arabic Language and director of the Arabic Language Center for Research and Development at Zayed University, UAE.

She designed the first system for leveling Arabic texts which is currently used by regional and international publishers to level their Arabic children's books with more than 8,000 books leveled using it. Dr. Taha Thomure developed the Arabic language arts standards that have been used by more than 100,000 students all over the Arab world. She is the senior author for Pearson's Arabic language Arts K–9, a state-of-the-art curriculum that is standards-, literature-, and inquiry-based. She has reviewed the national Arabic curricula for Morocco, Saudi Arabia, Jordan, the UAE, and Bahrain and is an adviser for Arab Thought Foundation, Queen Rania Foundation, USAID, DLI, World Bank, and many other entities across the region. Her research is in the field of Arabic language teaching and learning, oral reading fluency, Arabic children's literature and teacher preparation, and curriculum studies.

.